Accounting For Dummies

A Few Quick Tips about Accounting for Business Managers and Investors

1. **Business managers and investors need financial information.** Accounting's main function is to supply information about *profit, financial condition,* and *cash flow.* Managers and investors should meet accountants partway by having a basic understanding of the financial statements that report this information.

2. **The most important thing that accountants do is to measure profit — sales revenue minus expenses.** Accountants must decide which particular methods to use for recording sales and expenses. Profit measures are very dependent on which accounting methods are selected to measure expenses.

3. **Authoritative rules and standards have been established for measuring profit and presenting financial condition and cash flows** — these standards are called *generally accepted accounting principles,* or GAAP for short. Financial reports to investors must follow GAAP. Business managers must make sure that their financial reports follow GAAP.

4. **GAAP still leave room for manipulation of profit and financial condition numbers** — however, not of the numbers reported in the cash flow statement. A business can use very conservative or quite aggressive accounting methods to measure its *net income* (profit) and to value its assets and liabilities. Managers make these decisions, and investors should be alert to which accounting methods are used.

5. **The income statement is not the balance sheet** — the income statement reports bottom-line profit (net income) and the revenue and expenses leading down to this key figure. The balance sheet reports assets and liabilities at a moment in time. You cannot find profit for the most recent period in the business's balance sheet, no matter how hard you look. Even reporters in the financial press, who ought to know better, confuse these two financial statements — but you shouldn't!

6. **Bottom-line profit is not bottom-line cash flow for the year.** The actual cash flow generated from profit does not equal the amount of profit for the year. For one thing, you have to take into account depreciation expense. This return of cost though sales revenue provides cash flow in addition to the profit earned for the year. But the profit measure includes some sales revenue not collected by year-end and some expenses not paid by year-end. These and other changes make cash flow different from profit.

7. **Business managers need a basic profit accounting model,** both to focus on the key variables that determine profit performance and for making intelligent decisions about how best to protect and improve profit. The profit model, in the form of a management income statement, classifies expenses on the basis of whether they vary or are relatively fixed in nature, whether the expenses vary with sales volume (quantity sold) or sales revenue (total dollars of sales), and it also highlights profit margin.

8. **Profit margin and sales volume are the two most important factors in the profit model.** Profit margin equals sales price less product cost and less the variable expenses of making the sale. Even a small slippage in profit margin can have a devastating impact on profit; even a small gain in the profit margin can have a tremendous positive impact on profit.

...For Dummies®: Bestselling Book Series for Beginners

9. **A little more sales volume results in a lot more profit.** Businesses have *fixed expenses* for the year that are more or less locked in place and cannot be changed over the short-run. The business has to sell enough volume to earn total margin equal to its fixed expenses before it breaks into the profit zone. This cross-over volume is called the *break-even point*. After the business jumps over its fixed expenses hurdle, the margin on each additional unit sold goes entirely to profit (before income tax). The business starts making profit hand over fist above the break-even point.

10. **The profit-making activities of a business propels its balance sheet.** To understand a balance sheet, you must understand that sales revenue and expenses drive most of the assets and liabilities in the balance sheet. These vital connections between the income statement and the balance sheet are extraordinarily important for managers to understand in planning the capital needs of the business and in controlling the business's financial condition and cash flows.

11. **Business managers should closely scrutinize all cost figures.** Virtually every cost number that managers see in accounting reports and use in decision-making are based on choices between alternate accounting methods or on arbitrary methods of allocating costs. Managers should have a clear understanding of which choices were made and the justification of the allocation method.

12. **Some business ownership structures pay income tax, and some don't.** Corporations with more than 75 stockholders are taxed, but corporations with fewer stockholders, and partnerships and limited liability companies, don't have to pay income tax. They are *pass-through* tax entities; only the owners of these entities pay income tax, based on their respective ownership shares in the business. Cash dividends paid to stockholders by corporations that pay income tax are also taxable to the individual stockholders (which is called double taxation).

13. **Book values of two important assets are often less than their current replacement cost values.** Inventory is recorded at cost of acquisition and is not written up to recognize future increases in replacement cost. Likewise, fixed, or long-term, assets are recorded at cost and then depreciated to expense over their useful lives. No gains in replacement cost values are recorded. A business benefits from replacement cost increases only if it raises sales prices to its customers and earns higher profit when the inventory is sold and as fixed assets are used over time.

14. **Goodwill refers to the capability of a business to sustain above-average profit performance.** Unless it has actually been bought and paid for, goodwill is not recorded. Only when another business or group of investors pays cash for the goodwill already established by a business does goodwill show up as an asset in a balance sheet. Goodwill is written off to expense over its useful life.

15. **Audits by CPAs of the annual financial reports of public businesses are required.** Private businesses may have their annual financial reports audited to satisfy lenders or outside investors. CPA auditors don't necessarily catch everything, but a clean opinion in an auditor's report provides assurance that the financial statements are fairly presented and have been prepared according to GAAP. Investors should always read the auditor's report to make sure that a clean opinion is being expressed, and if not, then to find out what problems the auditor has with the financial statements.

16. **Business managers should not be intimidated by accountants.** Ask for clear, jargon-free explanations of terms and accounting methods. However, be prepared for the worst. Learning the basic language of accounting has many advantages (see Appendix A, the glossary).

Praise Praise Praise for Accounting For Dummies

"As one of the thousands of people taking graduate-level accounting management courses for the first time, I wanted a step-by-step guide that would quickly bring me up to speed on accounting concepts, approaches, and practices. *Accounting For Dummies* is essential reading for all of us who want to manage our business finances effectively and understand the financial health of companies we may deal with or invest in. I highly recommend it for managers and students of management."

— Mary Metcalfe, Partner, Envirocomm
Communications

"With a keen sense of wit and intelligence, John provides a wealth of practical information on understanding how to manage budgets and financial statements."

— Jack Rudolph, President, Colorado Community
First National Bank

"John has an uncanny knack for explaining complicated accounting and financial material to beginners as well as experts in the accounting field. I will definitely use *Accounting For Dummies* in my curriculum."

— G. Dale Meyer, Professor, College of Business,
University of Colorado

Praise Praise Praise for John A. Tracy's How to Read a Financial Report

"[If] you would like to have a minimal understanding of the numbers that make up a balance sheet, income, and cash flow statement . . . then *How to Read a Financial Report* might be just what you are looking for. Mr. Tracy's book explains in plain English the meaning of the major terms used in financial statements. . . ."

— *The Wall Street Journal*

"What distinguishes Tracy's efforts from other manuals is an innovative structure that visually ties together elements of the balance sheet and income statement by tracing where and how a line item in one affects an entry in the other."

— *INC. Magazine*

"An excellent job of showing how to separate the wheat from the chaff without choking in the process."

— *The Miami Herald*

". . . the best book this reviewer has seen in over 20 years of accounting education that is targeted to financial statement users who have little or no knowledge of accounting."

— *The Ohio CPA Journal*

"Tracy has overcome the traditional inability of accountants to talk or write about their subject in a way the layman can understand. . . ."

— *The Chicago Tribune*

". . . gives an easy-to-follow description of the purpose of each type of statement . . . A fine basic handbook for those beginning to perform due diligence on stocks and other investment offerings."

— *Financial Planning*

". . . precise and pragmatic . . . reads with clarity and conciseness, focusing on all business transactions. . . ."

— *Broward Review and Business Record*

". . . written for those non-financial people who would like to pass up all the complicated jargon to get to the real meat and potatoes."

— *Atlanta Business Chronicle*

"A major strength of this book is that it highlights relationships among financial reporting elements that often remain obscure to the non-accountant. It is clearly written and provides detailed guidelines for adjusting accounting numbers to determine cash flow."

— *Journal of Accountancy*

TM

References for the Rest of Us!™

1/99

ACCOUNTING

FOR

DUMMIES®

ACCOUNTING FOR DUMMIES®

by John A. Tracy, CPA

IDG Books Worldwide, Inc.
An International Data Group Company

Foster City, CA ◆ Chicago, IL ◆ Indianapolis, IN ◆ New York, NY

Accounting For Dummies®

Published by

IDG Books Worldwide, Inc.

An International Data Group Company
919 E. Hillsdale Blvd.
Suite 400
Foster City, CA 94404
www.idgbooks.com (IDG Books Worldwide Web site)
www.dummies.com (Dummies Press Web site)

Library of Congress Catalog Card No.: 97-71814

ISBN: 0-7645-5014-4

Printed in the United States of America

10 9

1B/TQ/QU/ZZ/IN

Distributed in the United States by IDG Books Worldwide, Inc.

Distributed by CDG Books Canada Inc. for Canada; by Transworld Publishers Limited in the United Kingdom; by IDG Norge Books for Norway; by IDG Sweden Books for Sweden; by Woodslane Pty. Ltd. for Australia; by Woodslane (NZ) Ltd. for New Zealand; by TransQuest Publishers Pte Ltd. for Singapore, Malaysia, Thailand, Indonesia, and Hong Kong; by ICG Muse, Inc. for Japan; by Norma Comunicaciones S.A. for Colombia; by Intersoft for South Africa; by Le Monde en Tique for France; by International Thomson Publishing for Germany, Austria and Switzerland; by Distribuidora Cuspide for Argentina; by Livraria Cultura for Brazil; by Ediciones ZETA S.C.R. Ltda. for Peru; by WS Computer Publishing Corporation, Inc., for the Philippines; by Contemporanea de Ediciones for Venezuela; by Express Computer Distributors for the Caribbean and West Indies; by Micronesia Media Distributor, Inc. for Micronesia; by Grupo Editorial Norma S.A. for Guatemala; by Chips Computadoras S.A. de C.V. for Mexico; by Editorial Norma de Panama S.A. for Panama; by American Bookshops for Finland. Authorized Sales Agent: Anthony Rudkin Associates for the Middle East and North Africa.

For general information on IDG Books Worldwide's books in the U.S., please call our Consumer Customer Service department at 800-762-2974. For reseller information, including discounts and premium sales, please call our Reseller Customer Service department at 800-434-3422.

For information on where to purchase IDG Books Worldwide's books outside the U.S., please contact our International Sales department at 317-596-5530 or fax 317-596-5692.

For consumer information on foreign language translations, please contact our Customer Service department at 1-800-434-3422, fax 317-596-5692, or e-mail rights@idgbooks.com.

For information on licensing foreign or domestic rights, please phone +1-650-655-3109.

For sales inquiries and special prices for bulk quantities, please contact our Sales department at 650-655-3200 or write to the address above.

For information on using IDG Books Worldwide's books in the classroom or for ordering examination copies, please contact our Educational Sales department at 800-434-2086 or fax 317-596-5499.

For press review copies, author interviews, or other publicity information, please contact our Public Relations department at 650-655-3000 or fax 650-655-3299.

For authorization to photocopy items for corporate, personal, or educational use, please contact Copyright Clearance Center, 222 Rosewood Drive, Danvers, MA 01923, or fax 978-750-4470.

 is a registered trademark or trademark under exclusive license to IDG Books Worldwide, Inc. from International Data Group, Inc. in the United States and/or other countries.

About the Author

John A. Tracy (Boulder, Colorado) is a Professor of Accounting for the College of Business and Administration at the University of Colorado in Boulder. He has served as a staff accountant at Ernst & Young and is the author of several books on accounting, including *The Fast Forward MBA in Finance* and *How to Read a Financial Report: Wringing Vital Signs Out of the Numbers*. Dr. Tracy received his MBA and Ph.D. degrees from the University of Wisconsin and is also a CPA in Colorado.

ABOUT IDG BOOKS WORLDWIDE

Welcome to the world of IDG Books Worldwide.

IDG Books Worldwide, Inc., is a subsidiary of International Data Group, the world's largest publisher of computer-related information and the leading global provider of information services on information technology. IDG was founded more than 30 years ago by Patrick J. McGovern and now employs more than 9,000 people worldwide. IDG publishes more than 290 computer publications in over 75 countries. More than 90 million people read one or more IDG publications each month.

Launched in 1990, IDG Books Worldwide is today the #1 publisher of best-selling computer books in the United States. We are proud to have received eight awards from the Computer Press Association in recognition of editorial excellence and three from Computer Currents' First Annual Readers' Choice Awards. Our best-selling ...*For Dummies*® series has more than 50 million copies in print with translations in 31 languages. IDG Books Worldwide, through a joint venture with IDG's Hi-Tech Beijing, became the first U.S. publisher to publish a computer book in the People's Republic of China. In record time, IDG Books Worldwide has become the first choice for millions of readers around the world who want to learn how to better manage their businesses.

Our mission is simple: Every one of our books is designed to bring extra value and skill-building instructions to the reader. Our books are written by experts who understand and care about our readers. The knowledge base of our editorial staff comes from years of experience in publishing, education, and journalism — experience we use to produce books to carry us into the new millennium. In short, we care about books, so we attract the best people. We devote special attention to details such as audience, interior design, use of icons, and illustrations. And because we use an efficient process of authoring, editing, and desktop publishing our books electronically, we can spend more time ensuring superior content and less time on the technicalities of making books.

You can count on our commitment to deliver high-quality books at competitive prices on topics you want to read about. At IDG Books Worldwide, we continue in the IDG tradition of delivering quality for more than 30 years. You'll find no better book on a subject than one from IDG Books Worldwide.

IDG BOOKS WORLDWIDE

John J. Kilcullen
John Kilcullen
Chairman and CEO
IDG Books Worldwide, Inc.

Steven Berkowitz
Steven Berkowitz
President and Publisher
IDG Books Worldwide, Inc.

Eighth Annual
Computer Press
Awards ≥1992

Ninth Annual
Computer Press
Awards ≥1993

Tenth Annual
Computer Press
Awards ≥1994

Eleventh Annual
Computer Press
Awards ≥1995

Dedication

For My Eight Grandchildren

Author's Acknowledgments

I'm deeply grateful to everyone at IDG Books Worldwide, Inc., who helped produce this book. Their professionalism and their unfailing sense of humor and courtesy were much appreciated. I supplied some raw materials (words), and then the outstanding editors at IDG Books Worldwide molded them into the finished product.

Out of the blue, I got a call one day from Kathy Welton, Vice President and Publisher for Dummies Trade Press. Kathy asked if I'd be interested in doing this book. It didn't take me very long to say yes. She can be very persuasive, and she certainly knows her stuff. Thank you, Kathy!

I can't say enough nice things about Pam Mourouzis, who worked with me as project editor on the book. The book is immensely better for her insights and advice. Pam started out as an accounting dummy, and she's now an accounting "smartie." The two copy editors on the book — Diane Giangrossi and Joe Jansen — made innumerable corrections and suggestions which were extraordinarily helpful. You two should also take a bow. I sincerely thank you two.

Also, Mark Butler gave me the right nudge when I needed it. Mary Metcalfe provided invaluable comments and suggestions on the manuscript as it worked its way through the development process. I don't know Mary personally, but in my mind's eye she is one tough cookie!

In short, it was my great privilege and pleasure to work with the IDG Books team on this book. I couldn't have done it without them.

Also, I owe a debt of gratitude to a faculty colleague at Boulder, an accomplished author in his own right, Professor Ed Gac. He offered very sage advice. Ed was always ready with a word of encouragement when I needed one, and I'm very appreciative.

I often think about why I like to write books. I believe it goes back to an accounting class in my undergraduate days at Creighton University in Omaha. In a course taught by the Dean of the Business School, Dr. Floyd Walsh, I turned in a term paper and he said that it was very well written. I have never forgotten that compliment. I think he would be proud of this book.

Publisher's Acknowledgments

We're proud of this book; please register your comments through our IDG Books Worldwide Online Registration Form located at http://my2cents.dummies.com.

Some of the people who helped bring this book to market include the following:

Acquisitions, Development, and Editorial

Senior Project Editor: Pamela Mourouzis

Acquisitions Editor: Mark Butler

Copy Editors: Diane L. Giangrossi, Joe Jansen

Technical Reviewer: Mary Metcalfe

Editorial Manager: Leah P. Cameron

Editorial Coordinator: Ann Miller

Production

Project Coordinator: Debbie Stailey

Layout and Graphics:
Brett Black, Cameron Booker, Elizabeth Cárdenas-Nelson, J. Tyler Connor, Angela F. Hunckler, Todd Klemme, Brent Savage, Kate Snell, Deirdre Smith, Rashell Smith

Proofreaders: Michelle Croninger, Joel K. Draper, Henry Lazarek, Jennifer Mahern, Robert Springer, Ethel M. Winslow

Indexer: Sharon Hilgenberg

Special Help

Diana R. Conover, Stephanie Koutek, Darren Meiss, Susan Diane Smith, Michael D. Sullivan

---

General and Administrative

IDG Books Worldwide, Inc.: John Kilcullen, CEO; Steven Berkowitz, President and Publisher

IDG Books Technology Publishing: Brenda McLaughlin, Senior Vice President and Group Publisher

Dummies Technology Press and Dummies Editorial: Diane Graves Steele, Vice President and Associate Publisher; Mary Bednarek, Director of Acquisitions and Product Development; Kristin A. Cocks, Editorial Director

Dummies Trade Press: Kathleen A. Welton, Vice President and Publisher; Kevin Thornton, Acquisitions Manager

IDG Books Production for Dummies Press: Michael R. Britton, Vice President of Production and Creative Services; Cindy L. Phipps, Manager of Project Coordination, Production Proofreading, and Indexing; Kathie S. Schutte, Supervisor of Page Layout; Shelley Lea, Supervisor of Graphics and Design; Debbie J. Gates, Production Systems Specialist; Robert Springer, Supervisor of Proofreading; Debbie Stailey, Special Projects Coordinator; Tony Augsburger, Supervisor of Reprints and Bluelines

Dummies Packaging and Book Design: Patty Page, Manager, Promotions Marketing

♦

The publisher would like to give special thanks to Patrick J. McGovern, without whom this book would not have been possible.

♦

Contents at a Glance

Cartoons at a Glance

By Rich Tennant

"OUR GOAL IS TO MAXIMIZE YOUR UPSIDE AND MINIMIZE YOUR DOWNSIDE WHILE WE PROTECT OUR OWN BACKSIDE."

page 85

"SINCE WE BEGAN ON-LINE SHOPPING, I JUST DON'T KNOW WHERE THE MONEY'S GOING."

page 293

They're moving on to chapter 2. That should daze and confuse them enough for us to finish changing the tire and get the heck out of here.

page 11

"COOKED BOOKS? LET ME JUST SAY YOU COULD SERVE THIS PROFIT AND LOSS STATEMENT WITH A FRUITY ZINFANDEL AND NOT BE OUT OF PLACE."

page 263

I'm mathematically dyslexic. But it's not that unusual - 100 out of every 15 people are.

page 171

Fax: 978-546-7747 • **E-mail:** the5wave@tiac.net

Table of Contents

· ·

Introduction

Welcome to *Accounting For Dummies*. Why would anyone in their right mind take the time to learn about accounting, you ask? The brief answer is that accounting is your window to the world of business and finance. Understanding accounting can be an excellent means for getting a handle on the financial aspects of your business, investments, income taxes, and personal financial management. Accounting paints a picture of financial condition — not in colors, but with numbers.

I've written this book for people who need to understand accounting information and financial reports — *not* for accountants and bookkeepers (although they should find this book very interesting and a good refresher course). This book is for people who need to use and understand accounting information — business managers, for example, who need to make profit, turn profit into cash flow, and control the assets and liabilities of their business. If you're a business manager, I'm preaching to the converted when I say that you need a basic familiarity with accounting and financial statements in order to make good business decisions.

Business investors, lawyers, business consultants — pretty much anyone who reads *The Wall Street Journal* — can also benefit from a solid understanding of how to read financial reports and how accounting works.

About This Book

Accounting For Dummies lifts the veil of obscure terminology and lays bare the methods of accounting. This book takes you behind the scenes and explains the language and methods of accounting in a down-to-earth and lighthearted manner — and *in plain English*.

Each chapter in this book is like a tub standing on its own feet — each is designed to stand on its own. Each chapter is self-contained, and you can jump from chapter to chapter as you please (although I encourage you to take a quick tour through the chapters in the order that I present them). I bet you'll discover some points that you may not have expected to find in a book about accounting.

Conventions Used in Financial Reports

Much of this book focuses on profit and how a business makes profit. Because profit and other financial aspects of a business are reported in *financial statements,* understanding some basic notations and conventions used in these financial reports is important.

I use the following income statement (stripped down to its bare essentials) to illustrate some conventions that you can expect to see when reading financial reports. These conventions are the common ways of showing figures in financial reports, like saying hello and shaking hands are common conventions that you can expect when you greet someone.

Sample Abbreviated Income Statement		
Sales revenue		$25,000,000
Expenses		
Variable expenses	(13,000,000)	
Fixed expenses	(7,000,000)	
Total expenses		(20,000,000)
Profit		$5,000,000

- You read a financial statement from the top down. In the preceding income statement, for example, Sales revenue is listed first, followed by Expenses, because expenses are deducted from revenue.

- Financial reports that show two or more categories with subtotals may appear with two columns, as shown in the preceding example. Simpler financial reports may display all figures in a single column.

- Figures that are deducted (or subtracted) from a total amount (like expenses deducted from sales revenue in the preceding example) may be indicated by parentheses around the figure. Some financial reports may make the assumption that you know that expenses are deducted from sales revenue — so no parentheses are put around the number. *Note:* You may see expenses represented both ways in financial reports. But you hardly ever see a minus or negative sign in front of expenses — it's just not done.

- Only the first number in a column is preceded by the dollar sign — not the following numbers. However, financial reporting practices are not uniform on this point. In some financial reports, dollar signs are in front of all numbers, but more often they are not.

✔ To indicate that a calculation is taking place on a column of numbers, a single underline is drawn under the number (as in the <u>20,000,000</u> expense total in the preceding example). Note that the dollar sign is not used for the expense number because it's not the first figure in the column.

✔ The final number in a financial report, the *bottom line,* appears with a dollar sign in front of it and the figure is <u>double underlined</u>, as you see in the preceding example. This is about as carried away as accountants get in their work — a double underline. Again, actual financial reporting practices are not completely uniform on this point — instead of a double underline on a bottom-line number, the number may appear in **bold.**

When I present an accounting formula that shows how financial numbers are computed, I show the formula in a different font with a gray screen, like this:

```
Assets = Liabilities + Owners' Equity
```

Terminology in financial reporting is reasonably uniform, thank goodness — although you may see a fair amount of jargon. When I introduce a new term in this book, I show the term in *italics* and flag it with an icon (see the section "Icons Used in This Book," later in this Introduction). You can also turn to Appendix A to look up a term that you're unfamiliar with.

Foolish Assumptions

This book is designed for all of you who have that nagging feeling that you really should know more about accounting. You don't want to be an accountant, nor do you have any aspirations of ever sitting for the CPA exam. But you worry that what you don't know about accounting may hamper your decision-making, and you know deep down that learning more about accounting would help.

Although I assume that you have a basic familiarity with the business world, I take nothing for granted in this book regarding how much accounting you know. Even if you have some experience with accounting and financial statements, I think you'll find this book useful — especially for improving your communication with real accountants.

This book is designed for people who need to *use* accounting information. Many different types of people need to understand accounting basics — not the technical stuff, just the fundamentals. They include the following:

- ✔ **Business managers** depend on accounting reports to know how much profit was earned and how it was earned, to see the financial impacts of profit, to determine whether the business is in good financial shape, and to identify the sources and uses of cash flows in the business. Without this kind of information, managers are at a serious disadvantage.

- ✔ **Investors** in securities (stocks and bonds), real estate, and other business ventures depend on financial reports to inform them about how things are going and where things stand with their investments. Investors are generally very interested in whether they are getting a fair shake or perhaps are being led down the primrose path. To know what they're getting into (and what happens if they want to get out of an investment), investors can benefit from knowing financial accounting basics.

- ✔ **Business professionals** need to know how to read financial statements, how accountants measure profit, and what the difference is between profit and cash flow. For example, lawyers who draw up contracts containing accounting terminology and provisions that depend on accounting numbers should definitely understand what the accounting terms and numbers mean.

- ✔ **Government regulators, public administrators, and managers in the nonprofit sector of the economy** need a solid underpinning of accounting knowledge. For example, when the U.S. Justice Department investigates a proposed merger of two competitors, they must examine financial statements of the businesses — one business may be in a precarious financial condition or not earning enough profit to remain a viable competitor.

- ✔ **Bankers and other lenders** depend heavily on financial statements and other accounting information in deciding whether to loan money to businesses and individuals for business and investment purposes. The character and collateral of the borrower count for a lot, but the accounting numbers also have to be in order.

- ✔ **Individuals who are trying to decipher their retirement fund reports,** but who can't get to first base on what it all means and what their future retirement benefits are, can benefit from a better understanding of accounting and of how things like compound interest work (see Chapter 4).

- ✔ **People who need to understand their personal investments and financial affairs,** such as CDs (certificates of deposit), real estate investments, 401(k) retirement plans, savings accounts, auto loans, home mortgages, and so on, can benefit from some basic accounting knowledge.

> ✓ **Individuals and families reading books and articles on personal financial planning** bump into accounting terms, concepts, and examples that they don't understand; frequently they are not certain about how things are being accounted for.

> ✓ **Politicians, social scientists, economists, journalists, and ordinary citizens** need a good understanding of how business and the investment markets work. Accounting provides the fundamental framework.

I assume that you want to know something about accounting because it's an excellent gateway for understanding how business works, and it gives you an indispensable vocabulary for moving up in the business and investment worlds. Finding out more about accounting helps you understand earnings reports, mergers and takeovers, frauds and Ponzi (pyramid) schemes, and business restructurings.

Let me point out one other very practical assumption that I have regarding why you should know some accounting — I call it the *defensive* reason. A lot of people out there in the cold, cruel financial world may take advantage of you, not necessarily by illegal means, but by withholding key information and by diverting your attention away from unfavorable aspects of certain financial decisions. These unscrupulous characters treat you as a lamb waiting to be fleeced. The best defense against such tactics is to learn some accounting basics, which can help you ask the right questions and understand the financial points that tricksters don't want you to know.

How This Book Is Organized

This book is divided into parts, and each part is further divided into chapters. The following sections describe what you can find in each part.

Part I: Accounting Basics

Part I of *Accounting For Dummies* introduces accounting to non-accountants and discusses the basic features of bookkeeping and accounting record-keeping systems. This part also talks about taxes of all kinds involved in running a business, as well as accounting in the everyday lives of individuals.

Part II: Getting a Grip on Financial Statements

Part II moves on to the end product of the accounting process — *financial statements*. Three main financial statements are prepared every period — one for each financial imperative of business: making *profit*, keeping *financial condition* in good shape, and controlling *cash flow*. The nature of profit and the financial effects of profit are explained in Chapter 5. Profit is more involved than you probably think, to say the least. The basic format of the profit report, called the *income statement,* is presented — including the topic of unusual gains and losses in addition to the normal revenue and expenses of a business.

Business managers and investors should understand the financial turbulence caused by profit-making activities, which can cause changes in a variety of assets and liabilities. A business has to invest in many different assets to support its profit-making activities. A business has to raise a substantial amount of capital either by borrowing money or by persuading owners to invest money in the business — not easy tasks to accomplish, especially for business managers who do not understand financial statement accounting. The assets, liabilities, and owners' capital invested in a business are reported in the *balance sheet,* which is discussed in Chapter 6.

Cash flow from profit and the *cash flow statement* are explained carefully in Chapter 7. The cash flow statement, which would seem to be the easiest financial statement to understand, is not so easy to grasp. Most people are irritated that profit doesn't simply generate cash flow of an equal amount. I am, too, but getting mad doesn't do any good. I can't think of a more important topic that business managers and investors need to understand clearly.

The last chapter in this part, Chapter 8, explains what managers have to do to get financial statements ready for the annual financial report of the business to its owners. This chapter explains the kinds of disclosures that are included in the annual financial report, in addition to the three financial statements. Also, I discuss frankly and openly the touchy topic of massaging the accounting numbers in financial statements.

Part III: Accounting Tools and Techniques for Business Managers

Business managers should know their financial statements like the backs of their hands. However, just understanding these reports is not the end of accounting for managers. Chapter 9 kicks off this part with an extraordinarily important topic — building a basic profit model that clearly focuses a business on the key variables that drive profit. This model is necessary, indeed absolutely critical, for decision-making analysis on topics such as changing sales prices, increasing sales volume, changing product costs, and the other factors for which managers are responsible. The importance of profit margin and sales volume is stressed in this chapter.

Chapter 10 discusses accounting-based planning and control techniques, especially *budgeting*. Business managers and owners have to decide on the best business ownership structure, which I discuss in Chapter 11. Managers in manufacturing businesses should be wary of how product costs are determined — as Chapter 12 explains. The broader topic of economic and accounting cost concepts is also discussed in that chapter.

Choosing accounting methods for recording expenses is not a cut-and-dried process; managers have to make tough decisions. Chapter 13 identifies and explains the alternative accounting methods for expenses and how the choice of method has a major impact on profit for the period, and on the cost of inventory and fixed assets reported in the balance sheet. This chapter covers how managers can work closely with accountants in select-ing the best accounting methods for their businesses — and how investors should be aware of which accounting methods are being used by the business in which they may want to invest.

Part IV: Financial Reporting to the Outside World

Part IV explains financial statement accounting for investors. Chapter 14 explains how to speed-read through a financial report. If you were a profes-sional investment manager of a mutual fund with a large staff of financial analysts, you and your staff would read carefully through the entire financial report of every business you've invested in or are thinking of investing in. You're talking about millions of dollars of investments. However, ordinary individual investors do not have this kind of time to spend. Instead, I present a speed-reading approach that concentrates on the key financial ratios to look for in a financial report.

Also, you should read the CPA auditor's report for assurance that the financial statements are reliable, or whether the auditor has some concerns that you should be aware of. The scope of the annual audit and what to look for in the auditor's report are explained in Chapter 15, which also explains the role of CPA auditors as enforcers of financial accounting and disclosure standards.

Part V: The Part of Tens

This part of the book presents two chapters — Chapter 16 presents some practical ideas for managers to help them put their accounting knowledge to use. Chapter 17 gives business investors some handy tips on things to look for in a financial report, tips that can make the difference between making a good investment and a not-so-good one.

Appendixes

At the back of the book, you can find two helpful appendixes that can assist you on your accounting safari. Appendix A, "Glossary: Slashing through the Accounting Jargon Jungle," provides you with a handy, succinct glossary of accounting terms. Appendix B, "Accounting Software," fills you in on the right questions to ask when deciding on an accounting software program for your business, and offers some suggestions on which software packages are best.

Icons Used in This Book

This icon calls your attention to particularly important points and offers useful advice on practical financial topics. This icon saves you the cost of buying a yellow highlighter pen.

This icon serves as a friendly reminder that the topic at hand is important enough for you to put a note about it in the front of your wallet. This icon marks material that your college professor might put on the board before class starts, noting the important points that you should remember at the end of class.

Accounting is the language of business, and, like all languages, the vocabulary of accounting contains many specialized terms. This icon identifies key accounting terms and their definitions. You can also check the glossary (Appendix A) to find definitions of unfamiliar terms.

This icon is a caution sign that warns you about speed bumps and potholes on the accounting highway. Taking special note of this material can steer you around a financial road hazard and keep you from blowing a fiscal tire. In short — watch out!

I use this icon sparingly; it refers to very specialized accounting stuff that is heavy-going, which only a CPA could get really excited about. However, you may find these topics important enough to return to when you have the time. Feel free to skip over these points the first time through and stay with the main discussion.

 This icon alerts you that I'm using a practical example to illustrate and clarify an important accounting point. You can apply the example to your business or to a business in which you invest.

 This icon points out especially important ideas and accounting concepts that are particularly deserving of your attention. The material marked by this icon describes concepts that are the undergirding and building blocks of accounting — concepts that you should be very clear about, and that clarify your understanding of accounting principles in general.

Where to Go from Here

If you're new to the accounting game, by all means, start with Part I. However, if you already have a good background in business and know something about bookkeeping and financial statements, you may want to jump right into Part II of this book, starting with Chapter 5. Part III is on accounting tools and techniques for managers and assumes that you have a handle on the financial statements material in Part II. Part IV stands on its own; if your main interest in accounting is to make sense of and interpret financial statements, you can read through Part II on financial statements and then jump to Part IV on reading financial reports. If you have questions about specific accounting terms, you can go directly to the glossary in Appendix A.

I've had a lot of fun writing this book. I sincerely hope that it helps you become a better business manager and investor, and that it aids you in your personal financial affairs. I also hope that you enjoy the book. I've tried to make accounting as fun as possible, even though it's a fairly serious subject. Just remember that accountants never die; they just lose their balance. Hey, accountants have a sense of humor, too.

Part I
Accounting Basics

In this part . . .

Accounting is important in all walks of life, and it's absolutely essential in the world of business. Accountants are the bookkeepers and scorekeepers of business. Without accounting, a business couldn't function; it wouldn't know whether it's making a profit, and it wouldn't know its financial situation. Book-keeping — the recording-keeping part of accounting — must be managed well to make sure that all the financial information needed to run the business is complete, accurate, and reliable, especially the numbers reported in financial statements and tax returns.

Speaking of taxes, you can't take more than three or four steps before bumping into taxes. No one likes to pay taxes, but managers must collect and pay taxes in running a business. In addition to income taxes, accounting plays a bigger role in your personal financial affairs than you might realize. This part of the book explains all this and more.

Chapter 1

Introducing Accounting to Non-Accountants

*M*ost medium to large businesses employ one or more accountants. Have you ever thought, why? What do these bean counters with the green eyeshades do, anyway? Probably the first thing you think of is that accountants keep the books — they keep the records of the financial activities of the business. But accountants perform other very critical, but less well-known, functions in a business:

✔ Accountants carry out vital back-office operating functions that keep the business running smoothly and effectively — including payroll, cash inflows and cash payments, purchases and inventory, and property records.

✔ Accountants prepare *tax returns,* including the federal income tax return for the business, as well as payroll and property tax returns.

✔ Accountants determine how to measure and record the costs of products and how to allocate common costs among different departments and other organizational units of the business.

✔ Accountants are the *professional profit scorekeepers* of the business world. They prepare reports for the managers of a business, which keep managers informed about costs and expenses, how sales are going, whether the cash balance is adequate, what's the inventory situation, and, the most important thing — accountants help managers understand on the reasons for changes in the bottom-line performance of a business.

✔ Accountants prepare *financial statements* that help the owners and stockholders of a business understand where the business stands financially. Stockholders wouldn't invest in a business without a clear understanding of the financial health business, which regular financial reports (which I sometimes just call *the financials*) provide.

In short, accountants are much more than bookkeepers — they provide the critical numbers to help business managers make good decisions, which keep a business on course toward its financial objectives.

Business managers, investors, and others who depend on financial statements should be willing to meet accountants halfway. People who use accounting information, like spectators at a football game, should know the basic rules of play and know how score is kept. The purpose of this book is to make you a knowledgeable spectator of the accounting game.

Accounting extends into virtually every walk of life. You're doing accounting when you make entries in your checkbook and fill out your federal income tax return. When you sign a mortgage on your home, you should know how the lender is going to account for your loan payments. Individual investors need to understand some accounting in order to figure the return on capital invested. And every organization, profit-motivated or not, needs to know how it stands financially. Accounting supplies all that information.

In your everyday business and personal life, many different kinds of accounting exist:

✔ There's accounting for organizations and accounting for individuals.

✔ There's accounting for profit-motivated businesses and accounting for non-profit-motivated organizations (such as hospitals, homeowners' associations, churches, credit unions, and colleges).

✔ There's income tax accounting while you're living and estate tax accounting after you die.

✔ There's accounting for farmers who grow their products, accounting for miners who extract their products from the earth, accounting for producers who manufacture products, and accounting for retailers who sell products that others make.

✔ There's accounting for businesses and professional firms that sell services rather than products, such as the entertainment, transportation, and health care industries.

✔ There's past-historical-based accounting and future-forecast-oriented accounting (that is, budgets and financial plans).

✔ There's accounting where periodic financial statements are mandatory (businesses are the primary example) and accounting where such formal accounting reports are not required.

✔ There's accounting that adheres to cost (most businesses) and accounting that records changes in market value (mutual funds, for example).

✔ There's accounting in the private sector of the economy and accounting in the public (government) sector.

✔ There's accounting for going-concern businesses that will be around for some time and accounting for businesses in bankruptcy that may not be around tomorrow.

Accounting is necessary in any free-market capitalist economic system. It's equally necessary in a centrally controlled, socialist economic system. All economic activity moves on information. The more developed the economic system, the more it depends on information. Much of the information comes from the accounting systems used by the businesses, individuals, and other institutions in the economic system.

Some of the earliest records of history are the accounts of wealth and trading activity. Scribes, the earliest names for the official bookkeepers and accountants of the day, were respected because they could read and write and knew how to keep records. The need for accounting information was a main incentive in the development of the numbering system we use today. In his classic textbook, Professor William A. Paton, a well-known accounting professor at the University of Michigan for many years (who lived to be over 100), put it very well in his classic book, *Essentials of Accounting* (published by the Macmillan Company):

> "In a broad sense accounting has one primary function: facilitating the administration of economic activity. This function has two closely related phases: (1) measuring and arraying economic data; [and] (2) communicating the results of this process to interested parties."

The Basic Elements of Accounting

I like Professor Paton's short definition because it strikes at the basic purpose of accounting. However, the definition does side-step around one aspect of accounting — *bookkeeping* (which you can find out more about in Chapter 2). Accounting certainly involves bookkeeping, which refers to the painstaking and detailed recording of economic activity and business transactions. But *accounting* is a much broader term that refers to the *design* of the bookkeeping system. It addresses the many problems in measuring the financial effects of economic activity and events and then communicating these economic measures of value and performance to non-accountants in a clear and concise manner — a diverse range of people need this accounting information to make good economic decisions.

Accountants design the *internals controls* in an accounting system, which serve to minimize errors in the large number of entries that a business records over the period. The internal controls that accountants design can detect and deter theft, embezzlement, fraud, and dishonest behavior of all kinds. In accounting, internal controls are the ounce of prevention that are worth a pound of cure.

Seldom does an accountant prepare a complete listing of all activities that took place during a period. Instead, he or she prepares a *summary financial statement,* which shows *totals,* not a complete listing of all the individual activities making up the total. Managers may occasionally need to search through a detailed list of all the specific transactions that make up the total, but this is not common. Most managers just want summary financial statements for the period — if they want to drill down into the details making up a total amount for the period, they can ask the accountant for this more detailed backup information. Also, outside investors usually only see these summary-level financial statements.

Financial statements are prepared at the end of each accounting period. A period may be one month, or one quarter (three calendar months), or one year. One basic type of accounting report prepared at the end of the period is a "Where do we stand at the end of the period?" type of report. This is called the *Statement of Financial Condition* or, more commonly, the *balance sheet.* A balance sheet shows two sides of the business. On the one side are listed in order the *assets* of the business, which are its economic resources being used in the business, and on the other side is a breakdown of where the assets came from, or the sources of the assets.

Assets are not like manna from the heavens. They come from borrowing money on the basis of loans that have to be paid back at a later date, and from owners' investment of capital (usually money) in the business. Also, making profit increases the assets of the business; profit retained in the business is the third basic source of assets. If a business has, say, $2.5 million in total assets (without knowing which particular assets the business holds), I know that the total of its liabilities, plus capital invested by its owners, plus its retained profit, adds up to $2.5 million.

This basic equality between total assets and total sources of assets is the foundation of *double-entry bookkeeping* and is the reason that the statement of financial condition is called the balance sheet. If students remember one thing from their introductory accounting course, it's that

```
Assets = Liabilities + Owners' Equity
```

The other financial statements are different than the balance sheet in one important respect: they summarize the significant *flows* of activities and operations over the period. For a business, accountants prepare two types of summary flow reports:

- ✔ The **income statement** summarizes the inflows of assets from the sale of products and services during the period. The income statement also summarizes the outflow of assets for expenses during the period — leading down to the well-known *bottom line,* or final profit or loss for the period.

- ✔ The **cash flow statement** summarizes the business's cash inflows and outflows during the period, starting with the net cash increase or decrease from the profit reported in the Income Statement. The cash flow statement also shows other sources of cash and uses of cash during the period.

Business entities need accounting reports for three essential purposes:

- ✔ **Tax returns** are prepared to determine the amount of tax owed for the period as required by income tax, payroll, and property tax laws.

- ✔ **Accounting reports keep managers informed** about what's going on and the financial position of the business. These accounting reports are absolutely essential to help managers control the performance of a business, identify problems as they come up, and plan the future course of a business.

- ✔ **External financial statements** go to those persons outside a business who need to stay informed about the business's financial affairs. These individuals may have invested capital in the business, or the business may owe them money, for example; therefore they have a financial interest in how well the business is doing.

The jargon jungle of accounting

Financial statements include many terms that are reasonably clear and straightforward, like cash, accounts receivable, fixed assets, and accounts payable. However, financial statements also use words like retained earnings, accumulated depreciation, accelerated depreciation, accrued expenses, reserve, allowance, accrual basis, and current assets. This type of jargon in accounting is like ugly on an ape: It's everywhere you look.

The real irony is that accounting is often called the "language of business." Accountants use some of the most baffling terminology you'll ever hear (well, medical terminology and some legal terms may be worse). Accountants know the definitions of their specialized vocabulary and they assume that non-accountants know all these terms as well. The result is that many financial statements seem to many business managers and investors to be written in Greek. Furthermore, financial statements do not come with a glossary — such as the one that you can find at the end of this book. If you have any doubt about a term as I go along in the book, please take a quick look in Appendix A, which defines many accounting terms in plain English.

Accounting and Financial Reporting Standards

Imagine if every business could invent its own accounting methods and terminology for measuring profit and for presenting financial statements. As an example from the academic world, what if I give a student an *A* for a course and a professor at another university gives a student a *K?* Keeping track of academic performance would be pretty tough without some recognized and accepted standards.

Experience and common sense have taught business and financial professionals that uniform financial reporting standards and methods are also critical in a free-enterprise, private, capital-based economic system. A common vocabulary, uniform accounting methods, and full disclosure in financial reports are the goals. How well the accounting profession performs in achieving these goals is an open question, but few disagree that these are worthy goals to strive for.

The supremacy of GAAP (Generally Accepted Accounting Principles)

The most important financial statement and financial reporting standards and rules are called *generally accepted accounting principles (GAAP),* which describe the basic methods to measure profit and to value assets and liabilities, as well as what information should be disclosed in external financial statements. If you're reading the financial statements of a business, you're entitled to assume that the business has used GAAP in providing adequate disclosure about its cash flows and profit, and its financial condition at the end of a financial period.

If financial statements violate GAAP and you suffer a loss because you took the financial information at face value (you made decisions based on the accounting information in the statements), you probably have grounds to sue the business for damages. For this reason, if no other, business managers should be aware of GAAP and should make certain that their accountants apply GAAP in preparing the business's financial statements.

A practical example of GAAP: Why the rules are important

Business managers should know the basic features of GAAP — though certainly not all the technical details — so that they understand how profit is measured. Managers get paid to make profit, and they should be very clear on how profit is measured and what profit consists of. Basically, what I'm saying here is that profit depends on how it's defined and measured.

For example, a business buys and holds products for sale; the stockpile of these products is called *inventory*. A business records the purchase of products at cost, which is the amount it paid for the products. Inventory is the stockpile of products being held for sale to customers. Examples include clothes in a department store, fuel in the tanks in a gas station, food on the shelves in a supermarket, books in a bookstore, and so on. The cost of products is put in the inventory asset account and kept there until the products are sold to customers. When the products are eventually sold, the cost of the products are recorded as the cost of goods sold expense, at which time a decrease is recorded in the inventory asset account. The cost of products sold is deducted from the sales revenue received from the customers, which gives a first-step measure of profit. (A business has many other expenses, which you can read about in later chapters.)

Now, assume that before the business sells the products to its customers, the replacement cost of many of the products being held in inventory awaiting sale increases. The replacement cost value of the products is now higher than the original, actual purchase cost of the products. The company's inventory is worth more, is it not? Perhaps the business could raise the sales prices that it charges its customers because of the cost increase, or perhaps not. In any case, should the increase in the replacement cost of the products be recorded as profit? The manager may think that this holding gain should be recorded as profit. But accounting standards (GAAP) say that no profit is earned until the products are sold to the customers.

What about the opposite movement in replacement costs of products — when replacement costs fall below the original purchase costs? Should this development be recorded as a loss, or should the business wait until the products are sold? As you'll see, the accounting rule that applies here is called *lower of cost or market,* and the loss is recorded. So the rule requires one method on the upside but another method on the downside. See why business managers and investors need to know something about the rules of the game?

Income tax and accounting rules

Generally speaking (and I'm being very general when I say the following), the federal income tax accounting rules for determining the annual taxable income of a business are in agreement with GAAP. This makes sense because having two entirely different sets of methods of measuring profit would be very inefficient and impractical. In short, accounting for taxable income and accounting for business profit before income tax are in general agreement. Having said this, I should point out that differences do exist here and there. A business may use one accounting method for filing its annual income tax returns and a different method of measuring its profit both for management reporting purposes and for preparing its external financial statements to outsiders.

Flexibility in accounting standards

An often-repeated accounting story concerns a CPA interviewing for an important accounting position with a business. The CPA is asked one key question: "What's 2 plus 2?" Candidate #1 answers 4, and is told, "Don't call us, we'll call you." Candidate #2 answers, "Well, most of the time the answer is 4, but sometimes it's 3 and sometimes it's 5." Candidate #3, being very shrewd, answers: "What do you want the answer to be?" Guess who got the job?

The point is that GAAP are not entirely airtight or cut-and-dried. Many accounting standards leave a lot of room for interpretation. *Guidelines* would be a better way to describe some accounting rules. Deciding how to account for certain transactions and situations requires flexibility, seasoned judgment, and careful interpretation of the rules.

Sometimes, accountants use what's called *creative accounting* to make profit for the period look better. Like lawyers who know where to find loopholes, accountants sometimes come up with "inventive" solutions, but still stay within the guidelines of GAAP. I warn you about these creative accounting techniques — also called *massaging the numbers* — at various points in this book.

Enforcing Accounting Rules

As I mentioned in the preceding sections, when preparing financial statements, a business must follow generally accepted accounting principles (GAAP) — the authoritative ground rules for measuring profit and for putting values on assets and liabilities. Everyone reading a financial report is entitled to assume that GAAP have been followed.

The basic idea behind GAAP is to measure profit and to value assets and liabilities *consistently* from business to business — to establish broad-scale uniformity in accounting methods for all businesses. The idea is to make sure that all accountants are singing from the same hymnal and the same tune, so to speak. Also, the purpose is to establish realistic and objective methods for measuring profit and putting values on assets and liabilities. The authoritative bodies write the songs that accountants have to sing.

GAAP also include minimum requirements for *disclosure,* which refers to how information is classified and presented in financial statements and to the types of information that have to be added to the financial statements in the form of footnotes. Chapter 8 explains these disclosures that are required in addition to the three primary financial statements of a business (the income statement, balance sheet, and cash flow statement).

The official GAAP rule book is *big* — more than a thousand pages! These rules have evolved over many decades — some rules remaining the same for many years, some being superseded and modified from time to time, and new rules being added. Recently, official pronouncements have been coming out at the rate of four or five a year from the Financial Accounting Standards Board, the body that generates the GAAP.

Changes in accounting rules can have big effects. Consider that recently, the accounting methods for post-retirement medical and hospital benefits paid by businesses to their retired employees were recently changed (after much rancor and heated debate). This new accounting standard resulted in billion-dollar, one-time, catch-up charge-offs by many large corporations for the years of expenses that they had not recorded before. You may also find it interesting that the cash flow statement was made mandatory in 1987. You may have thought that this important financial statement had been around a long time, but it became a required statement only recently.

How do you know if businesses actually follow the rules faithfully? I think it boils down to two factors. First is the competence and ethical standards of accountants who prepare financial reports. No substitute exists for the expertise and integrity of the accountants who prepare financial reports. But accountants often come under intense pressure from the higher-level executives they work for in business organizations.

Which leads to the second factor — that businesses have their financial statements audited by independent CPAs. In fact, public businesses are required to have annual audits by outside CPAs; many private businesses hire CPAs to do an annual audit, even if not legally required. Chapter 15 explains audits and why investors should read carefully the auditor's report on the financial statements.

The Accounting Department: Behind the Scenes in the Back Office

As I discussed earlier in this chapter, bookkeeping (or record-keeping) and financial reporting to managers and investors are the core functions of accounting. In this section, I explain another basic function of a business's accounting department: the "back-office" functions that keep the business running smoothly.

Most people don't realize the importance of the accounting department's functions. That's probably because accountants do many of the back-office operating functions in a business — as opposed to sales, for example, which is front-line activity, out in the open and in the line of fire. Go into any retail store, and you're in the thick of sales activities. But have you ever seen a company's accounting department in action?

Folks may not think much about these back-office activities, but they would sure notice if those activities didn't get done. On payday, a business had better not tell its employees, "Sorry, but the accounting department is running a little late this month; you'll get your checks later." And when a customer insists on up-to-date information about how much he or she owes to the business, the accounting department can't very well say, "Oh, don't worry, just wait a week or so and we'll get the information to you then."

Typically, the accounting department is responsible for:

✔ **Payroll:** The total wages and salaries earned by every employee every pay period, which are called *gross wages* or *gross earnings,* have to be determined. Based on detailed private information in personnel files and earnings-to-date information, the correct amount of income tax, social security tax, and several other deductions from gross wages have to be determined.

Next, accountants prepare payroll checks, which must also include various information that has to be reported to employees every pay period. The total amounts of withheld income tax and social security taxes, plus the employment taxes imposed on the employer, have to be paid over to federal and state government agencies right away. Retirement, vacation, sick pay, and other benefits earned by the employees also have to be updated every pay period. In short, payroll is a complex and critical function that the accounting department performs.

✔ **Cash inflows:** All cash received from sales to customers and from all other sources has to be carefully identified and recorded, not only in the cash account but also in the appropriate account for the source of the cash received. The accounting department makes sure that the cash is deposited in the appropriate checking accounts of the business and that an adequate amount of coin and currency is kept on hand for making change for customers. Accountants balance the checkbook of the business and control who has access to incoming cash receipts. (In larger organizations, the *Treasurer* may be responsible for some of these cash flow and cash-handling functions.)

✔ **Cash payments:** In addition to payroll checks, a business writes many other checks during the course of a year — to pay for a wide variety of purchases, for property taxes, to pay off loans, and to distribute some of its profit to the owners of the business, for example. The accounting department prepares all these checks for the signatures of the designated business officers of the business who are authorized to sign checks. The accounting department keeps all the supporting business documents and files to know when the checks should be paid, makes sure that the amount to be paid is correct, and forwards the checks for signature.

✔ **Purchases and inventory:** Accounting departments usually are responsible for keeping track of all purchase orders that have been placed for inventory (products to be sold by the business) and all other assets and services that the business buys — from postage stamps to forklift trucks. A typical business makes many purchases during the course of a year, many of them on credit, which means that the items bought are reveived today but paid for later. So this area of responsibility includes keeping files on all liabilities that arise from purchases on credit so that cash payments can be processed on time. The accounting department also keeps detailed records on all inventory of products held for sale by the business and, when the products are sold, records the cost of the goods sold.

✔ **Property accounting:** A typical business holds many different assets called *property* — including office furniture and equipment, retail display cabinets, computers, machinery and tools, vehicles (autos and trucks), buildings, and land. Except for relatively small-cost items, such as screwdrivers and pencil sharpeners, a business has to maintain detailed records of its property, both for controlling the use of the assets and for determining personal property and real estate taxes. The accounting department keeps these property records.

The accounting department may be assigned other functions as well, but I think that this list gives you a pretty clear idea of the back-office functions that the accounting department performs. Quite literally, a business could not operate if the accounting department did not do these functions efficiently and on time.

Focusing on Business Transactions and Other Financial Events

It's very important to understand that a great deal of accounting focuses on business *transactions,* which are economic exchanges between a business and the persons and other businesses with which the business deals. Transactions are the lifeblood of every business, the heartbeat of activity that keeps the business going. Understanding accounting to a large extent means understanding how transactions are accounted for.

A business carries on economic exchanges with six basic groups:

✔ Its **customers,** who buy the products and services that the business sells.

✔ Its **employees,** who provide services to the business and are paid wages and salaries and provided with a broad range of benefits, such as a retirement plan, health and medical insurance, workers' compensation, and unemployment insurance.

✔ Its **suppliers** and **vendors,** who sell to the business a wide range of things, such as legal advice, electricity and gas, telephone service, computers, vehicles, tools and equipment, furniture, and audits.

✔ Its **debt sources of capital,** who loan money to the business, charge interest on the amount loaned, and have to be repaid at definite dates in the future.

✔ Its **equity sources of capital,** or individuals and financial institutions who invest money in the business and expect the business to earn profit on the capital they invested.

✔ The **government,** or the federal, state, and local agencies who collect income taxes, payroll taxes, and property taxes from the business.

Figure 1-1 illustrates the interactions between the business and the other parties in the economic exchange.

Figure 1-1:
The six-spoke wheel of business transactions between a business and the parties with which it engages in economic exchanges.

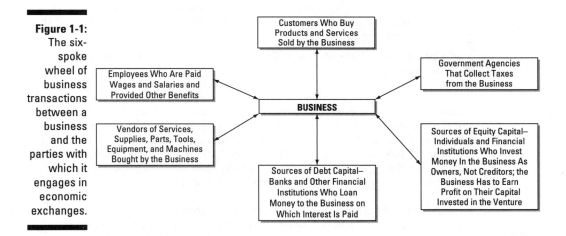

Even a relatively small business generates a surprisingly large number of transactions, and all transactions have to be recorded. Certain other *events* that have a financial impact on the business have to be recorded as well. These are called events because they are not based on give-and-take bargaining — unlike the something-given-for-something-received nature of economic exchanges. Developments such as the following cause economic impact on a business and have to be recorded as events:

✔ A business may lose a lawsuit and be ordered to pay damages. The liability to pay the damages has to be recorded.

✔ A business may suffer a flood loss that is uninsured. The assets have to be written off and removed from the account kept for the asset. For example, products that were being held for sale to customers (until they floated down the river) must be removed from the inventory account.

✔ A business may decide to shut down a major product line and downsize its workforce, requiring that severance be paid to laid-off employees.

Taking a Closer Look at Financial Statements

As I mentioned in the preceding sections, accountants prepare certain basic financial statements for a business. The three basic financial statements are the following:

- ✔ **Statement of financial condition (or balance sheet):** A summary of the financial situation of the business at the end of the period.

- ✔ **Income statement:** A summary of sales revenue and expenses that determines the profit (or loss) for the period just ended. In the old days, this was called the *profit and loss statement,* or simply the *P&L statement.* (Alternate titles include the statement of operations and the statement of earnings.)

- ✔ **Cash flow statement:** A summary of cash inflows and cash outflows for the period just ended.

This section gives you a preview of these statements, which constitute a business's financial center of gravity. I show you the general format and content of these three accounting reports. The president and chief executive officer of a business (plus other top-level managers and financial officers) are responsible for seeing that the financial statements are prepared according to financial reporting standards and that proper accounting methods have been used to prepare the financial statements.

If a business's financial statements are discovered later to be seriously in error or misleading, the business and its top executives can be sued for damages suffered by lenders and investors who relied on the financial statements. For this reason, business managers should understand their financial statements and the accounting methods used to prepare the statements. In a court of law, they can't plead ignorance.

I frequently meet managers who don't seem to have a clue about the three primary financial statements. This situation is a little scary; a manager who doesn't understand financial statements is like an airplane pilot who doesn't understand the instrument readouts in the cockpit. A manager *could* run the business and "land the plane safely," but knowing how to read the vital signs along the way is much more prudent.

Understanding financial reports is so important that *Business Week* magazine featured a cover story on the topic. In the November 25, 1996, issue, the magazine cited the National Association of Corporate Directors' new guidelines for enhancing the professionalism of board of director members. One of the key recommendations says:

"Directors should know how to read a balance sheet, an income statement, and a cash flow statement, and they should understand the use of financial ratios and other indices for evaluating company performance."

In short, business managers at all levels — from the board of directors down to the lower rungs on the management ladder, and especially managers of smaller businesses who have to be a jack-of-all-trades in running the business — need to understand financial statements and the accounting methods used to prepare the statements. Also, lenders to business, investors in business, business lawyers, government regulators of business, entrepreneurs, employees who depend on the continued financial success of the business for their jobs, anyone thinking of becoming an entrepreneur and starting a business, and, yes, even economists should know the basics of financial statement accounting. I've noticed that even experienced business journalists, who ought to know better, sometimes refer to the balance sheet when they're talking about profit performance. The bottom line is found in the income statement, not the balance sheet!

The common meeting ground for these different groups are the three primary financial statements that accountants prepare, which are the touchstones for every business.

The balance sheet (or statement of financial condition)

This essential financial statement summarizes the *assets* owned by a business on one side and the sources of its assets on the other side. Sources of assets divide into two basic categories: *liabilities* and *owners' equity*. Some of the total assets of a business are from borrowing money or buying things on credit that haven't been paid for yet. Collectively, these are called liabilities. So a part of a business's total assets comes from its liabilities.

The remainder of total assets comes from *owners' equity,* which is a collective term for two quite different things:

- ✔ Money invested in a business by its owners
- ✔ Profit that the business has earned and retained

You generally see the balance sheet in the following layout:

Basic Format of the Balance Sheet

List of **Assets**, or the economic resources the business owns; examples are cash on deposit in bank checking accounts, products held for sale to customers, and buildings.	List of **Liabilities**, which arise from borrowing money and buying things on credit.
	Owners' Equity, which arises from two sources: money invested by the owners, and profit earned and retained by the business.
Total Assets =	*Total Liabilities + Owners' Equity*

Owner's equity is sometimes referred to as *net worth*. You compute net worth as follows:

```
Assets - Liabilities = Net Worth
```

Net worth is not a good term, because it implies that the business is worth the amount recorded in its owners' equity accounts. Though the term may suggest that the business could be sold for this amount, nothing is further from the truth. (Chapter 6 presents more information about the recorded, or book value of owners' equity reported in the balance sheet, and why current replacement costs of some assets may be higher than the book values of these assets. Chapter 14 discusses the market prices of stock shares, which are units of ownership in a business corporation.)

The income statement

This all-important financial statement summarizes the profit-making activities of a business over a period. In very broad outline, this statement is reported like this:

Basic Format of the Income Statement

Sales Revenue (from the sales of products and services to customers)

− **Expenses** (which include a wide variety of costs paid by the business, including the cost of products sold to customers, wages and benefits paid to employees, occupancy costs, administrative costs, and income tax)

= **Net Income** (which is referred to as the "bottom line" and means final profit after all expenses are deducted from sales revenue)

The income statement gets the most attention from business managers and investors — not that they ignore the other two financial statements. The very abbreviated versions of income statements that you see in the financial press, such as in *The Wall Street Journal,* report only the top line (sales revenue) and the bottom line (net income). The income statement in actual practice is more involved than the basic format shown here. (See Chapter 5 for more information on income statements.)

The cash flow statement

This very important financial statement presents a summary of the sources and uses of cash in a business during a financial period. Smart business managers hardly get the word *profit* out of their mouths before mentioning *cash flow.* Successful business managers can tell you that they have to manage both profit *and* cash flow; you can't do one and ignore the other. Business is a two-headed dragon in this respect. Ignoring cash flow can pull the rug out from under a successful profit formula. Still, some managers become preoccupied with making profit and overlook cash flow. Managers should know better, but they may assume that profit equals cash flow. It doesn't!

For financial reporting, cash flows are divided into three basic categories:

Basic Format of the Cash Flow Statement

(1) Cash flow from the profit-making activities, or **operating activities,** for the period (*Note: Operating* means the profit-making transactions of the business.)

(2) Cash inflows and outflows from **investing activities** for the period

(3) Cash inflows and outflows from the **financing activities** for the period

You determine the bottom-line net increase (or decrease) in cash during the period by summing the three types of cash flows shown in the preceding list.

Part (1) is an important part of the cash flow statement because it explains why net cash flow from sales revenue and expenses — the business's profit-making operating activities — is more or less than the amount of profit reported in the income statement. The basic reasons are that the *actual* cash flow and expenses from sales run on a different timetable than when the sales revenue and expenses are recorded on the books. It's like two different trains going to the same destination — the second train (the cash flow train) runs on a later schedule than the first train (the recording of sales revenue and expenses in the accounts of the business). As I mention earlier, the cash flow analysis of net income, or cash flow from profit, as it's also called, is a little complicated. Chapter 7 explains the cash-flow analysis of profit as well as the other sources of cash and the uses of cash.

Part (2) of the cash flow statement sums up the major long-term investments of capital made by the business during the year, such as constructing a new production plant or replacing machinery and equipment. If the business sold any of its long-term assets, it reports the cash inflows from these divestments in this section of the cash flow statement.

Part (3) sums up the financing activities of the business during the period — borrowing new money from lenders and raising new capital investment in the business from its owners. Cash outflows to pay off debt are reported in this section, as well as cash distributions from profit paid to the owners of the business.

The last line of the cash flow statement reports the net increase or net decrease in cash during the year, caused by the three types of cash flows. By the way, the last line in the cash flow statement is never referred to as *the bottom line*. This term is strictly limited to the last line of the income statement, which reflects net income — the final profit after all expenses are deducted. It's all right to say that the bottom line in the cash flow statement is the net increase in cash during the year, but if you just used the term *bottom line* without any further reference to what you mean, an accountant would assume that you mean the bottom line of the income statement.

I should point out that the profit performance of a public business is big news and gets most of the attention in the financial press and in the annual financial report of a business. Everyone looks at how the business did profit-wise first, and then they look at the other information in the financial statements. This can be compared with how most people read their daily newspaper — they turn to the sports page headline or favorite comic strip first, and then they move on to reading the rest of the newspaper. The net increase or net decrease in cash is seldom in the spotlight. However, the amount of cash flow from profit — reported in Part (1) of the cash flow statement — is getting more and more attention these days, and for good reason. Chapter 7 explains why this internal source of cash is so important.

Accounting as a Career

In our highly developed economy, many people make their living as accountants — and here I'm using the term *accountant* in the broadest possible sense. According to the *1995 Statistical Abstract of the United States* (Table No. 649, page 411), about 1.5 million people in the United States work force are accountants and auditors. A little more than half are women, which is quite an improvement compared to a generation ago. About one-third of these accountants work for independent establishments that offer their accounting and auditing services to the public. The other two-thirds are employed by businesses, government agencies, nonprofit organizations, and other organizations and associations.

Certified Public Accountants

In the accounting profession, the mark of distinction is the *CPA,* which stands for *Certified Public Accountant.* The term *Public* means that the person has had some practical experience working for a CPA firm; it does not necessarily indicate whether that person is presently in *public* practice (as an individual CPA or as an employee or partner in a CPA firm that offers services to the public at large) rather than working exclusively for one organization.

To become a Certified Public Accountant (CPA), you go to college, graduate with an accounting major in either a four-year or a five-year program, and pass the two-day national CPA exam, which is prepared and graded by the American Institute of Certified Public Accountants. You also must satisfy professional employment experience; this requirement varies from state to state but generally is one or two years. After satisfying the education, exam, and experience requirements, you get a CPA certificate to hang on your wall. More important, you get a permit from your state to practice as a CPA and offer your services to the public. States now require continuing education hours to be satisfied to maintain their active CPA permits.

The Controller: the top accountant in an organization

After working for a CPA firm in public practice for a few years, most CPAs leave public accounting and go to work for a business or other organization. Usually, they start at a mid-level accounting position with fairly heavy accounting responsibilities, but some step in as the top accountant in charge of all accounting matters of a business. The top-level accountant in a business organization is usually called the *Controller.*

The Controller designs the entire accounting system of the business and keeps it up-to-date with changes in the tax laws and changes in the accounting rules that govern reporting financial statements to outside lenders and owners. Controllers are responsible for hiring, training, evaluating, promoting, and sometimes firing the persons who hold the various book-keeping and accounting positions in an organization — which range from payroll functions to the several different types of tax returns that have to be filed on time with different government agencies.

The Controller is the lead person in the financial planning and budgeting process of the business organization. Furthermore, the Controller designs the accounting reports that all the various managers in the organization receive — from the sales and marketing managers to the purchasing and procurement managers. These internal reports should be designed to fit the authority and responsibility of each manager, and should provide information for their decision-making analysis needs.

The Controller also designs and monitors the accounting reports that go to the business's top-level vice presidents, president, chief executive officer of the business, and board of directors. All tough accounting questions and problems get referred to the Controller. The Controller needs good people management skills, should know how to communicate with all the non-accounting managers in the organization, and at the same time should be an "accountant's accountant" who has deep expertise in many areas of accounting.

Smaller businesses may have only one or two accountants. The full-charge bookkeeper or office manager may carry out many of the duties of the Controller in a larger organization. Smaller businesses often call in a CPA in public practice to advise their accountants. The CPA may function more or less as a part-time Controller for a small business, preparing the income tax returns and helping to prepare the business's external financial reports of the business.

Chapter 2

Bookkeeping 101: From Shoe Boxes to Computers

- -

In This Chapter

▶ Understanding the bookkeeping cycle

▶ Keeping a bookkeeping checklist

▶ Getting down the basics of double-entry bookkeeping

▶ Sniffing out fraudulent bookkeeping

- -

Most folks are lousy bookkeepers just because they really don't do much bookkeeping. Admit it: Maybe you balance your checkbook against your bank statement every month and somehow manage to pull together all the records you need for your annual federal income tax return. But you probably stuff your bills in a drawer and just drag them out once a month when you're ready to pay them. (Hey, that's what I do.) And you almost certainly don't have a detailed listing of all your assets and liabilities (even though a listing of assets is a good idea for fire insurance purposes).

I don't prepare a summary statement of my earnings and income for the year, nor a breakdown of what I spent my money on and how much I saved. Why not? Because I don't need to! Individuals can get along quite well without much bookkeeping — but the exact opposite is true for a business.

One key difference between individuals and businesses is that a business must prepare periodic financial statements, the accuracy of which is critical to the business's very survival. The business uses the accounts and records generated by its bookkeeping process to prepare these statements; if the accounting records are incomplete or inaccurate, the financial statements are incomplete or inaccurate. And inaccuracy simply won't do.

Obviously, then, business managers have to be sure that the company's bookkeeping system is adequate and reliable. This chapter shows you managers what your bookkeepers and accountants do, mainly so that you can make sure that the information coming out of your accounting system is complete and accurate.

Bookkeeping versus Accounting

Bookkeeping is essentially the act of recording all the information regarding the transactions and financial activities of a business — the record-keeping aspects of *accounting*. Bookkeeping is an indispensable subset of accounting. The term *accounting* goes much further, into the realm of designing the bookkeeping system in the first place, establishing controls to make sure that the system is working well, and analyzing and verifying the information recorded. Bookkeepers follow orders; accountants give the orders.

Accounting takes over where bookkeeping ends. Accountants prepare reports based on the information accumulated by the bookkeeping process — financial statements, tax returns, and various confidential reports to managers. Measuring profit is a very important task that accountants perform, a task that depends on the accuracy of the information recorded by the bookkeeper. The accountant decides how to measure sales revenue and expenses to determine the profit or loss for the period. The tough questions about profit — where it is and what it consists of — can't be answered through bookkeeping alone.

The rest of this book doesn't discuss bookkeeping in any detail — no talk of debits and credits and all that stuff. All you really need to know about bookkeeping, as a business manager, is contained in this chapter alone.

Pedaling through the Bookkeeping Cycle

Figure 2-1 presents an overview of the bookkeeping cycle. The basic steps in the sequence are as follows (see "Managing the Bookkeeping System: A Checklist," later in this chapter, for more details on some of these steps):

1. **Record *transactions* — the economic exchanges between a business and the other persons and businesses that it deals with.**

   Transactions have financial effects that must be recorded — the business is better off, worse off, or at least "different off" as the result of its transactions. Examples of typical business transactions include paying employees, making sales to customers, borrowing money from the bank, and buying products that will be sold to customers. The bookkeeping process begins by identifying all transactions and capturing the relevant information about each transaction.

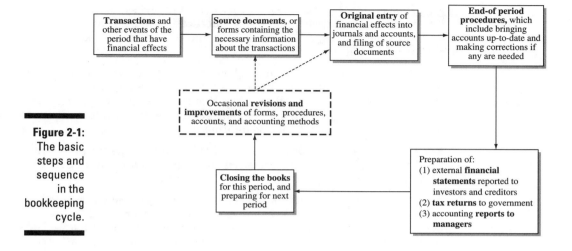

Figure 2-1:
The basic
steps and
sequence
in the
bookkeeping
cycle.

2. Collect *source documents* — transaction documentation that the bookkeeper uses to record the transactions.

When buying products, a business gets a *purchase invoice* from the supplier. When borrowing money from the bank, a business signs a *note payable,* a copy of which is kept by the business. When a customer uses a credit card, such as MasterCard or Visa, to buy the business's product, the business gets the *credit card slip* as evidence of the transaction. When preparing payroll checks, a business depends on *salary rosters* and *time cards* for its employees. These key business forms serve as the source of information into the bookkeeping system, for the bookkeeper to use in recording the financial effects of the transaction.

3. Record original entries (the financial effects of the transactions) into journals and accounts.

The bookkeeper uses the source document to make an original (or initial) entry into a journal and then into the business's accounts. A *journal* is a chronological record of transactions in the order in which they occur — like a personal diary or journal for everything you did day by day. In contrast, an *account* is a separate record for each asset, each liability, and so on. One transaction affects two or more accounts. The journal entry records the whole transaction in one place; then each piece is recorded in the two or more accounts changed by the transaction. In ancient days, bookkeepers had to record these entries by hand, and even today there's nothing wrong with a good hand-entry (manual) bookkeeping system. But bookkeepers now have personal computer accounting software available to take over many of the tedious chores of bookkeeping. Computers have come to the rescue — of course, typing has replaced hand cramps with carpal tunnel syndrome, but at least the work gets done more quickly and with fewer errors! (See Appendix B for more about popular accounting software packages for personal computers.)

I can't exaggerate the importance of entering transaction data correctly and in a timely manner. For example, an important reason that most retailers these days use cash registers that read bar-coded information on products is to more accurately capture the necessary information and to speed up the entry of this information.

4. **Perform end-of-period procedures — preliminary steps for preparing the accounting reports and financial statements at the end of every period.**

   A *period* can be any stretch of time — from one day to one month to one quarter (three months) to one year — and is determined by the needs of the business. A year is the longest period of time that a business would wait to prepare its financial statements. As a matter of fact, most businesses need accounting reports and financial statements at the end of each quarter, and many need monthly financial statements.

   Before the accounting reports can be prepared at the end of the period, the bookkeeper needs to bring the accounts of the business up-to-date and complete the bookkeeping process. One step, for example, is recording the *depreciation expense* for the period (see Chapter 5 for more on depreciation), and another step is getting an actual count of the business's inventory so that the inventory records can be adjusted to account for shoplifting, employee theft, and so on.

   The accountant needs to take the final step and check for errors in the business's accounts. Data entry clerks and bookkeepers may not fully understand the unusual nature of some business transactions and may have entered transactions incorrectly. One reason for establishing *internal controls* (discussed in "Protect the family jewels: internal controls," later in this chapter) is to keep errors to an absolute minimum. Ideally, accounts should contain very few errors at year-end, but the accountant can't be too sure about that and should make a final check for any errors that fell through the cracks during the period.

5. **Prepare reports.**

   The three main types of accounting reports, shown in Figure 2-1, are the result of and the main reason for the time, trouble, and costs of bookkeeping:

   • *Tax returns,* including federal and state income tax returns, payroll tax returns, and property tax returns, all of which are based on the accounting records of the business

   • *Accounting reports to managers,* to provide the information that the managers need for decision-making

- *External financial statements,* which the business sends to the outside world (or, more accurately, to the business's lenders and owners) and which the business may make available to its employees

6. *Close the books* — **bring the bookkeeping for the fiscal year just ended to a close and get things ready to begin the bookkeeping process for the coming fiscal year.**

   Books is the common term for *accounts.* A business's transactions are a constant stream of activities that don't end tidily on the last day of the year, which can make preparing financial statements and tax returns challenging. The business has to draw a clear line of demarcation between activities for the year ended and the year yet to come by *closing the books* for one year and starting with fresh books for the next year.

7. **Revise and improve the bookkeeping procedures and accounting methods, based on a very careful review of the current system.**

   The business may have an *accounting manual* that spells out in great detail the specific accounts and procedures for recording transactions. But all businesses change over time, and they occasionally need to review their accounting system and make revisions. Companies do not take this task lightly; discontinuities in the accounting system can be major shocks and have to be carefully thought out.

The test of a good bookkeeping system is whether all the necessary accounting reports and financial statements are on time, complete, accurate, and reasonably easy to read and interpret. The second test is whether the system enables the accounting department to carry out its support functions effectively and efficiently (see Chapter 1 for more information on these "back-office" functions).

In short, the accounting department has daily, weekly, and monthly operating functions to perform, as well as the preparation of the end-of-period accounting reports to managers, the business's financial statements, and its tax returns.

Managing the Bookkeeping System: A Checklist

In my experience, far too many business managers either ignore their bookkeeping systems or take them for granted — unless something obvious goes wrong. The managers assume that if "the books are in balance," everything is okay. The section "The accounting equation: debits and credits," later in this chapter covers just exactly what "the books being in balance" means — but it does *not* mean that everything is necessarily okay.

To determine whether your bookkeeping system is up-to-snuff, check out the following sections, which taken as a whole provide a checklist of the nine most important elements of a good system.

Categorize your financial information: the chart of accounts

Suppose that you're the accountant for a business corporation and you're faced with the daunting task of preparing the annual federal income tax return for the business, which demands that you report the following kinds of expenses (and the following is only a minimum list!):

- ✔ Advertising
- ✔ Bad debts
- ✔ Charitable contributions
- ✔ Compensation of officers
- ✔ Cost of goods sold
- ✔ Depreciation
- ✔ Employee benefit plans

- ✔ Interest
- ✔ Pension, profit-sharing plans
- ✔ Rents
- ✔ Repairs and maintenance
- ✔ Salaries and wages
- ✔ Taxes and licenses

In addition, you must supplement some of these expenses with additional information. For example, the cost of goods sold expense is determined in a schedule that also requires inventory cost at the beginning of the year, purchases during the year, cost of labor during the year (for manufacturers), other costs, and inventory cost at year-end.

Where do you start? Well, if it's March 1 and the tax return deadline is March 15, you start with panicking — unless you were smart enough to think ahead about the kinds of information your business would need to report. In fact, when your accountant first designs your business's accounting system, he or she should dissect every report to managers, the external financial statements, and the tax returns, breaking down all the information into categories such as those I just listed.

For each category, you need an *account,* a record of the activities in that category. An account is basically a focused history of a particular dimension of a business. Individuals can have accounts, too — for example, your checkbook is an account of the cash inflows and outflows and the balance of your checking account (assuming that you remember to record all activities and balance your checkbook against your bank statement). I doubt that you keep a written account of the coin and currency in your wallet, pockets, car glove compartment, and sofa cushions, but a business needs to.

Note: The term *account* in the bookkeeping sense means a basic category of information in which the financial effects of transactions are recorded and which serves as the source of information for preparing financial statements, tax returns, and reports to managers. In general usage, the term refers to a personal checking account in a bank, or a charge account you have at a store, or an investment account you have established for saving money for your retirement. In the following discussion, I use the term in its bookkeeping sense.

The term *general ledger* refers to the complete set of accounts established and maintained by a business. The *chart of accounts* is the formal index of these accounts — the complete listing and classification of the accounts used by the business to record its transactions. *General ledger* usually refers to the actual accounts and often to the balances in these accounts at some particular time.

The chart of accounts, even for a relatively small business, normally contains 100 or more accounts. Larger business organizations need thousands of accounts. The larger the number, the more likely that the accounts are given number codes according to some scheme — all assets may be in the 100 to 300 range, all liabilities in the 400 to 500 range, and so on.

As the business manager, you should make sure that the person in charge of accounting (or perhaps an outside CPA) reviews the chart of accounts every so often, to determine whether the accounts are up-to-date and adequate to the needs of the business. Over time, income tax rules change, the company goes into new lines of business, the company adopts new employee benefit plans, and so on. The business world is in constant flux, and the chart of accounts has to keep up with these changes.

Standardize forms and procedures: source documents

Businesses move on paperwork. Placing an order to buy products, selling a product to a customer, determining the earnings of an employee for the month — virtually every business transaction needs documentation, known as *source documents*. Source documents serve as evidence of the terms and conditions agreed upon by the business and the other person or organization that it's dealing with. Both parties receive some kind of source document (for example, for a sale at a cash register, the customer gets a sales receipt, and the business keeps a running tape of all transactions in the register).

More than you want to know right now about account classes and types

Accounts fall into two basic *classes,* with three *types* of accounts in one class and two in the other:

✔ **Balance sheet accounts:** Assets, liabilities, and owners' equity accounts

✔ **Income statement accounts:** Revenue and income accounts and expense and loss accounts

In other words, the accounts are divided between those that constitute the financial condition of the business (assets, liabilities, and owners' equity accounts) and those that summarize the profit-making operations of the business (revenue and expenses, plus income and loss accounts). Business managers and investors are mainly interested in the two financial statements that report the financial position of the business and its profit performance. You should be clear about how accounts shake out between these two key financial statements.

Note: Although your business reports a cash flow financial statement in addition to the financial condition and profit statements, the cash flow amounts that are reported in the cash flow statement are prepared from information already included in the balance sheet and income statement accounts (see Chapter 7). So, rest assured that the balance sheet and income statement accounts taken together are all the accounts a business needs.

Clearly, an accounting system needs to use standardized forms and procedures for all normal, repetitive transactions and effectively control the generation and handling of these source documents.

From the bookkeeping point of view, these business forms and documents are very important because they provide the input information needed for recording transactions in the business's accounts. Sloppy paperwork leads to sloppy accounting records, and sloppy accounting records just won't do when the time comes to prepare tax returns and financial statements.

Check out a business office-supply store to see the kinds of forms that you can buy right off the shelf. You can find many — maybe all — of the basic forms and documents that you need for recording business transactions, although most firms have to design at least some of their own forms.

Don't be penny-wise and pound-foolish: the need for competent, trained personnel

What good is meticulously collecting source documents if the information on those documents isn't entered into your system correctly? Bookkeepers and accountants, like all other employees in a business, should have the level of skills and knowledge needed to perform their functions. No-brainer, right? Well, determining what that level is *can* be difficult. You shouldn't try to save a few bucks here by hiring the lowest-paid people you can find. Here are some guidelines for choosing the right people to enter and manipulate your business's data and for making sure that those people *remain* the "right people":

- ✓ **College degree:** Many accountants in business organizations have a college degree with a major in accounting. However, as you move down the accounting department, you find that more and more employees do not have a college degree and perhaps not even any courses in accounting — they learned bookkeeping methods and skills through on-the-job training. Although these employees may have good skills and instincts, my experience has been that they tend to do things by the book; they often lack the broader perspective necessary for improvising and being innovative. So your best bet is to at least look twice at a potential employee who has no college-based accounting background.

- ✓ **CPA or CMA:** The more responsibility an accountant has in a business, the more important it is to ask whether he or she should be a certified public accountant (CPA). Most larger businesses insist on this credential along with a specific number of years' experience in public accounting. The other professional credential is the *CMA,* or *certified management accountant,* sponsored by the Institute of Management Accountants (IMA). Unlike the CPA license, the CMA designation of professional achievement is not regulated by the state. The CMA is evidence that the person has passed tough exams and has a good understanding of business accounting and income tax. In my opinion, a business is prudent to require the CPA or CMA credential for its chief accountant (who usually holds the title of Controller), or a business should regularly consult with a CPA in public practice for advice on its accounting system and on accounting problems that come up.

- ✓ **Continuing education:** Bookkeepers and accountants need continuing education to keep up with changes in the income tax law and financial reporting requirements as well as changes in how the business operates. Ideally, bookkeepers and accountants should be able to spot needed improvements and implement these changes — to make accounting reports to managers more useful, for example. Fortunately, many short-term courses, home study programs, and the like are available at very reasonable costs for keeping up on the latest accounting developments. States require that CPAs in public practice must take 30 to 40 hours per year of continuing education in approved courses to keep their licenses.

✔ **Integrity:** What's possibly the most important quality to look for is also the hardest to judge. Bookkeepers and accountants need to be honest people because of the control they have over your business's financial records. Do a very careful background check when hiring new accounting personnel. After you hire them, periodically (and discreetly) check whether their life-styles match their salaries. Of course, you can't invade their privacy, and you have to be extremely careful in accusing them of anything. Small-business owners and managers have closer day-in and day-out contact with their accountants and bookkeepers, which can be a real advantage — they get to know their accountants and bookkeepers on a personal level.

Protect the family jewels: internal controls

Every accounting system should establish and vigorously enforce *internal controls* — basically, additional forms and procedures, over and above what's strictly needed just to move operations along, that serve to deter and detect errors (honest mistakes) and all forms of dishonesty by employees, customers, suppliers, and even by managers themselves. Internal controls are like highway truck weigh stations, which make sure that the truck's load doesn't exceed the limits and that the truck has a valid plate. You're just checking that your staff is playing by the rules.

For example, to prevent or minimize shoplifting, most retailers now have video surveillance, tags that set off the alarms if the customer leaves the store with the tag still on the product, and so on. Likewise, a business has to implement certain procedures and forms to prevent as much as possible any theft, embezzlement, kickbacks, and fraud (and simple mistakes) by its own employees and managers.

I've played poker every month with the same bunch of guys for 30 years. We all trust each other, I'm sure. But before every hand is dealt, we still cut the deck. Remember that line in the movie *The Godfather?* "It's not personal; it's only business." Indeed, it's good business to put checks and balances into place to both discourage dishonest practices and discover any fraud and theft as soon as possible.

New perspective on paperwork: controlling against mistakes and theft

Accounting is characterized by a lot of paperwork — forms and procedures are plentiful. Most business managers and employees have their enthusiasm under control when it comes to the paperwork and procedures that the accounting department requires. One reason for this attitude, in my experience, is that non-accountants fail to appreciate the need for the accounting controls that are an essential part of many forms and procedures.

These controls are designed to minimize errors in bookkeeping, which has to process a great deal of detailed information and data. Equally important, controls are necessary to deter employee fraud, embezzlement, and theft, as well as fraud and dishonest behavior against the business from the outside. Unfortunately, every business is a target for fraud and theft, such as customers who shoplift; suppliers who deliberately ship less than the quantities invoiced to a business, hoping that the business won't notice the difference (called *short-counts*); and even dishonest managers themselves, who might pad expense accounts or take kickbacks from suppliers or customers.

A business has to avoid being an easy target for dishonest behavior by its employees, customers, and suppliers. Every business should institute and enforce certain control measures; many of these controls are designed into the accounting process. Following are five common examples of control measures:

- Requiring a second signature on cash disbursements over a certain dollar amount

- Matching up receiving reports based on actual counts and inspections of incoming shipments with purchase orders before preparing checks for payment to suppliers

- Requiring both a sales manager's and a second high-level manager's approval for formal *write-offs* of customers' overdue receivable balances (that is, closing the accounts on the assumption that they won't be collected), including a checklist of collection efforts that were undertaken

- Having auditors or employees who do not work in the warehouse take surprise counts of products stored in the company's warehouse and compare the counts with inventory records

- Requiring mandatory vacations by every employee, including bookkeepers and accountants, during which time someone else does that person's job (a second person may notice irregularities or deviations from company policies)

Keep the seesaw in balance: debits and credits

A business needs to be sure that *both* the debit side and the credit side, not just one or the other side, of all transactions are recorded. Economic exchanges involve a give and take, or something given for something received. See "The accounting equation: debits and credits," later in this chapter for more details.

Check your figures: end-of-period procedures checklist

Like an airplane pilot before takeoff, the accountant should have a clear-cut checklist to follow at the end of each period and especially at the end of the accounting year. Two main things have to be done at the end of the period:

- ✓ **Normal, routine *adjusting entries* for certain expenses:** For example, depreciation isn't a transaction as such and therefore hasn't been recorded as an expense in the flow of transactions recorded in the day-to-day bookkeeping process. (Chapter 5 explains depreciation expense.) Similarly, certain other expenses and some revenues may not have been associated with a specific transaction and have not been recorded. These kinds of adjustments are necessary for providing complete and accurate reports.

- ✓ ***Careful sweep of all matters* to check for other developments that may affect the accuracy of the reports:** For example, the company may have discontinued a product line, and the existing inventory of these products may have to be removed from the asset account, with a loss recorded in the period. Or the company may have settled a long-standing lawsuit, and the amount of damages needs to be recorded. Layoffs and severance packages are another example of what the chief accountant needs to look for before preparing reports.

Lest you still think of accounting as dry and dull, let me tell you that end-of-period accounting procedures can stir up controversy of the heated-debate variety. These procedures require that the accountant make decisions and judgment calls that upper management may not agree with. For example, the accountant may suggest recording major losses that would put a big dent in profit for the year or cause the business to report a loss. The outside CPA auditor, assuming that the business needs an audit of its financial statements, often gets in the middle of the argument. These kinds of debates are precisely why you business managers need to know some accounting: to hold up your end of the argument and participate in the great sport of yelling and name-calling — strictly on a professional basis, of course.

Keep good records: happy audit trails to you!

The happy trails that accountants like to walk are called *audit trails*. Good bookkeeping systems leave good audit trails. An audit trail is a clear-cut path of the sequence of events leading up to an entry in the accounts; an accountant starts with the source documents and follows through the bookkeeping steps in recording transactions to reconstruct this path. Even if a business doesn't have an outside CPA do an annual audit, the accountant has frequent occasion to go back to the source documents and either verify certain information in the accounts or reconstruct the information in a different manner. For example, suppose that a salesperson is claiming some suspicious-looking travel expenses; the accountant would probably want to go through all this person's travel and entertainment reimbursements for the past year.

If the IRS (Internal Revenue Service) comes in for a field audit of your business, you'd better have good audit trails to substantiate all your expense deductions and sales revenue for the year. The IRS has rules about saving source documents for a reasonable period of time and having a well-defined process for marking bookkeeping entries and keeping accounts. Think twice before throwing away source documents. Also, ask your accountant to demonstrate and lay out for your inspection the audit trails for key transactions — such as cash collections, sales, cash disbursements, inventory purchases, and so on.

Look out for unusual events and developments

Business managers should encourage their accountants to be alert to anything out of the ordinary that may require attention. Suppose that the accounts receivable balance for a particular customer is rapidly increasing — that is, the customer is buying more and more from your company on credit. Maybe the customer has switched more of his or her company's purchases to your business and is buying more from you only because he or she is buying less from other businesses. But maybe the customer is planning to stiff your business and take off without paying his or her debts. Or maybe the customer is secretly planning to go into bankruptcy soon and is stockpiling products before the company's credit rating heads south.

Don't forget internal time bombs: A bookkeeper's refusal to take a vacation could mean that he or she is reluctant to let anyone else look at the books.

To some extent, the accountants have to act as the eyes and ears of the business. Of course, that's one of your main functions as business manager, but your accounting staff can play an important role as well.

Control the design of accounting reports to managers

I have to be careful in this section; I have strong opinions on this matter. I have seen too many off-the-mark accounting reports to managers — difficult to decipher and not very useful or relevant to the manager's decision-making needs.

Part of the problem lies with the managers themselves. As a business manager, have you told your accounting staff what you need to know, when you need it, and how to present it in the most efficient manner? Probably not. When you stepped into your position, you probably didn't hesitate to rearrange your office and maybe even insist on hiring your own support staff. Yet you most likely lay down like a lapdog regarding your accounting reports. Maybe you've assumed that the reports have to be done that way and that arguing for change is no use.

On the other hand, accountants bear a good share of the blame for the poor reports, too. Accountants should proactively study the manager's decision-making functions and provide the information that is most useful, presented in the most easily digestible manner.

But another barrier to more-relevant and easier-to-use management accounting reports is the chart of accounts, discussed in "Categorize your financial information: the chart of accounts," earlier in this chapter. The chart of accounts for most businesses reflects mainly what's required for preparing the company's federal income tax return and its external financial statements.

These two reporting demands on the accounting system are, by and large, in agreement, so a single chart of accounts can serve both purposes pretty well. In designing the chart of accounts, the accountant should also keep in mind the type of information needed for management reports. To exercise control, managers need much more detail than what's reported on tax returns and external financial statements. And as Chapter 9 explains, expenses should be regrouped into different categories for management decision-making analysis. A good chart of accounts looks ahead to both the external and the internal (management) needs for information.

 So what's the answer for the manager who receives poorly formatted reports? Demand a report format that suits your needs! See Chapter 9 for some useful formats to use for your management accounting reports (and make sure that your accountant reads that chapter as well).

Double-Entry Bookkeeping for Nonbookkeepers

A business entity is a *two-sided* creature: It sells goods and services in return for payment. Naturally, the actual cost to the business of the goods and services is lower than what the customer pays — that's where profit comes in, and I'm sure that you won't be surprised to hear that profit is what motivates business (see Chapter 5 for more about profit). The core of profit is an increase in wealth, and the wealth of a business is its *assets,* such as cash, inventory (products held for sale to customers), buildings, equipment, and tools, to name some of the most common kinds of business assets.

To calculate how much profit is left over after the bills are paid and to keep complete records of its other transactions, a business uses the *double-entry bookkeeping system,* which tracks the two sides of the business: its assets and the sources of those assets, as described in the following section.

Assets and sources of assets

Putting values on a business's assets is one of the key accounting functions. Generally speaking, asset values are the costs of the assets (although some exceptions do exist). Of course, the business should keep accounts for all its assets — an account for cash, an account for inventory, an account for buildings, and so on. But asset-side accounting is only half the accountant's job.

Complete accounting for business requires that the *sources of the assets* also be accounted for. You need to establish an account for each source, and for every transaction, you record the changes to the assets and to the sources of the assets, if those sources were involved in the transaction. For example, suppose a business buys products for resale to its customers and pays the supplier of the products in cash for the purchase. One asset, inventory, increases, and another asset, cash, decreases.

Now suppose that your business purchases a product on credit, meaning that you promise to pay for the product at some point in the future rather than right away. You record the increase in the inventory asset account, of course, *and* you record an increase in the liability to be paid later (called an *account payable*). The account payable is the *source* of this addition to your inventory asset account.

Read on to find out how you balance things out by using the accounting equation, which is the foundation of double-entry bookkeeping.

The accounting equation: debits and credits

Double-entry bookkeeping means that you record both sides of every business transaction. This method of accounting, used by all businesses, rests on the *accounting equation:*

```
Assets = Liabilities + Owners' Equity
```

Every dollar of assets must come from somewhere, and the accountant's job is to keep track of the *sources* of assets as well as the assets themselves. For every increase in total assets, you're adding to either your *liabilities* (what you owe) or your *owners' equity* (the investment that others have made in your business). Total assets can also be increased by making a profit, as Chapter 5 explains. When profit is the reason for the increase in assets, an owners' equity account is increased. In other words, profit is a source of assets.

In the world of *debits and credits,* the technique for keeping both sides of the accounting equation in balance, the recording of every transaction requires an equality of debits on the one side and credits on the other side. Just think back to your math classes in your school days: What you have on one side of the equal sign (in this case, in the accounting equation) must equal what you have on the other side of the equal sign.

Here's how you record debits and credits:

- ✓ **Increases in assets:** Record as debits in the appropriate accounts.

- ✓ **Decreases in assets:** Record as credits in the appropriate accounts.

- ✓ **Increases in liabilities and owners' equity:** Record as credits in the appropriate accounts.

- ✓ **Decreases in liabilities and owners' equity:** Record as debits in the appropriate accounts.

Note: Sales revenue and expense accounts, which are not listed here, also follow debit and credit rules for entering increases and decreases.

As a business manager, you don't need to know all the mechanics and technical aspects of using debits and credits. Here's what you do need to know:

- ✓ **The basic premise of the accounting equation:** Assets equal the sources of the assets. That is, the total of assets on the one side should equal the sum of total liabilities and total owners' equity on the other side.

- ✓ **The important differences between liabilities and owners' equity accounts:** Because liabilities need to be paid off at definite due dates in the future but owners' equity has no such claims for definite payments at definite dates, these two accounts must be kept separate.

- ✓ **That balanced books don't necessarily mean correct balances:** If debits equal credits, the entry for the transaction is correct as far as keeping the accounting equation in balance. However, even if the debits equal the credits, other errors are possible. The bookkeeper may have recorded the debits and credits in a wrong account, or may have entered wrong amounts, or may have missed recording an entry altogether. Having balanced books simply means that the total of accounts with debit balances equals the total of accounts with credit balances. The important thing is whether the books (the accounts) have *correct* balances, which depends on whether all transactions and other developments have been accounted for and accounted for correctly.

✔ **That the system of debits and credits has been around for more than 500 years:** Okay, you don't really need to know this bit of trivia. But to impress your accounting staff with the depth of your accounting knowledge, you may want to casually mention that a book published in 1494 described how business traders and merchants of the day used debits and credits in their bookkeeping. Stops 'em cold every time.

Being Aware of Fraud in Bookkeeping

One of the problems I have as a business professor is what to say about fraud and dishonest practices in the business world. Accounting textbooks say little about these negative topics — which is kind of like a marriage textbook not mentioning adultery. I certainly don't encourage students to commit fraud, but my obligation is to point out that these things happen in the business world. Even people you know and like may engage in fraud of one kind or another. The large majority of business managers and employees don't commit fraud, in my opinion, but a significant minority do, that's for sure.

Fraud is a catch-all term; I'm using the term in its broadest sense to include any type of dishonest, unethical, immoral, or illegal practice. My concern here is with the effects of fraud on the business's accounting records, not with the broader social and criminal aspects of fraud.

A business should capture and record faithfully all transactions in its accounting records. Having said this, I have to admit that some business activities are deliberately *not* accounted for or are accounted for in a way that disguises their true nature.

Fraud occurs in big business corporations and one-owner/manager-controlled small businesses — and every size business in between. Some types of fraud are more common in small businesses, including *sales skimming* (not recording all sales revenue, to deflate the taxable income of the business and its owner) and the recording of personal expenses through the business (to make these expenses deductible for income tax). Some kinds of fraud are committed mainly by large business organizations, including paying bribes to public officials and entering into illegal conspiracies to fix prices or divide the market. The purchasing managers in any size business can be tempted to accept kickbacks and under-the-table payoffs from vendors and suppliers.

Some tricks of the trade in bookkeeping

Bookkeeping for even a relatively small business requires recording a large number of transactions over the course of one year. A few errors and mistakes are normal. Here are some ways in which a bookkeeper can find the errors and correct them:

✔ At the end of the period, take a *trial balance,* which is a listing of all accounts that puts debit accounts in one column and credit accounts in a second column, to check whether the total of all debit balance accounts equals the total of all credit balance accounts. The two totals may not agree. One trick is to divide the difference by 9. If the answer is a whole number (no digits needed after a decimal point), chances are good that a *transposition error* was made. Suppose that the actual $34,564.60 balance in an account was transposed as $35,464.60. Notice that the $900.00 error is divisible by 9 to give the whole number 100.

If this step doesn't find the answer, try dividing the amount of imbalance by 2 and then searching for any accounts that have a balance of this one-half amount. Perhaps a debit balance was listed wrongly as a credit balance, or vice versa, which would cause the trial balance to have a difference twice the balance of the account.

✔ Sometimes a business receives money without any clear indication of why the money was sent (some people just like to part with their money for no reason, maybe). My wife, Fay, who does bookkeeping for her employer, calls this money "mystery checks." You increase the cash account when you deposit the money, but what account do you credit? The answer is to create what's called a *suspense* account (also known as a *clearing* or *wash* account) as a temporary holding place for the credit so that the books stay in balance. Of course, you should find out as soon as possible the reason behind the cash receipt. When you do, credit the appropriate account and reduce the suspense account to a zero balance.

✔ I have fun in my accounting classes teasing the students with the following question: What's the *WITTB* account? Of course, they haven't seen such an account title in their textbooks. WITTB stands for "what it takes to balance." You use this account to force the trial balance into balance, meaning that if you have an unaccounted-for credit, you put a balancing debit in the WITTB account, and if you have an unaccounted-for debit, you put a balancing credit in the WITTB account. This account should serve as just a temporary means of balancing the accounts until you can find the error at a more convenient time. I don't recommend this technique if the trial balance is out of balance by a large difference, in which case you should immediately do some serious studying of the accounts to get them reconciled.

I should mention here another problem that puts accountants on the hot seat: In many situations, two or more businesses are controlled by the same person or the same group of investors. Revenue and expenses can be arbitrarily shifted among the different business entities under common control. One person having a controlling ownership interest in two or more businesses is perfectly legal, and such an arrangement often makes good business sense. For example, a business rents a building from another business corporation that owns the building, and the same person is the majority owner in both businesses. The problem arises when that person arbitrarily sets the monthly rent to shift profit between the two businesses; a high rent generates more profit for the real estate business and lower profit for the other business. This kind of thing may be perfectly legal, but it raises a fundamental accounting issue.

Readers of financial statements are entitled to assume that all activities between the business and the other parties it deals with are based on what's called *arm's-length bargaining,* meaning that the business and the other parties have a purely professional relationship. When that's not the case, the financial report should — but usually doesn't — use the term *related parties* to describe persons and organizations who are not at "arm's length" with the business. According to financial reporting standards, your accountant should advise you, the business manager, to disclose any material amounts of related-party transactions in your external financial statements.

In short, fraud goes on in the business world, and most of these schemes require *cooking the books* — which means altering entries in the accounts to cover the fraud or simply not recording certain entries that should be recorded. Of course, if you were to see an expense account called *bribes,* you would want to be a little suspicious, but unethical bookkeepers and accountants are usually just a tad more clever than that. You can find several tips on uncovering and preventing fraud in "Managing the Bookkeeping System: A Checklist," earlier in this chapter.

When the books have been cooked, the financial statements prepared from the accounts are distorted, incorrect, and probably misleading. Lenders, other creditors, and the owners who have capital invested in the business rely on the company's financial statements. Also, a business's managers and board of directors (the group of people who oversee a business corporation) may be misled — assuming that they're not a party to the fraud, of course — and may also have liability to third-party creditors and investors for their failure to catch the fraud: Creditors and investors who end up suffering losses have legal grounds to sue the managers and directors (and perhaps the auditors who did not catch the fraud) for damages suffered.

Persons engaging in fraud generally cheat on their federal income taxes; they don't declare the ill-gotten income. Needless to say, the Internal Revenue Service is on constant alert for fraud in federal income tax returns — both business and personal returns. The IRS has the authority to come in and audit the books of the business and also the personal income tax returns of its managers and investors. Conviction for income tax evasion is a felony, I might point out.

Chapter 3

Taxes, Taxes, and More Taxes

In This Chapter

▶ Paying taxes as an employer and a property owner

▶ Putting on your tax agent hat and collecting sales tax

▶ Determining how much of your profit goes to the government

▶ Looking at the ways taxes work for different legal business structures

A s an employer, a business pays taxes. As a property owner, a business pays taxes. As a retailer, a business collects sales taxes paid by customers and remits the amounts to state and local governments. And, of course, a business pays federal income tax. Yikes! Is there no escaping the tax millstone?

Nope, afraid not (short of resorting to illegal activity or a sly move to another country — you'll have to find another book to tell you about those options). But you can take advantage of the many options in tax laws that can minimize how much you pay and to delay your payment (a perfectly legal strategy known as *tax avoidance*). This chapter starts you on your way by explaining all the various types of taxation that a business faces.

I say that this chapter "*starts* you on your way" because I can't possibly provide you with exhaustive detail in one chapter, and besides, no one can give you good tax advice without first looking at your specific situation — consult a professional tax expert for that.

Some critics say that income tax is a real disincentive to investing in business. But you can also look at how much income tax you pay as a measure of your success. One of my colleagues says that he'd love to pay a million dollars of income tax every year. He's got a good point. Hey, you can't get away from taxes (you know the old saying about death and taxes), so you may as well try for a positive outlook.

Taking a Bite Out of Wages and Property

Even if you don't earn a profit in your business, you still have to pay certain taxes. Unlike income tax, which is a *contingent* or *conditional* tax that depends on whether a business earns taxable income for the year, the two major types of non-income taxes — *employer* or *payroll taxes* and *property taxes* — always have to be paid. (See "Taxing Your Bottom Line: Income Taxes," later in this chapter, for more about income tax.)

Putting Uncle Sam on the payroll: employer taxes

In addition to deducting federal, state, and local taxes from employees' wages and remitting those amounts to the proper government agencies, businesses need to pay the following employee-related taxes: social security and Medicare taxes, unemployment tax, and workers' compensation insurance (actually, that last one isn't really a tax, but don't get technical).

Social security and Medicare tax

Most folks don't realize that they pay only half of their social security tax — the employer picks up the rest of the tab. The social security law stipulates that the tax burden be divided 50-50 between an employee and an employer.

I don't want to get into a debate about the social security system and the financial problems it's facing; let me just say that the amount you pay in social security taxes almost certainly won't go down. Here's an idea of what a business pays in social security taxes: In 1997, the first $65,400.00 of annual wages were taxed at 6.20 percent on the employee and 6.20 percent on the employer, for a maximum of $4,054.80 paid by each. Wages above this level are not subject to the social security tax but continue to be taxed 1.45 percent on both the employee and the employer for the Medicare program. (Wages subject to Medicare taxes have no ceiling.)

So for employees who earn less than $65,400.00, the total tax rate for social security and Medicare is 7.65 percent. A business pays this 7.65 percent tax in addition to the wages that it pays an employee in this wage range. That is, for every $100.00 paid to an employee, the employer's total cost is $107.65. (Tell *that* to Pat in Marketing the next time he gripes about the tax deductions in his paycheck!)

The way to an employee's heart is through the payroll department

Remember the first time you received a real paycheck? Your jaw dropped when you compared the *gross wages* (the amount before deductions) and the *net pay* (the amount you actually received), right? A business's accountants need to track how much of the following, by law, to deduct from employees' paychecks:

- ✔ Social security tax

- ✔ Medicare tax

- ✔ Federal, state, and local income taxes

- ✔ Other, nontax-related withholdings that the employee agrees to (such as union dues, retirement-plan contributions, and health insurance costs paid by the employee)

- ✔ Other nontax-related withholdings required by a court order (for example, a business may be ordered to withhold part or all of an employee's wages and remit the amount to a legal agency or a creditor to which the employee owes money)

For all these deductions, a business serves as a collection agent and remits the appropriate amount of wages to the appropriate party. As you can imagine, this task requires lots of additional accounting and record keeping. *Tip:* Don't underestimate the cost and importance of an experienced, well-trained payroll accounting staff to keep all the necessary records, file all the required reports on time, answer questions from employees, and make corrections for the inevitable errors that occur. Employee morale is very important, and one surefire way to screw it up is to have a lousy payroll department that makes many mistakes and is short-tempered with employees.

You can't do anything to answer your employees' gripes about how much tax is deducted, but you can certainly do your best to make the whole payroll system as painless for them as possible.

Unemployment tax

Another tax that an employer pays is the *unemployment tax*, which provides funds for individuals thrown out of work through no fault of their own. A worker who is laid off because of downsizing is entitled to unemployment benefits, for example, but a worker who was fired *for cause* is not (the specific rules about who qualifies and for how long vary from state to state).

The unemployment tax rate (in 1997 and 1998) is 6.2 percent on a maximum of $7,000 wages paid to each employee, or a maximum of $434 per employee (note, however, that unlike with social security, employees don't pay anything for this tax). This program is a joint federal-state venture, so the employer pays part of the unemployment tax to the state in which its employees work and part to the federal government.

Whereas the social security and Medicare taxes are *flat* taxes — the rates are fixed and cannot be reduced — the unemployment tax rate is reduced for employers that have a stable work force and do not lay off employees very often. It's never reduced all the way to zero, though; every business pays *some* unemployment tax.

Workers' compensation insurance

Although, strictly speaking, workers' compensation insurance isn't a tax, state laws require that every business purchase it. The purpose of this insurance coverage is to provide replacement income to employees who suffer work-related injuries and other job-related disabilities that keep them from performing their normal duties for a specified period of time. Employees don't pay for the insurance; the employer bears all the cost.

Unfortunately, collecting workers' compensation benefits has become a cottage industry for some dishonest employees and their unscrupulous doctors and lawyers who help them submit bogus claims for faked or exaggerated injuries. These false or exaggerated claims drive up the costs of providing benefits to honest employees who suffer actual injuries on the job and who should be compensated for the weeks they miss a paycheck.

A business owner friend had serious problems with employees filing false claims and driving up the premiums for his workers' compensation insurance. He decided to start screening job applicants more carefully by sending their information to a company that maintains a national database on people who have filed workers' compensation claims (as well as people with driving violations and other criminal convictions). My friend has to ask for permission from the job applicants before submitting their information to the company. He won't hire job applicants with too many workers' compensation claims or other bad marks on their records. He's very careful to conduct this background check on all job applicants — without regard to gender, minority ethnic status, age, and so on. Employers are permitted to ask directly relevant questions about the background and experience of job applicants.

Taxing everything you can put your hands on: property taxes

Businesses may have to pay two types of property taxes:

- **Real estate tax:** Owners of land and buildings and other permanent improvements on the land (such as a concrete driveway or a paved parking lot) pay annual taxes to county and other local-level governments.

✔ **Tangible personal property tax:** Some states and localities tax *inventory* (products held for sale) and *portable assets* (office furniture, computers, cars and trucks, and so on). Property taxes on vehicles are universal; the other items are taxed in some states and not in others.

Property taxes are *ad valorem,* or "according to value." These taxes are based on *assessed values* of assets. The main thing you have to do is make sure that the assessed values of your real estate and personal property assets are correct and not higher than they should be. Believe it or not, the government has been known to make mistakes (say it isn't so!); in fact, government assessment methods are always open to question and challenge. Your assets may qualify for exemption under various state and local laws or may be eligible for special reductions *(abatements).* Property taxation is a legal thicket — laws, terminology, procedures, and forms differ a great deal from state to state and county to county — so consult your tax advisor.

Generally speaking, only personal property physically located within the jurisdiction of the government entity on a specific tax assessment date is taxed. If the property happens to be outside the vicinity on the assessment date, it may not be subject to the property tax. Many companies let their inventory levels drop as low as possible on the tax assessment date — by delaying incoming shipments or delaying purchase orders. However, a business should be careful not to illegally move property out of the state on the tax date if the only reason is to avoid the tax. Talk to a good property tax lawyer first.

Property taxes can take a big chunk out a business's profit if not managed well. In large organizations, an in-house accountant who deals with property taxes and knows the tax law language and methods is responsible for developing strategies to minimize property taxes. You small-business owners may want to consult with a CPA or an attorney who specializes in property tax law — it may be money well spent.

'Cause I'm the Tax Man: Collecting Sales Tax

Most states, counties, and municipal governments levy *retail sales taxes* on certain products and services sold within their jurisdictions. The final consumer of the product or service pays the sales tax — in other words, the sales tax is tacked on to the product's price tag at the very end of the economic chain. The business that is selling the product or service collects the tax and remits it to the appropriate tax agency. Businesses that operate earlier in the economic chain (that is, those that sell products to other businesses that in turn resell the products) generally do not pay sales tax.

For example, when you run to your local bookstore to buy *Taxes For Dummies* because you simply can't get enough of this tax business, you pay the bookstore the cost of the book plus sales tax. But the bookstore did not pay sales tax when it bought the book from IDG Books Worldwide, Inc. Only you, the final consumer, pay sales tax (lucky you).

Businesses that make retail sales must register with a government agency and obtain a *retail sales tax number,* thus becoming a designated sales tax collector. As a designated sales tax collector, the business does not pay sales tax on products that it buys from other businesses for resale to its customers. If you're a small-business owner/manager, be aware that if you overlook this role imposed on your business by the state, you're still responsible for paying over the sales tax to government. Suppose that you make a sale for $100 but don't add the $6 sales tax into the total amount you collect from the customer. Big Brother says that you did collect the sales tax, whether you think you did or not. So you still have to pay the government $6, which leaves you only $94 sales revenue.

As anyone who has traveled to various U.S. states knows, sales tax is anything but nationally uniform. In addition to the differences in sales tax rates from state to state, the following issues complicate state sales tax:

✔ Some products, such as clothing, are subject to sales tax in some states and not others.

✔ Some products and services are always taxed — namely, sales of liquor, beer, and cigarettes, the taxes that are referred to as *sin taxes.*

✔ Many products and services, such as prescription drug sales and medical and hospital charges, are specifically exempted from retail sales taxes.

✔ Sales of professional services (lawyers and CPAs, for example) generally are not taxed, though some states have considered doing so.

Tracking and recording retail sales tax is a big responsibility for many businesses, especially if the business operates out of more than one state. Having a well-trained accounting staff manage this side of the business is well worth the cost.

Taxing Your Bottom Line: Income Taxes

You may think that Uncle Sam is a trusting soul; after all, he doesn't send any bills for income tax. Instead, he trusts that individuals and businesses will determine their taxable income honestly and will file the appropriate, accurately filled-out tax returns to the IRS (Internal Revenue Service) yearly.

But just like your seemingly trusting spouse who expects that you'll do your chores without being asked, Uncle Sam will raise Cain if you don't do what you're supposed to.

A business's tax return reports its *gross income,* which is very broadly defined to include sales revenue, investment income, and any other cash inflow or realized increase in wealth. Gross income is either *exempt,* meaning that it's not subject to taxation, or *taxable,* the meaning of which should be painfully obvious. To determine your *taxable income,* you deduct certain allowed expenses from gross income. Income tax law rests very roughly on the premise that all income is taxable unless expressly exempted and nothing can be deducted unless expressly allowed.

Although you determine your business's taxable income as an annual amount (for 12 consecutive months, which can end March 31 or September 30, instead of December 31), you don't wait until you file your tax return to make that calculation and payment. Instead, you estimate your income tax for the year and make four (quarterly) installment payments during the year. When you file the final tax return — with the official, rather than the estimated, taxable income amount disclosed — after the close of the year, you pay the final quarterly installment, adjusted to reflect the actual taxable income amount (which may be more than or less than you estimated).

You must keep *adequate accounting records* to determine your business's annual taxable income. If you report the wrong taxable income amount, you can't plead that the bookkeeper was incompetent or that your accounting records were inadequate or poorly organized — in fact, good old Uncle Sam may decide that your poor accounting was intentional and is evidence of income tax evasion. If you underreport your taxable income, you may have to pay interest and penalties in addition to the tax that you owe.

I'm not talking about the accounting *methods* that you select to determine annual taxable income — Chapter 13 discusses choosing among alternative accounting methods for certain expenses. After you've selected which accounting methods you'll use for these expenses, your bookkeeping procedures must follow these methods faithfully. Choose the accounting methods that minimize your current year's taxable income — but make certain that your bookkeeping is done accurately and on time and that your accounting records are complete. If your business's income tax return is audited, the IRS agents first look at your accounting records and bookkeeping system.

Furthermore, you must stand ready to present evidence for expense deductions. Be sure to hold on to receipts and other relevant documents. In an IRS audit, the burden of proof is on *you.* The IRS doesn't have to disprove a deduction; you have to prove that you were entitled to the deduction. *Tip: No evidence, no deduction* is the rule to keep in mind.

Tax law can be very . . . well . . . *taxing!*

Did I mention that I can't possibly do justice to tax law in just a single chapter? The federal income tax law is extraordinarily complex and is constantly evolving. Most businesses hire tax professionals to

- Keep the business in compliance with the tax law and regulations.

- Help the business prepare and file all the necessary returns and schedules completely, correctly, and on time.

- Give advice on the many options in the tax law for minimizing taxable income and for doing general tax planning.

Congress is under constant pressure to simplify the tax law, but the pressure to promote certain expenditures (contributions to churches, for example) is equally great. For example, a *flat tax,* where you pay a standard tax rate without having to make all sorts of mind-numbing calculations, seems like a great idea — until you realize that a flat tax won't let you deduct your home mortgage interest anymore.

Behind the flat tax idea is the concept that all taxpayers should be treated exactly the same regardless of whether they earn $10,000, $100,000, or $1 million annual income. Incomes are not flat, so don't pin your hopes on a flat tax anytime soon. Maybe someday you'll be able to figure your annual income tax in one short, simple calculation, but — and I hate to sound like a sourpuss — I don't think anyone will ever see that day.

The following sections paint a rough sketch of the main topics of business income taxation (I *don't* go into the technical details of determining taxable income, however).

Profit accounting and taxable income accounting

You're probably thinking that this section of the chapter is about how a business's bottom-line profit — its net income — drives its taxable income amount. Actually, I want to discuss the exact opposite: how income tax law drives a business's profit accounting. That's right: Tax law can play a large role in how a business determines its profit figure.

Before I explain that relationship, let me discuss profit briefly. As I mention in Chapter 13, no single accounting method is "correct"; accountants have a certain amount of legitimate leeway in measuring and reporting the revenue and expenses that drive the profit figure. Therefore, two different accountants, recording the same profit-making activities during the period, would most likely come up with two different profit figures.

And that's fine — as long as the differences are due to legitimate reasons. I'd like to be able to report to you that in measuring profit, accountants always aim right at the bull's-eye, the dead center of the profit target. One commandment in the accountants' bible is that annual profit should be as close to the truth as can be measured; accounting methods should be objective and fair. As the late Howard Cosell used to say, "Tell it like it is." Well, in the real world, profit accounting doesn't quite live up to this ideal.

Be aware that a business may be tempted to *deliberately overstate* or *understate* its profit. The bigger problem, of course, is overstating profit. When a business overstates its profit, it reports, in its income statement, profit that it hasn't entirely earned, at least not yet, by recording sales revenue too soon or expenses too late. Overstating profit is a dangerous game to play because it deceives investors and other interested parties into thinking that the business is doing better than it really is. Audits of financial reports by CPAs (as discussed in Chapter 15) keep such financial reporting fraud to a minimum but don't catch every case.

More to the point of this chapter is the fact that most businesses are under some pressure to *understate* the profit reported in their annual income statements. Businesses generally record sales revenue correctly but record some expenses sooner than these costs should be deducted from sales revenue. Why? Businesses are preoccupied with minimizing income tax, which means minimizing taxable income. To minimize taxable income, a business chooses accounting methods that record expenses as soon as possible. Keeping two sets of books (accounting records) — one for external financial reporting, like tax returns, and one for internal profit accounting, for the benefit of managers — would be impractical, so the business operates according to the books used for external financial reporting. And that's how a business's profit figure can be driven by tax concerns.

In short, the income tax law permits fairly conservative expense accounting methods — expense amounts can be *front-loaded,* or deducted sooner rather than later. The reason, of course, is to give a business the option to minimize its current taxable income (even though this course has a reverse effect in later years). Many businesses select these conservative expense methods — both for their income tax returns and their financial statements. Thus, financial statements of many businesses tilt to the conservative side.

Of course, I feel that a business should report a correct, accurate figure as its net income, with no deliberate fudging. If you can't trust that figure, who knows for sure exactly how the company is doing? Not the owners, the value of whose investment in the business depends mostly on profit performance, and not even the business's managers, whose business decisions depend mostly on profit performance. Every business needs a reliable profit compass to navigate its way through the competitive environment of business — that's just practical common sense and doesn't even begin to address ethical issues.

Other reasons for understating profit

Minimizing taxable income is a strong motive for understating profit, but businesses have other reasons as well. Imagine for the moment that business profit isn't subject to income tax (you wish!). Even in this hypothetical no-tax world, many businesses probably would select accounting methods that measure their profit on the low side rather than the high side. I see two possible reasons behind this decision:

✔ **Don't Count Your Chickens before They Hatch philosophy:** Business managers and owners tend to be financially conservative; they prefer to err on the low side of profit measurement rather than on the high side.

✔ **Save for a Rainy Day philosophy:** A business may want to keep some profit in reserve so that during a future downturn, it has a profit cushion to soften the blow.

The people who think this way tend to view *overstating profit* as a form of defrauding investors but view *understating profit* as simply being prudent. Frankly, I think that putting a thumb on either side of the profit scale (revenue being one side and expenses the other) is not a good idea. *Let the chips fall where they may* is my philosophy. Adopt the accounting methods that you think best reflect how you operate the business. The income tax law has put too much downward pressure on profit measurement, in my opinion, which causes noise in the financial statement communication process.

I should say that many businesses do report their annual profit correctly — sales revenue and expenses are recorded properly and without any attempt to manipulate either side of the profit equation.

See Chapter 13 for more about how choosing one expense accounting method over another method impacts profit. (***Note:*** The following sections, which discuss expenses and income that are not deductible or only partially deductible, have nothing to do with choosing accounting methods.)

Nondeductible expenses

To be deductible, business expenses must be *ordinary and necessary* — that is, regular, routine stuff that you need to do to run your business. You're probably thinking that you can make an argument that *any* of your expenses is "ordinary and necessary." And you're mostly right — almost all business expenses meet this twofold test.

However, the IRS considers certain business expenses to be anything but ordinary and necessary; you can argue about them until you're blue in the face, and it won't make any difference. Here's a list of expenses that are *not* deductible or only partially deductible:

✔ **Customer entertainment expenses and gifts to customers:** You can generally deduct only 50 percent of your customer entertainment expenses, and only a very low amount of what you spend on gifts is deductible.

✔ **Bribes, kickbacks, fines, and penalties:** Oh, come on, did you really think that you could get rewarded for doing stuff that's illegal or, at best, undesirable? If you were allowed to deduct these costs, that would be tantamount to the IRS encouraging such behavior — a policy that wouldn't sit too well with the general public.

✔ **Lobbying costs:** You can't deduct payments made to influence legislation. Sorry, but you can't deduct the expenses you ran up to persuade Senator Hardnose to give your bicycle business special tax credits because riding bicycles is good exercise for people.

✔ **Start-up costs:** A new business is not permitted to deduct these costs immediately. You divide these costs over five years or longer and take a fractional deduction each of those years.

✔ **Unreasonable compensation:** The IRS doesn't generally question salaries and wages, but a special rule applies to all publicly owned corporations. If one or more of their top five executives (CEO, president, executive president, and so on) are paid more than $1 million in annual wages, the compensation over that amount must be based on objective performance criteria, or else the excess is not deductible. The IRS doesn't question the first $1 million. Likewise, *golden parachute payments* — generous severance packages given to executives who were suddenly dismissed (because of a merger, for example) — may not be fully deductible.

Also, anyone from the business owner's family who's on the payroll must be paid an amount that's consistent with that person's actual contribution to the business. An IRS auditor will laugh herself silly while she disallows a huge salary paid to your nephew who just makes coffee and copies.

✔ **Life insurance premiums:** A business may buy life insurance coverage on key officers and executives, but if the business is the beneficiary, the premiums are not deductible. The proceeds from a life insurance policy are not taxable income to the business if the insured person dies, because the cost of the premiums was not deductible. In short, premiums are not deductible, and proceeds upon death are excluded from taxable income.

✔ **Travel and convention attendance expenses:** Cruise ship conventions and some other types of travel have been abused by businesses and are subject to strict limits and documentation requirements.

✓ **Transactions with related parties:** Income tax law takes a special interest in transactions where the two parties are related in some way. For example, a business may rent space in a building owned by the same people who have money invested in the business; the rent may be artificially high or low in an attempt to shift income and expenses between the two tax entities or individuals. In other words, these transactions may not be based on what's known as *arm's-length bargaining.* A business that deals with a related party must be ready to show that the price paid or received is consistent with what the price would be for an unrelated party.

Nontaxable income

Whereas having some nondeductible or partially deductible expenses is common for a business, having income that's not taxable or only partially taxable isn't all that common. The two sources of nontaxable income are

✓ Interest income from municipal bonds (bonds issued by state and local governments)

✓ Cash dividends received from other corporations in which the business owns stock

Not many businesses invest in municipal bonds, but a fair number own stock in other corporations, either as investors or as members of an affiliated group of corporations. A business can deduct 70, 80, or 100 percent of the dividends, depending on how many shares it owns. The purpose of this *dividend-received deduction* is to avoid taxing the receiving corporation again on money earned by the paying corporation, which has already paid income tax on its profit. In other words, the dividends received have already been taxed once, and the idea is to avoid double taxation among the two corporations. But when a corporation pays dividends to its individual stockholders (real-live persons such as you and I), the dividends are taxed a second time as income to the individuals. This is called the *double taxation* of corporate profit — once in the hands of the corporation and once again in the hands of the individual stockholders.

Consider this example: Say that a business called Mary Muffet's Tuffets (MMT) is a stockholder in Spiders Corp. Without the dividend-received deduction, MMT would have to pay the following taxes:

✓ MMT pays income tax on its taxable income, before counting in the cash received as dividends from Spiders Corp.

✓ MMT pays income tax on dividends received from Spiders Corp. — even though Spiders Corp. has already paid income tax on its profit and is simply transferring some of its after-tax net income to another corporation.

✓ MMT's owners pay a *third* tax on the dividends they received from MMT.

To avoid such triple taxation, MMT reduces or eliminates altogether (depending on how many shares in Spiders Corp. it owns) the second tax I've listed with the dividend-received deduction. So if MMT owns enough stock in Spiders Corp., none of the cash dividends from it is taxed, and you're back to "only" the double taxation of its profit — which is bad enough, of course.

Equity capital disguised as debt

Debt is money borrowed from lenders who require that the money plus interest be paid back by a certain date. *Equity* is money invested by owners (stockholders) in a business in return for hoped-for, but not guaranteed, profit returns. Interest is deductible, but cash dividends paid to stockholders are not — which gives debt capital a big edge over equity capital at tax time.

Not surprisingly, some businesses try to pass off equity capital as debt on their tax returns so that they can deduct the payments on the equity capital. Don't think that the IRS is ignorant of these tactics: Everything that you declare as interest on debt is examined carefully, and if the IRS determines that what you're calling "debt" is really equity capital, it disallows the "interest" deduction. In short, debt must really be debt and must have few or none of the characteristics of equity. Drawing a clear-cut line between debt and equity has been a vexing problem for the IRS, and its rules are complex. You'll probably have to consult a tax professional if you have any question about this issue. Be warned that if you attempt to disguise equity capital as debt, your charade may not work — and any "interest" payments you have made may be later disallowed by the IRS.

Who Pays the Income Tax?

One final word. You may not know this, but many businesses do not pay income tax on their taxable incomes. No — these businesses are not breaking the law and evading income tax. Whether a business actually pays income tax depends on its legal organizational structure. A business may be organized as a corporation and have more than 75 owners (called stockholders). This type of business entity does not have a choice — it pays the income tax on its annual taxable income.

But corporations with 75 or fewer owners, as well as other types of noncorporate businesses, do not pay income tax. Don't jump to the conclusion that this is a big loophole in the tax law. These non-taxpaying kinds of business entities pass the amount of their annual taxable income through to their owners, who must include their respective shares of the business's taxable income on their individual tax returns. Chapter 11 explains income taxation of different types of business entities.

A word on cash basis accounting

Cash basis accounting (also known as *checkbook accounting*) isn't generally acceptable in the world of business but is permitted by income tax law for some businesses. The key factor for determining which businesses may use this method is inventory. The business must meet the following criteria:

- Does not deal in inventories (products sold to customers).

- Keeps accounting records for cash receipts and cash payments only, even though it may buy some things on credit that it doesn't pay for right away and even if it allows its customers to pay a few weeks after the sales to them. (As long as the business does not formally record these payables and receivables in its bookkeeping process, the IRS will not insist that it do so.)

- Has no more than $5 million in annual sales revenue.

For the great majority of businesses, cash basis accounting is not acceptable, neither for reporting to the IRS nor for preparing financial statements. This method falls short of the information needed for even a relatively small business. Accrual basis accounting, described in Chapters 6 and 7, is the only real option for most businesses. Even small businesses that don't sell products should carefully consider whether cash basis is adequate for

- Preparing external financial statements for borrowing money and reporting to owners

- Dividing profit among owners

For all practical purposes, only sole proprietorships (one-owner businesses) that sell just services and no products can use cash basis accounting. Other businesses must use accrual basis — which provides a much better income statement for management control and decision making, and a much more complete picture of the business's financial condition.

Chapter 4

Accounting in Your Everyday Personal Financial Tasks

. . . .

In This Chapter

▶ Boiling down income tax into a simple model

▶ Determining the real before-tax cost of things

▶ Making sure you know how interest works when borrowing

▶ Accounting for how your money grows when saving and investing

. . . .

*B*efore moving on to the world of business, in this chapter I look at you as an *individual*. I look over your financial shoulder at four different roles in which some accounting smarts can help you on a daily basis — as a taxpayer, a spender, a borrower, and an investor. Knowing a little accounting makes you a more rational economic decision-maker in these different financial roles.

Individuals as Taxpayers

It's hard to think of anything involving money for which the tax angle is not important. When you consider all the different kinds of taxes — either the taxes you pay yourself or the taxes that are built into the prices of things you buy — middle- and upper-income earners have a tax load of about 50 percent of annual income. The major types of taxes include income taxes (federal and state), social security and Medicare taxes, sales taxes, real estate and personal property taxes, and fuel taxes. (It's a discouragingly long list, isn't it?) The one tax you have the most control over is the income tax.

The federal income tax law is sometimes called the "Accountants' Relief and Welfare Act" because it provides employment for a large number of accountants who are hired to prepare the annual tax returns of individuals and businesses. Sure, the income tax law is complex and frustrating; no wonder so many people use an accountant to prepare their annual income tax returns. The alternative is to grit your teeth and do your own taxes. Either way, I strongly suggest that you see the forest and not get lost in all the trees. A thumbnail-size model of how the income tax law works helps you in making many important financial decisions and is very useful for mapping your overall financial strategy.

The basic income tax model is also useful for testing investment opportunities that seem too good to be true. I have seen too many people get suckered into questionable investments because of alleged income tax advantages. I'm sure you've heard the often-repeated warning, "There's a sucker born every minute."

Don't let the extraordinary complexity of the federal income tax law stop you from trying to understand how it works. Here's a basic income tax model that is very useful, even though just four factors (numbered 1 through 4) drive income tax in this example:

Basic Income Tax Model

(1)	Annual Income, Profit, and Gains	$62,200
(2)	Less Personal Exemptions	(5,300)
(3)	Less Standard Deduction for a Married Couple	(6,900)
	Equals Taxable Income	$50,000
(4)	Times the Tax Rates (15% on first $41,200 and 28% on excess)	
	Equals Income Tax Amount	$8,644

Note: Some sources of income are not taxable or are subject to a more favorable tax treatment. Some expenditures are deductible, and some are not. Persons over 65 or blind get. . . . Hold on! Once you start getting into technical details, you're on a slippery slope and there's no turning back. My purpose here is not to provide a detailed tax guide but to provide a simple, hands-on income model to show the basic income tax effects of your financial decisions. Several good tax guides are available, including *Taxes For Dummies,* by Eric Tyson and David Silverman (published by IDG Books Worldwide, Inc.).

Following is a brief — and I do mean *brief* — explanation of each factor in the basic income tax model:

✔ **(1) Income, Profit, and Gains:** Money flowing your direction from working or owning assets is subject to income tax — unless the income tax law specifically makes the inflow not subject to income tax (two examples are interest income on municipal bonds and insurance proceeds received upon death of the insured). A good general rule is that every dollar of income comes with a potential income tax burden.

✔ **(2) Personal Exemptions:** The income tax law gives every individual a so-called *personal exemption*. The term *exemption* means that a certain amount of income is excused from income tax. For 1996 (the amount changes from year to year), the personal exemption was $2,650 per person, or $5,300 for a married couple filing a joint return (one combined income tax return for both persons, as shown in the preceding basic income tax model).

✔ **(3) Deductions:** In writing the income tax law, Congress decided that you can deduct certain expenditures — but not others — to determine taxable income. For example, you can deduct interest paid on home mortgages, charitable contributions, and property taxes. In lieu of itemizing deductions, the income tax law allows a *standard deduction* of a flat amount. For 1996, a married couple filing a joint return could deduct a $6,900 standard deduction instead of itemizing specific expenditures, whether or not they made deductible-type expenditures.

✔ **Taxable Income:** The first $12,200 of income earned by the married couple in the basic income tax model shown is *not* subject to income tax — equal to the personal exemption of $5,300 plus the standard deduction of $6,900. Income above this amount is the taxable income for the year. The married couple's taxable income is "only" $50,000 because the first $12,200 is offset by exemptions and deductions. You multiply the taxable income by the tax rates — one rate for the first layer of taxable income and a higher rate for the excess — to determine the income tax amount.

✔ **(4) Tax Rate:** The federal income tax law is based on the *progressive taxation* philosophy — as your income progresses, your tax rate progresses. (This is progress?) Taxable income is subdivided into *brackets;* each higher bracket is subject to a higher income tax rate. The lowest rate is 15.0 percent; the top rate is 39.6 percent on taxable income in excess of $271,050. The brackets and rates can change from year to year, but don't worry — Uncle Sam keeps you informed in the booklet that comes with your annual income tax forms.

✔ **Income Tax Amount:** In 1996, the tax rate on $50,000 taxable income is 15 percent on the first $41,200 and then almost doubles to 28 percent on the next bracket of taxable income. As you can see in the example, the income tax on the $50,000 taxable income is $8,644.

The income tax of $8,644 is 17.3 percent of the $50,000 taxable income and 13.9 percent of the $62,200 gross income. However, the *marginal tax rate* gets the most attention. The marginal tax rate is the rate that applies to an increase or decrease in taxable income on the margin; the margin in this example is $50,000. For example, by earning $5,000 more or $5,000 less taxable income, the married couple's income tax amount would change by 28 percent of the change. Their marginal tax rate is 28 percent.

I find that using a total federal and state marginal income tax rate of $1/3$, which is based on a 28 percent federal income tax plus a 5 percent state income tax, is generally accurate and computationally convenient. This number may be too high or too low for a specific individual or married couple, but it's reasonably accurate for a broad range of taxpayers. (If you're a multimillionaire, you probably should shift up to a 45 percent marginal tax rate.)

Individuals as Spenders

From an income tax point of view, your expenses are either *deductible* or *nondeductible*. The cost difference between the two types is significant, as the following sections explain. This discussion assumes that your annual income puts you in a marginal income tax bracket of about $1/3$, which is typical. If you have a very low income or very high deductions, your marginal tax rate is less. If you have a taxable income of more than quarter of a million dollars and don't have high deductions, you may want to use a higher marginal tax rate.

The before-tax cost of nondeductible expenditures

You should get into the good habit of thinking in terms of the *before-tax income* required for nondeductible expenditures such as a loaf of bread, a new coat, a Caribbean vacation, or a new car. Multiply the cost of the nondeductible expenditure by $3/2$ (or 150 percent) to determine the amount of income you *really* have to earn to pay for the item (assuming a $1/3$ tax rate). For example, if I want to take a $2,000 vacation with my wife, I immediately think about the $3,000 before-tax income I have to earn (that is, I give up $1,000 in income tax and have $2,000 left over for our vacation).

Suppose you just bought a new car for personal and family use and paid $24,000. Do you know the *cost* of your new car?

You say $24,000? I disagree. Your actual cost is the *amount of income* you have to earn to have $24,000 after tax to pay for the car. You need to earn income to buy things, so the cost of what you buy is the amount of income you need to earn to buy it. To buy a $24,000 car, you have to earn $36,000 before income tax, on which you pay $12,000 income tax ($1/3 \times \$36,000$) to have $24,000 after-tax disposable income to pay for the car. Your before-tax income cost of the car is $36,000, because the car is for personal use and is not deductible.

The before-tax cost of deductible expenditures

Suppose that you just received a $6,000 year-end bonus, which is considered income. You decide to make a $6,000 contribution to your church for its building fund drive. Contributions to churches and other qualified nonprofit organizations are *deductible*. In this situation, you probably would be itemizing your deductions for income tax (instead of taking the standard deduction). By making the contribution to the church, you increase your total deductions by $6,000. Therefore, your taxable income does not increase. The additional $6,000 in income is offset by the additional $6,000 deduction. The before-tax cost of your generous contribution is $6,000. You had to earn only $6,000 to make this expenditure.

Cost equals income when you spend income on *deductible* expenditures. For example, you need $2 income to have $2 for deductible expenditures. Assuming that you itemize deductions, the before-tax cost or before-tax income you have to earn to pay $2,000 property tax on your home is just $2,000, because real estate taxes are deductible. In contrast, you need $3 income to have $2 for a nondeductible expenditure. (Remember that I'm assuming a $1/3$ marginal income tax rate.)

If you had not donated the $6,000 to the church, your income tax amount would have been $2,000 higher, based on the $1/3$ marginal income tax rate. In other words, you would have had only $4,000 after-tax for a nondeductible expenditure — such as paying college tuition for your son or daughter.

What interest on consumer debt really costs

Some years ago, all interest paid by individuals, including interest on consumer debt, was deductible. But today, only interest paid on home mortgages is deductible. Removing the deductibility of interest paid on credit cards and other consumer debt increased the before-tax cost of this interest. In the old days, paying $240 interest on a credit card during the year required $240 of income. Today, you need $360 in income to pay $240 in credit card interest ($360 income × $1/3$ = $120 income tax, leaving only $240 for interest). In effect, Congress increased the cost of credit card interest by 50 percent.

Individuals as Borrowers

Everyone borrows money — for car loans, for home mortgages, on unpaid credit card balances, and so on. In my experience, everyone knows that interest is the extra amount you have to pay the lender in addition to paying back the amount you borrowed. But most people (including even experienced business people) are not entirely clear on how interest is figured. They worry that they may be getting the short end of the stick or that a lender may be taking advantage of them. You should be clear on the following points:

✔ If you make more than one loan payment per year, divide the annual interest rate by the number of loan payments to determine the interest rate per period, which usually is a month or a quarter. In other words, the quoted annual rate is simply the number to divide by to get the real interest rate per month or per quarter.

✔ When you make two or more loan payments, each payment goes first to the interest amount; the remainder is deducted from the loan balance, called the *principal*. The amount of the principal paydown each period is referred to as the *amortization* of the loan. Accounting for loan payments is based on this breakdown of loan payments.

✔ Shortening the term of a long-term loan, say from 30 years to 15 years, results in a dramatic decrease in the total interest paid over the life of the loan but a relatively small increase in the monthly loan payment amount.

✔ A monthly interest rate should not be multiplied by 12 to determine the *effective annual interest rate;* likewise, a quarterly interest rate should not be multiplied by 4 to determine the effective interest rate. Annual effective rates assume the *compounding* of interest during the year. Compounding means paying interest on interest; it is an extremely important building block for understanding financial matters.

A good example to illustrate several of these points is a typical home mortgage loan.

Home mortgage example

The biggest loan in most individuals' financial lives is a home mortgage. Compared with a short-term auto loan, a home mortgage loan runs up to 30 years, and the amount borrowed is usually much larger (unless you buy a Ferrari).

Suppose that you just bought the home of your dreams and qualified for a $200,000 first mortgage loan for 30 years at a 9.0 percent annual interest rate. The loan requires equal monthly payments, so you divide the annual interest rate by 12 to determine the monthly rate, which is 0.75 percent (or ³/₄ of 1 percent) per month. How much would each of your 360 loan payments be? How do you determine this amount? You probably would assume that the lender's quoted amount is correct — and you'd be pretty safe in this assumption. But I would pull out my hand-held calculator and punch in the key numbers as follows:

- ✔ **N** = number of periods — 360 months in this example

- ✔ **INT** = interest rate per period — 0.75 percent per month in this example

- ✔ **PV** = present value, or amount borrowed today (the present time) — $200,000 in this example

- ✔ **FV** = future value, or principal amount owed after all loan payments are made — $0 in this example (which means that the loan is fully amortized and paid off after the final monthly loan payment)

- ✔ **PMT** = payment per period given the data just listed — $1,609.25 in this example, which is the amount you solve for

The big advantage of a business/financial hand-held calculator is that you can punch in the known numbers (the first four) and then simply hit the button for the unknown number, which then appears instantly on the screen. Another big advantage is that you can keep all these numbers in the calculator and make "what if" changes very, very quickly. For example, what if the annual interest rate was 8.4 percent? Just re-enter the new interest rate (0.7 percent per month) and then call up the new monthly payment amount, which is $1,523.68. The monthly payment difference times the 360 payments is $30,803 less interest over the life of the loan. So you might decide to shop around for a lower rate.

Or you can do a "what if" for a 15-year loan and see how much more the monthly payment would be — which may come as a big surprise. Later in this chapter, I show you an example of how shortening a loan payment period can save you money; but first, take a look at the 30-year loan.

Each mortgage payment is divided between interest and principal reduction (paydown). For the first month, the interest amount is $1,500.00 ($200,000 loan balance × 0.75 percent monthly interest rate = $1,500.00). Therefore, the principal paydown is only $109.25. Right off, you can see that the loan's principal balance is going to go down very slowly — and that a 30-year mortgage loan involves a lot of interest. Lenders provide you with a loan payoff (amortization) schedule. I encourage you to take a look — although trying to follow down a table of 360 rows of monthly payments is tough going.

Figure 4-1 presents the annual amounts of interest and principal reduction for this mortgage loan. (I generated this data from a Microsoft Excel spreadsheet amortization schedule for the loan and used the built-in chart functions.) I present annual amounts instead of monthly amounts to help you see the basic contrast between interest and principal paydown. Note that the annual principal paydown doesn't overcome annual interest until the *23rd year*. In other words, you pay mostly interest during the first 22 years!

One alternative that you should definitely consider when taking out a home mortgage is a 15-year loan instead of a 30-year loan. For this home mortgage example, the monthly payment on a 15-year loan is $2,028.53, which is an additional $419.28 per month. The total interest over the life of the 15-year loan is about $165,000, compared with $379,000 on the 30-year loan. The 15-year loan saves you about $214,000 total interest over the life of the mortgage, and you own your home free and clear 15 years sooner. Of course, you have to come up with $419.28 more per month, which may not be possible in the short run. But after a few years of paying the 30-year amount, you can step up the amount you pay each month and pay off your mortgage sooner. Figure 4-1A (A is for *alternative*) shows the annual interest and principal payments for the 15-year mortgage.

You may be tempted to focus on the amount of the monthly payment and how this amount fits into your personal budget. But you should also look closely at the pattern of interest versus principal payments over the life of the loan. In my experience, overlooking interest versus principal payments is the biggest mistake borrowers make. You should always know how fast you are paying off principal, and you should keep track of your loan balance.

Tools of the trade

I advise everyone to "invest" the time and effort (plus a relatively small cost) and learn how to use one of two indispensable tools of the trade for analyzing savings and investments: a hand-held calculator and a personal computer spreadsheet program, such as Excel, Quattro Pro, or Lotus 1-2-3.

A powerful business/financial hand-held calculator costs under $100. I use a financial calculator every day. You have to take some time and go through a few examples to learn how to operate the thing — but I think the time is well spent. The owner's manuals for the Hewlett Packard hand-held business/financial calculators are very well written and have good practical examples. When negotiating my most recent home mortgage, I brought my HP calculator along and caught the loan officer in a major error.

If you already use a computer spreadsheet program, take advantage of its financial functions. For example, you can easily print out loan payoff schedules, savings plans, retirement fund accumulations, estimated retirement income, and many more useful tables and schedules and convert these into charts for easier viewing. The spreadsheet owners' manuals are terrible, I know. I suggest buying one of the *...For Dummies* books for the spreadsheet program you use.

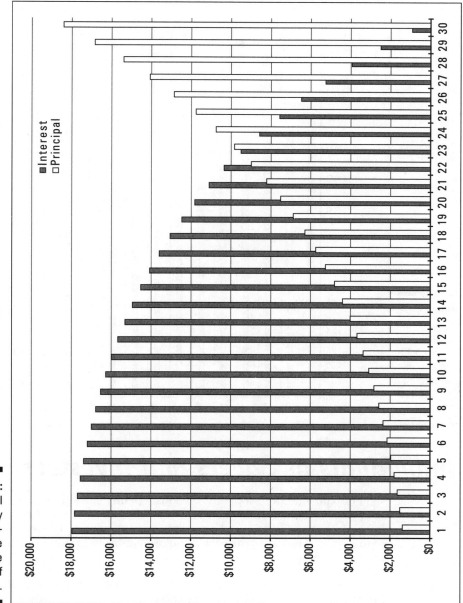

Figure 4-1:
Annual
summary
for a 30-
year home
mortgage
payoff
schedule.

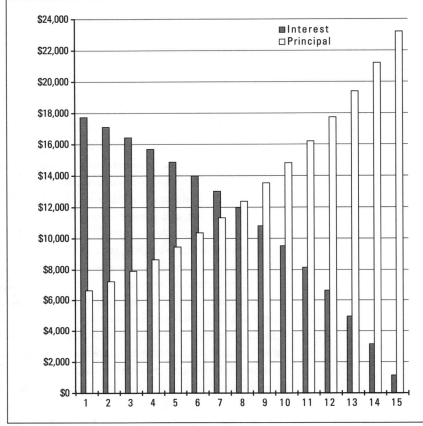

Figure 4-1A:
Annual
summary
for a 15-
year home
mortgage
payoff
schedule.

Individuals as Savers and Investors

Ben Franklin said that "a penny saved is a penny earned." His point is that one penny not spent today is a penny kept for another day. Until that later day arrives, the penny saved can earn interest income. These days, 100 pennies saved for one year earn about 6 pennies in interest income, or 6 percent per year.

Saving is done for income and safety of principal and not for market value appreciation. Suppose you save $10,000 for one year. You expect to earn the going interest rate, *and* you expect to have very little or no risk of losing any of your capital during the year. You do not expect your savings to appreciate in value other than from interest income. Assuming that the going interest rate is 6 percent, you expect that your savings will grow to $10,600 by the end of the year — the $10,000 you started with plus 6 percent interest earned on that money.

The power of compounding

Suppose that you have some money that you want to save. You can deposit your money in a savings account at a savings and loan association, a bank, or a credit union. Or you can buy a CD — not the music kind or the kind you insert into a computer compact disc drive, but a certificate of deposit issued by a bank or other financial institution. Or you can put your money in a money market fund. You can save money through many different types of vehicles and instruments, which are explained in Eric Tyson's excellent book *Personal Finance For Dummies* (IDG Books Worldwide, Inc.). My purpose is to demonstrate how your savings grows or does not grow depending on what you do with the interest income each period.

Suppose that you have $100,000 in savings (larger amounts of money are more interesting than smaller amounts). You leave the money alone for one year, and at the end of the year your savings balance has grown to $106,000. Therefore, you earned a 6 percent annual interest or earnings rate:

```
$6,000 increase in savings balance ÷ $100,000 balance at
        start of year = 6%
```

Now you have a critical choice to make: Should you withdraw the $6,000 earnings and spend the money, or should you leave the $6,000 in savings? Many people depend on income from their savings for living expenses. Others want to build up their capital over time. Suppose that you're in the second group; you leave the earnings in savings for a second year.

At the end of the second year, your savings amount is $112,360 — $6,360 more than at the start of the year. Therefore, for the second year, you also earned a 6 percent annual interest rate:

```
$6,360 increase in savings balance ÷ $106,000 balance at
        start of year = 6%
```

You made more earnings (interest income) in the second year because you had more in savings at the start of the year.

If you continue to plow back annual earnings for 20 years, how much do you have at the end of the 20 years — starting with $100,000, earning 6 percent per year, and resaving earnings every year? Your savings balance would grow to $320,714, more than three times the amount you started with. This projected amount is called the *future value* and depends on the interest rate per period and the number of periods.

Note: I use the terms *plow back* and *resaving* in order to avoid the term *reinvesting*. Reinvesting implies an investment, which, strictly speaking, involves market value fluctuation risk. Saving does not involve this risk. (I should warn you that there is always a small risk that part of the money in a savings account or instrument will be lost or will be delayed in being returned to you — witness the savings and loan association scandals of a few years ago.)

Figure 4-2 illustrates how your savings balance would grow year by year, assuming a 6 percent annual interest rate for all 20 years. This growth comes at a price — you cannot take out annual earnings. Not withdrawing annual earnings is called *compounding;* the term *compound interest* refers to not withdrawing interest income. Compounding means that you save more and more each year.

Unfortunately, compounding of earnings is often touted as a sort of magical way to build wealth over time. Don't be suckered by this claim. You sacrifice 20 years of earnings to make your money grow; you don't get to spend the interest income on your savings for 20 years. I don't call this magic; I call it *frugal*.

In your economic life, you constantly make many spend-versus-save decisions. I didn't have to take my wife out to a nice dinner on her birthday. If I had saved the $100 and earned a 6 percent annual interest rate and compounded the earnings for 20 years, I would have $320.71 (exactly one-thousandth of the preceding savings example). By then, I'd be in my 80s. Compounding is not magical — it's a conservative way to build wealth that requires you to forgo a lot of spending along the way.

The rule of 72

A very handy trick of the trade is called the rule of 72. In Figure 4-2, at the end of the 12th year, notice that your savings balance is sitting right on $200,000 — exactly twice what you started with. This is a good example of the rule of 72. The rule states that if you take the periodic earnings rate as a whole number and divide it into 72, the answer is the number of periods it takes to double what you started with. Sure enough: 72 ÷ 6 = 12. Doubling your money at 6 percent per year takes 12 years.

The rule of 72 assumes compounding of earnings. It's amazingly accurate over a broad range of earnings rates and number of periods. For example, how long does it take to double your money at an 8 percent annual earnings rate? It takes nine years (72 ÷ 8 = 9). If you earn 18 percent per year, you double your money in just four years.

One caution: For very low and very high earnings rates, the rule is not accurate and should not be used.

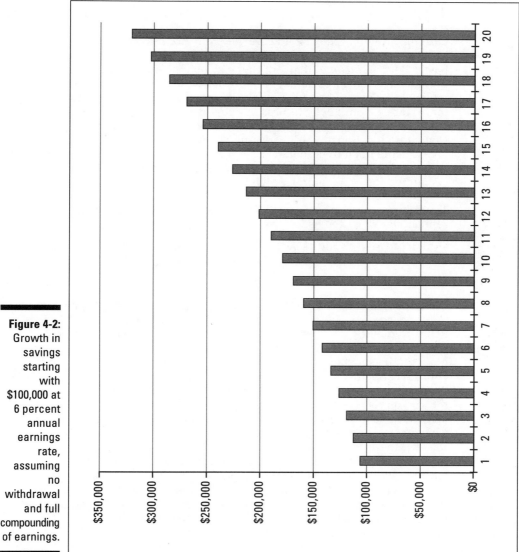

Figure 4-2:
Growth in savings starting with $100,000 at 6 percent annual earnings rate, assuming no withdrawal and full compounding of earnings.

The twofold nature of return on investment

Earnings from *investing* capital are generally not referred to as earnings on investment, but rather as *return on investment* (ROI). ROI consists of two parts: (1) *cash income* (if in fact there is cash income during the period), and (2) *market value appreciation or depreciation.* When you invest, you put your money in stocks and bonds (which are called *securities*), or mutual funds, or real estate, or pork belly futures, or whatever. The range of possible investments is diverse, to say the least. I recommend Eric Tyson's *Investing For Dummies* (IDG Books Worldwide, Inc.). He explains the wide range of investments open to individuals, from mutual funds to real estate and most things in between. Investors should understand how *return on investment* is accounted for — no matter which type of investment they choose.

The return on investment, or ROI, for a period is expressed as a percent or rate and is computed as follows:

```
Return for Period ÷ Amount Invested at Start of Period =
          Rate of Return on Investment (ROI), usually
                expressed as a percentage
```

Often, people use the term *ROI* when they really mean *rate,* or *percent* of ROI. Like some words that have a silent character that is not pronounced, ROI is frequently used without rate or percent. Anytime you see the % symbol, you know that the *rate* of ROI is meant. In any case, the ROI rate is not a totally satisfactory measure. For instance, suppose you tell me that your investments earned an 18 percent ROI last year. I know your wealth, or capital, increased 18 percent — although I don't know how much of this return you received in cash income and how much was an increase in the market value of your investment, and I don't know whether you spent your cash income or reinvested it.

The cash income component of investment return is always accounted for by individuals, financial institutions, and businesses. However, the market value gain or loss during the period may or may not be recorded. Most individuals who invest in real estate, farms, and stocks and bonds do not record the gain or loss in the market value of their investment during the period. So they do not have a full and complete accounting of ROI for the period.

My father-in-law has owned a farm in Iowa since 1940. He keeps very good accounting records for the revenue and expenses of the farm so that he can determine net income (or loss) for the year, which he reports in his annual income tax return. But he does not record a gain or loss from changes in the market value of the farm from year to year. He knows the approximate market value of the farm, but he does not account for changes in the market value. Only the original 1940 cost is on his books.

He doesn't plan on selling the farm. For one thing, he would have to pay a big amount of income tax on the gain over original cost if he did. He plans to leave the farm in his estate. In short, accounting for the return on his farm investment is restricted to cash income (or loss) for the year. Only mentally does he compare the cash income against the current market value of the farm — which is as close as he gets to calculating a ROI rate for the year.

The investment accounting that's done by most individuals is governed largely by what's required for income tax purposes. Unrealized market value gains are not taxed; not until the investments are actually sold at a gain do individuals have to pay income tax. So they do not record market value gains. Nevertheless, they keep an eye on market value ups and downs, in addition to their cash income. For example, real estate investors generally do not measure and record market value changes each year, although they keep an eye on the prices of comparable properties.

In contrast, financial institutions, including banks, mutual funds, insurance companies, and pension funds, are governed by generally accepted accounting principles (GAAP). Accounting for their investments in marketable securities that are held for sale or trading or that are available for sale requires that changes in market value be recognized. On the other hand, accounting for investments in fixed-income debt securities (for example, bonds and notes) that are held until maturity does not recognize market value gains and losses.

The main point of this discussion is that you should be very clear about what's included and what's not included in ROI. As just discussed, many individuals do not capture market value changes during the year in accounting for the return, or earnings on their investments — they account for only the cash income part, which gives an incomplete measure of ROI. On the other hand, when a mutual fund advertises that its annual ROI has been 18 percent over the last five years, you can be sure that it *does* include the market value gains in this rate (as well as cash income, of course).

A real-world example of ROI accounting

Suppose that you invest $94,757.86 today in a U.S. Treasury Note that has three years to go until its maturity date. The face, or par, value of this debt security is $100,000.00, which is its maturity value three years hence and also is the basis on which interest is computed. (U.S. debt securities issued with less than ten years to maturity are called *notes* instead of bonds.) This note pays 6 percent annual interest, which is paid semiannually. Every six months, the U.S. Treasury Department sends you $3,000.

Assume that you spend the $3,000 semiannual interest income. So far, so good. But now a tough question: What's your ROI rate on this investment?

By paying $94,757.86, you buy the Treasury Note at a *discount* from its $100,000.00 maturity value. The discount provides part of your return on investment in addition to your cash flow interest income. Most of your ROI consists of cash income every six months. But part consists of *market value appreciation* as the note moves closer to its maturity date. This second component does not provide cash flow until the maturity date is reached. Taking both parts into account, your ROI rate is more than the 6 percent interest rate based on the par value of the note.

Tell you what: Guess that the correct ROI rate is 4 percent per period (six months), and see whether this rate is correct. I'll walk you quickly through the accounting in this example to test out the 4 percent ROI rate. Indeed, this is the correct rate. Figure 4-3 demonstrates that in each period, the return on the investment equals 4 percent of the amount invested at the start of the period. The investor receives only $3,000 per period of cash income. The gain in the value of the note each period as it moves towards its maturity value provides the remainder of the ROI.

Figure 4-3:
Buying debt security at a discount from maturity value to illustrate a higher ROI than the interest rate.

		ROI @ 4.0%	At End of Period		
Period	Beginning Balance	on Beginning Balance	Cash Received	Gain in Value	Ending Balance
1	$94,757.86	$3,790.31	$3,000.00	$790.31	$95,548.18
2	$95,548.18	$3,821.93	$3,000.00	$821.93	$96,370.10
3	$96,370.10	$3,854.80	$3,000.00	$854.80	$97,224.91
4	$97,224.91	$3,889.00	$3,000.00	$889.00	$98,113.91
5	$98,113.91	$3,924.56	$3,000.00	$924.56	$99,038.46
6	$99,038.46	$3,961.54	$3,000.00	$961.54	$100,000.00
				$5,242.14	Maturity Value

Revealing the implicit assumption in annual ROI rates

The investment in the U.S. Treasury Note is really two investments in one. For the $3,000 semiannual interest income, you invest $75,000 to earn 4 percent each six-month period:

```
$3,000 interest income ÷ $75,000 investment = 4%
```

The additional $19,757.86 invested in the note ($94,757.86 total cost – $75,000 for the interest income) does not yield cash income each period. Instead, this part of your investment in the note increases 4 percent in value each period. For the first period:

```
$19,757.86 invested × 4% ROI = $790.31 (check this amount
        in Figure 4-3)
```

Because this amount is not received in cash, it is reinvested, or compounded, to determine the amount invested next period. Therefore, the gain-in-value amount is larger from period to period, as shown in Figure 4-3.

One final question: What is the *annual* ROI rate on this investment? The answer is not simply 8 percent (4 percent semiannual ROI × 2). The $3,000 semiannual interest income could have been reinvested in another investment for the second six months of the year, or *compounded*. In fact, the other part of your investment return (that is, the gain in value each period as the note moves towards its maturity date) is compounded, as just explained.

The standard practice in the finance world is to compound investment income that is received in cash during the year to determine the annual ROI rate on the investment. Assume that you did not spend the $3,000 interest income but instead invested it for the second six months of the year at 4 percent. This additional investment would yield:

```
$3,000 invested × 4% ROI = $120 investment income
```

So your total return for the year would be $6,120 — your two $3,000 interest receipts from the note plus the $120 on the $3,000 that was reinvested for the second half of the year. The annual ROI rate is calculated as follows:

```
$6,120 total return ÷ $75,000 invested = 8.16% annual ROI
        rate
```

Annual ROI rates quoted by financial institutions, for stock index ROI annual rates, and for almost every type of investment make this critical assumption. In short, any cash income received during the year is assumed to be compounded (reinvested) for the rest of the year to determine the annual ROI rate.

Part II
Getting a Grip on Financial Statements

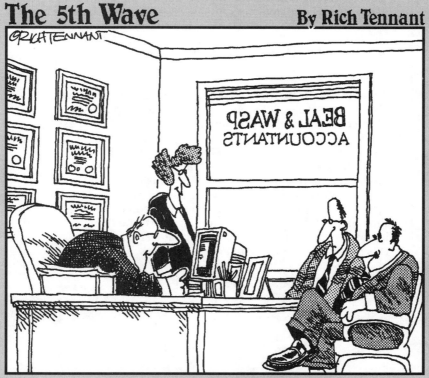

The 5th Wave   By Rich Tennant

BEAL & WASP
ACCOUNTANTS

"OUR GOAL IS TO MAXIMIZE YOUR UPSIDE AND MINIMIZE YOUR DOWNSIDE WHILE WE PROTECT OUR OWN BACKSIDE."

In this part . . .

Financial statements are like the tip of an iceberg —
the only visible part, underneath which are a lot of
record-keeping and accounting methods. The managers
of a business, the investors in a business, and the lenders
to a business need a firm grasp on these accounting
communications. They need to know which handles to
grab hold of and how to find both the good and bad
signals in financial statements.

Accountants prepare three primary financial statements.
The *income statement* reports the profit-making activities
of the business and how much profit or loss the business
made. (Sounds odd, doesn't it, to say a business *made a
loss?* But to make profit, a business has to take the risk
that it may suffer a loss.) The *balance sheet* reports the
financial situation and position of the business. The *cash
flow statement* reports how much cash was actually
realized from profit and other sources of cash, and what
the business did with this money. In short, the financial
life of a business is revealed in its financial statements, as
this part of the book uncovers.

Chapter 5

Making Profit and Knowing Where It Is

*P*rofit is the main financial goal of a business, of course. Accountants are the professional *profit measurers* in the business world — measuring profit is their expertise. I find profit accounting a really fascinating challenge. You have to understand the way a business operates and its profit-making strategies to account for its profit. At first glance, making profit may seem fairly simple — make sales and control expenses. Bring in more dollars from sales revenue than the dollars paid out for expenses. The excess of revenue over expenses is profit. What's the problem?

Well, making and accounting for profit is not nearly as simple as it might appear. Managers have the very demanding tasks of making sales and controlling expenses — and accountants have the tough tasks of measuring revenue and expenses and preparing profit reports that summarize the profit-making activities each period. Also, accountants have to explain to managers where profit went if the cash account doesn't increase by the same amount as profit.

This chapter starts with the simple case in which the increase in cash is equal to profit — the business collects cash for all its sales during the period and pays out cash for all its expenses, and profit equals the cash left over. But alas, the business world is not so simple. So the chapter continues one step at a time to build a realistic profit model. Your business is very much like this real-world example. Walking through this example lets you answer one very important question: Where exactly is my profit that I worked so hard to earn?

Profit in One Fell Swoop: Measuring Profit with the Profit Equation

For a business that sells products, its profit equation is simply Profit = sales revenue – expenses, commonly presented like this:

Sales revenue	$xx,xxx,xxx
Expenses	(xx,xxx,xxx)
Profit	$ x,xxx,xxx

Businesses that sell services instead of products also use the term *sales revenue* for the *gross income* (total income, before deducting expenses) from sales of their services — but you also see slight variations on this term. Businesses that don't sell anything as such — financial institutions that earn investment income, for example — use other terms for their gross income.

Notice the following about this equation:

✔ Even though you're deducting expenses from sales revenue, you generally don't use a minus sign or parentheses to indicate that the expenses amount is a negative number (although some people do).

✔ Using a double underline under the profit number is common practice but not universal. Some people use bold type. You generally don't see anything as garish as a fat arrow pointing to the profit number or a big smiley encircling the profit number — but again, tastes vary.

✔ Profit isn't usually called *profit*. It's called *net income* or the *bottom line* or — particularly on financial reports intended for people outside the business — *net earnings*. (Can't accountants agree on *anything?*) Throughout this book, I use the terms *net income* and *profit* pretty much interchangeably.

✔ *Sales revenue* is the total amount of money or other assets received from sales of the company's products for the entire year. The number used in the profit equation represents all sales — you can't tell how many different sales were made, or how many different customers the company sold products to, or how the sales were distributed over the 12 months of the year.

Sales revenue is strictly what belongs to the business and doesn't include money that anyone else can claim (for example, sales tax that the business collects from customers and then remits to the government).

Note: A business may have other sources of income, in addition to the sales revenue from its products. One common example is interest earned on investments, which gives the business excess money that it doesn't need for its profit-making assets. In the profit report, investment income goes on a separate line and is not included with sales revenue — to make clear that this source of income is secondary to the mainstream sales revenue of the business.

✔ *Expenses* consist of a wide variety of different costs, starting with the cost of the goods (products) sold to the customers and including many other costs of operating the business:

- Payroll costs (wages, salaries, and benefits paid to employees)
- Insurance costs
- Property taxes on buildings and land
- Cost of gas and electric utilities
- Telephone and Internet charges
- Depreciation of operating assets that last more than one year (such as buildings, cars and trucks, computers, office furniture, tools and machinery, and shelving)
- Advertising
- Office supplies
- Legal and audit costs
- Interest paid on loans
- Income taxes

As is the case with sales revenue, you can't tell from the amount reported as an expense how much was spent on each component making up the total of expense. For example, the total depreciation expense amount doesn't tell you how much was for buildings and how much for trucks. Sales tax that the company collects from customers and then remits to the government is not included as an expense.

To better understand the whole sales tax thing, suppose you have a business with the following profit equation for the year:

Sales revenue	$1,000,000
Expenses	(900,000)
Profit	$100,000

The P word: profitable terminology

I'm sure you won't be surprised to hear that the financial objective of every business is to make profit. In the pursuit of profit, a business should behave ethically, stay within the law, care for its employees, and be friendly to the environment. I don't mean to preach here. But the blunt truth of the matter is that *profit* is a dirty word to many people, and the profit motive is a favorite target of many critics who blame it for unsafe working conditions, exploitation of child labor, wages that are below the poverty line, and other ills of the economic system. The profit motive is blamed for how incomes and wealth are distributed in our economic system as well.

Businesses should find that earning profit by doing things the right way rather than by cutting corners is in their own interest. But even on their best behavior, businesses will continue to come under the fire of criticism for the profit motive. It's certainly an easy target.

You hear a lot about the profit motive of business, but you hardly ever see the *P* word in external financial reports. In the financial press, the most common term you see instead is *earnings*. Both *The Wall Street Journal* and *The New York Times* cover the profit performance of public corporations and use the term *earnings reports*. If you look in financial statements, the term *net income* is used most often for the bottom-line profit that a business earns. Accountants prefer *net income,* though they also use other names, like *net earnings* and *net operating earnings.*

In short, *profit* is more of a street name; in polite company, you generally say *net income.*

Assume that all sales were subject to a 7 percent sales tax. The company collected another $70,000 from its customers (7% × $1,000,000 = $70,000), in addition to the $1 million sales revenue amount shown. This $70,000 does not belong to the business and is soon paid over to the government sales tax agencies. The main point is that the $70,000 sales tax is not included in sales revenue, nor is it included in expenses.

By the way, notice that only one total amount is shown for all the business's expenses — to keep the profit equation as short as possible. However, when preparing a formal profit report — which is called the *income statement* — expenses are broken down into several basic categories (see "Reporting Profit: The Income Statement" at the end of the chapter).

Measuring the Effects of Profit

Your business earned $100,000 profit for the year. (See the profit equation in the preceding section.) That means you're a hundred grand richer now, right? Well, that could happen in a make-believe world, and I start this section with a hypothetical profit example in which your business checking account *does* increase by $100,000 — but this example is extremely oversimplified. In the real world, nothing is that simple.

The financial effects of profit on a business go far beyond a fatter bank account. To get a clear picture of these effects, you use a *balance sheet* — a summary of assets on one side and liabilities and owners' equity on the other — to report the business's financial condition at the end of the profit period. The general format of a balance sheet is as follows:

```
Assets = liabilities + owners' equity
```

See Chapter 2 for more information about this equation.

Profit is essentially an increase in a business's assets — or to be more precise, its *net assets,* which is total assets less total liabilities. To whom does profit belong? The owners, of course. A business's *creditors* — those to whom the business owes money, as recorded in the liability accounts — don't benefit from profit; the amounts owed to the creditors don't increase with the profit earned by the business, just as those amounts wouldn't decrease if the business suffered a loss.

So profit has no impact on the liabilities part of the equation but has a big impact on the owners' equity part (and, of course, a corresponding impact on assets). Profit increases the owners' share of the company's assets; the retained earnings account records this increase. *Retained earnings* is one of two sources of owners' equity — the other is money invested in the business by its owners. In other words, owners' equity is increased both by profit and by additional money that owners pour into the business. Owners' equity is like a tub that has two inflow spigots — capital invested by owners is one spigot, and profit is the other. Profit is accumulated in the retained earnings account.

Please pay attention here: The retained earnings account is *not* — I repeat, *not* — an asset, even though its name suggests that it refers to assets. It is a *source*-of-assets account, not an assets account. The retained earnings account is part of the broad category of owners' equity, so it appears as owners' equity on the right side of the balance sheet (the right side of the equal sign in the equation), opposite assets. *Remember:* Assets appear on the left side of the balance sheet, and the two sources of the assets — owners' equity and liabilities — appear on the right side. The two sides do *not* mingle. Imagine a Chinese wall or an iron curtain between them. See the "So why is it called *retained earnings?*" sidebar for more information about the retained earnings account.

So why is it called *retained earnings?*

The retained earnings account, like all balance sheet accounts, reports the net balance in the account after recording both the increases *and the decreases* in the account through the end of the period. The retained earnings account increases when the business makes a profit, and it then decreases when the business distributes some of the profit to the owners. That is, the total amount of profit paid out to the owners is recorded as a decrease in the retained earnings account. (Exactly how the profit is divided among the owners depends on the ownership structure of the business — see Chapter 11.)

The net balance in the account is the amount of profit increases less the amount of distribution decreases — that is, the net amount of profit retained in the business. That's why the account is called *retained earnings*.

Bonus question: Why doesn't a business pay out *all* its profit to owners? One reason is that the business may not have converted all the profit into cash by the end of the year and may not have enough cash to distribute the profit to the owners (in fact, the increase in cash seldom equals the amount of profit). Or the business may have had the cash but needed it for other purposes, such as growing the company by buying new buildings and equipment, or spending the money on research and development of new products. Reinvesting the profit in the business in this way is often referred to as *plowing back earnings*. A business should always make good use of its profit cash flow instead of just letting the cash pile up in the cash account. See Chapter 7 for more on cash flow from profit.

Here's a simple, if unrealistic, example: Suppose that your business collected all sales revenue for the year in cash and paid out all expenses for the year in cash. No liabilities are involved, so the increase in net assets consists entirely of the increase in cash. Your profit for the year was $100,000. Here's how that profit affects the financial condition of your business (in the following examples, I use + and – in the equations, which you won't see in regular financial reports):

Assets	=	Liabilities	+	Owners' Equity
Cash: +$100,000		No impact		Retained earnings: +$100,000

So the cash asset account increases by $100,000, the net difference between sales revenue and expenses — your business checking account balance is $100,000 higher at the end of the year than at the beginning of the year. You haven't distributed any of the profit to the owners, so the retained earnings account also increases by $100,000 (if you had distributed some of the profit, the balance of the retained earnings account would equal $100,000 less the amount you distributed, and your cash would be lower by the same amount). Of course, other factors may be involved here — for example, you may have other cash receipts and cash disbursements to record — but I want to keep this example simple. Read on for a more complex situation.

Exploring Profit One Step at a Time

I don't mean to scare you off, but the profit picture gets more complex than the simple cash-increase example just discussed. Many businesses sell their products on credit rather than cash, for example, and usually don't collect all their sales revenue by year-end. Expenses are even more complicated. Each of the following sections adds a basic layer of reality one at a time, to bring the profit picture into more realistic focus. To appreciate profit, you need to have a grip on these factors.

Making sales on credit

When a business allows customers to buy its products or services on credit — using a credit card, such as American Express, or using a line of credit that the business personally extended to the customer — you need to add an asset account called *accounts receivable,* which records the total amount owed to the business by its customers who made purchases on credit and haven't paid up yet. You probably would not have collected all your receivables by the end of the year, especially for purchases that occurred in the last weeks of the year. However, you still record the sales revenue and the cost of goods sold expense for these sales in the year in which the sale occurred.

To build on the example from earlier in this chapter, say that your business had sales revenue of $1 million and total expenses of $900,000, making for a bottom-line profit of $100,000. But now assume that $80,000 of the sales revenue came from credit sales that haven't been paid off yet. Here's what the financial effects of your $100,000 profit look like now:

Assets	=	Liabilities	+	Owners' Equity
Cash:	+$20,000	No impact		Retained earnings: +$100,000
Accounts receivable:	+$80,000			

As in the simple cash example from the preceding section, the $100,000 profit increases retained earnings and has no impact on liabilities. But assets is now divided into cash and accounts receivable. The cash account has increased only $20,000, though the other $80,000 is basically cash waiting in the wings to be collected in the near future (assuming that all your customers pay their debts).

Can you distribute the $100,000 profit in cash to the owners? Obviously not. Even if your cash balance is more than $100,000, only $20,000 of it came from profit for the year; the rest comes from other sources and can't be treated as profit gains.

Notice that profit and sales revenue are the same — $100,000 and $1 million, respectively — whether the business example makes all sales on cash or makes sales on credit. But the financial effects are quite different. When you make sales on credit, you count the sales as part of your profits, but you don't have that cash available to pay your bills or reinvest in your business. So to make sales and earn profit, you basically need to finance your accounts receivable by borrowing money or raising capital from your business's owners. Remember that the accounting equation has to balance — higher total assets means that the total of liabilities and owners' equity has to be higher.

Depreciation expense

Depreciation expense means spreading out the cost of a fixed asset instead of charging the entire cost to the year of purchase; that way, each year of use bears a share of the total cost. *Fixed assets* are long-lived operating assets — buildings, machinery, office equipment, vehicles, computers and data-processing equipment, shelving and cabinets, and so on. Of course, depreciation applies only to fixed assets that you buy, not those you rent or lease. (If you lease or rent fixed assets, which is quite common for some fixed assets, the rent you pay each month is charged to *rent expense*. Rent expense is the substitute for depreciation expense when you rent rather than buy your fixed assets.)

For example, cars and light trucks are depreciated over five years for income tax purposes (businesses apply the five-year rule to other kinds of assets as well). The basic idea of depreciation is to charge a fraction of the total cost to your depreciation expense account for each of the five years (the actual fraction each year depends on which method of depreciation you choose, which is explained in Chapter 13).

Suppose that your business has the same amount of profit and sales revenue — $100,000 and $1 million, respectively — as in the previous example, with $80,000 still in accounts receivable. Expenses still total $900,000, but in this example, the total of expenses includes $25,000 depreciation for fixed assets (assume that you bought these assets for $125,000 and are charging one-fifth of the cost each year for five years). Because you didn't actually pay anything for the fixed assets this year — the assets were bought in previous years — the cash account balance in this example is now $45,000 instead of $20,000 (see the "Appreciating the positive impact of depreciation on cash flow" sidebar if you're confused about this point). *Remember:* Depreciation is a real expense, but not a *cash* expense after the fixed assets are already bought and paid for.

Appreciating the positive impact of depreciation on cash flow

Whereas making sales on credit has a negative impact on your cash flow, depreciation is good news for cash flow. This concept gets a little complex, so stay with me here:

Fundamentally, a business sets its sales prices high enough to recover its expenses plus provide a profit. In a real sense, the business is passing on the cost of its fixed assets to its customers and recovering some of the cost of the fixed assets each year though sales revenue. The example that I use in class to illustrate this critical point is a taxicab owner and driver. She sets her fares high enough to pay for her time; to pay for the insurance, license, gas, and oil; and to recover the cost of the cab. Included in each fare is a tiny fraction of the cost of the cab, which over the course of the year adds up to the depreciation expense that she passed on to her passengers and collected in fares. At the end of the year, she has collected a certain amount of money that pays her back for part of the cost of the cab.

In short, fixed assets are gradually *liquidated*, or turned back into cash, each year. Part of sales revenue recovers a fraction of the cost of fixed assets, which is why the decrease in the fixed assets account to record depreciation expense has the effect of increasing cash. What the company does with this cash recovery is another matter. Sooner or later, you need to replace the fixed assets to continue in business. In this chapter, I do not look beyond the immediate impacts of the sales revenue and expenses of this period.

Here's what the financial effects for that profit look like:

Assets	**=**		**Liabilities**	**+**	**Owners' Equity**
Cash:	+$45,000		No impact		Retained earnings: +$100,000
Accounts receivable: +$80,000					
Fixed assets:	−$25,000				

The $100,000 profit for the year now consists of two asset increases totaling $125,000 ($45,000 cash + $80,000 accounts receivable = $125,000), less one asset decrease of $25,000. Total assets increase by $100,000 — the profit for the year.

Remember, nothing has changed in the income statement; sales revenue and total expenses are the same. But the financial effects from profit are getting more spread out in the balance sheet.

Unpaid expenses

A business often pays many of its expenses some time after the period benefited by the expense. For example, your business hires a law firm that does a lot of legal work for the company during the year, but you don't pay the bill until the following year. Your business may match retirement contributions made by employees, but you may not pay your share until the following year. Or your business may have unpaid bills for telephone, gas, electricity, and water that it has used during the year.

You use three different liability accounts to record three different types of unpaid expenses:

- ✔ **Accounts payable:** For items that the business buys on credit and for which it receives an invoice (a bill). For example, your business receives an invoice from its lawyers for legal work done. As soon as you receive the invoice, you record in the accounts payable liability account the amount that you owe. Later, when you pay the invoice, you subtract that amount from the accounts payable account — and your cash goes down by the same amount, of course.

- ✔ **Accrued expenses:** For unpaid costs that a business generally has to estimate because it doesn't receive an invoice for them. Some examples of accrued expenses are unused vacation and sick days that your employees are carrying over to the following year, which you will have to pay for in the coming year; unpaid bonuses to salespeople; the cost of future repairs and part replacements on products that customers have bought and haven't returned for repair yet; and the daily accumulation of interest on borrowed money that won't be paid until the end of the loan period.

  As you can imagine, without invoices to refer to, you have to examine your business operations carefully to determine which liabilities of this sort to record.

- ✔ **Income tax payable:** For income taxes that a business still owes the IRS. At the end of the year, your business may not have paid all its income tax expense for the year — it may still owe a fraction to the IRS. You record the unpaid amount in the income tax payable account, and you record the full amount of the income tax on the taxable income earned for the year (including the paid and unpaid portions) as an expense. In other words, the income tax expense for the year is the total amount based on the taxable income for the entire year — most of which is paid by year-end, but part of which is still unpaid at year-end. This unpaid part is recorded in the income tax payable liability account.

> *Note:* A business may be organized as a *pass-through tax entity* for income tax purposes, which means that it doesn't pay income tax itself but instead passes its taxable income through to its owners. Chapter 11 explains these types of business entities. This example assumes that the business is a corporation that pays income tax.

The following balance sheet continues the example that I've used throughout this chapter. This time, I add the financial effects of unpaid expenses. I also add totals at the bottom of the balance sheet for total assets on one side and the total of liabilities and owners' equity on the other side. Eyeballing the situation to make sure that the accounting equation is in balance is getting more and more difficult with each new account that you add.

Assets	=	Liabilities	+	Owners' Equity
Cash: +$115,000		Accounts payable: +$30,000		Retained earnings: +$100,000
Accounts receivable: +$80,000		Accrued expenses: +$35,000		
Fixed assets: −$25,000		Income tax payable: +$5,000		
Totals: $170,000	=	**$70,000**	+	**$100,000**

Adding unpaid expenses to the balance sheet causes the cash increase to go up again, just like when I add depreciation expense in the preceding section. The cash increase was $45,000 with the depreciation expense factored in, and now it's $115,000 — an additional $70,000. The reason is that the three unpaid expenses amount to $70,000 ($30,000 accounts payable + $35,000 accrued expenses + $5,000 income tax payable). In short, the business did not pay $70,000 of its expenses by the end of the year, and its cash balance is higher by this amount — you get to hang on to the cash until you pay the liabilities. Of course, you have to pay these liabilities next year, but isn't it nice to have your balance sheet show a big, fat cash increase for this year?

Prepaid expenses

Prepaid expenses are the opposite of unpaid expenses. For example, a business buys fire insurance and general liability insurance (in case a customer who slips on a wet floor or is insulted by a careless salesperson sues the business). You pay insurance premiums ahead of time, before the period in which you're covered, but you charge that expense to the actual period benefited. At the end of the year, the business may be only halfway through the insurance coverage period and so it charges off only half the premium cost as an expense (for a six-month policy, you charge one-sixth of the premium cost to each of the six months covered). So at the time you pay the premium, you charge the entire amount to the prepaid expenses asset account, and for each month of coverage, you transfer the appropriate fraction of the cost to the insurance expense account.

Another example of when to use a prepaid expenses asset account is when your business pays cash to stock up on office supplies that it may not use for several months. You record the cost in the prepaid expenses asset account at the time of purchase; then when you finally use the supplies, you subtract the amount from the prepaid expenses asset account and add the expense to the office supplies expense account.

Using the prepaid expenses asset account is not so much for the purpose of reporting all assets of a business, because the balance in the account compared to other assets and total assets is typically small. Rather, using this account is another example of allocating costs to expenses in the period benefited by the costs and not necessarily in the period in which the business pays for the costs.

Here's that same example I've been using throughout the chapter, with the financial effects of prepaid expenses through the end of the year factored in:

Assets	=	Liabilities	+	Owners' Equity	
Cash:	+$100,000	Accounts payable:	+$30,000	Retained earnings:	+$100,000
Accounts receivable:	+$80,000	Accrued expenses:	+$35,000		
Fixed assets:	−$25,000	Income tax payable:	+$5,000		
Prepaid expenses:	+$15,000				
Totals:	**$170,000**	=	**$70,000**	+	**$100,000**

This time, adding an account to the balance sheet has a negative impact on the business's cash increase. Whereas the cash increase was $115,000 after I factored in unpaid expenses (see the preceding section), it's now only $100,000 — $15,000 less because of the new, $15,000 prepaid expenses account.

Again, remember that although your business is $15,000 cash poorer, the profit remains the same ($100,000) as it is in the previous examples. The difference lies in the way the profit is spread out over the balance sheet.

Inventory increase (cost of goods sold)

Cost of goods sold is one of the primary expenses of businesses that sell products. It's just what its name implies: what the business paid for the products that it sells to customers. A business makes profit by setting its prices high enough to cover the actual cost of the product, the costs of operating the business, interest on borrowed money, and income taxes (assuming that the business pays income tax), with a little (or a lot) left over for profit.

When the business acquires a product, the cost of the product goes into an *inventory asset account* (and, of course, the cost is either deducted from the cash account or added to a liability account, depending on whether the business paid with cash or bought on credit). When a customer buys that product, you transfer the cost of the product from the inventory asset account to the cost of goods sold expense account because the product is no longer in your inventory but you still have to account for the cost that you put out.

The first step in determining profit for the period is deducting the cost of goods sold expense from the sales revenue for the goods sold. Most income statements report the cost of goods sold as a separate expense (see "Reporting Profit: The Income Statement," later in this chapter).

In a very simple but unlikely scenario, a business starts off the year with no inventory (no stock of products on hand); this business buys and pays for all the products that it sells during the year. In this hypothetical situation, the business pays out cash equal to its cost of goods sold expense. In a more realistic setting, the business starts the year with one or two months' quantity of inventory on hand, ready for sale to its customers — it bought its beginning inventory in the preceding year.

So assume that your business in this profit example did, in fact, start the year with a sizable stock of products, whose cost is recorded in the inventory asset account. As your business sold the products early in the year, it removed the cost of the goods sold from the inventory account and charged that cost to expense.

These goods seemingly did not require any cash outlay *this* year because the products were purchased *last* year. But — and this is the key point — the company has to replace the goods sold to maintain its stock of inventory ready to be sold to customers. So the company did have cash outlays — for the replacement of the products sold.

In many cases, the business is on a growth curve, steadily increasing sales month to month or year to year. Higher sales levels require higher inventory levels, meaning that in addition to replacing the products sold, the business increases its inventory in anticipation of higher sales in the coming months. That's the assumption in this profit example. So at the end of the year, the financial effects of the profit-making activities of your business are as follows:

Assets	=	Liabilities	+	Owners' Equity
Cash: +$35,000		Accounts payable: +$30,000		Retained earnings: +$100,000
Accounts receivable: +$80,000		Accrued expenses: +$35,000		
Fixed assets: −$25,000		Income tax payable: +$5,000		
Prepaid expenses: +$15,000				
Inventory: +$65,000				
Totals: <u>**$170,000**</u>	=	<u>**$70,000**</u>	+	<u>**$100,000**</u>

Notice the $65,000 increase in inventory. The company not only replaced the products sold to customers but also bought additional products that cost $65,000. This additional layer of inventory buildup takes cash — notice that the cash increase is now $35,000, which is $65,000 less than when I factor in prepaid expenses in the preceding example. The increase in inventory may be a smart move, but it did use $65,000 in cash.

An increase in the accounts payable liability account may provide part of the inventory increase because most businesses that have established good credit histories buy their inventory on credit. However, I didn't want to add another change in the accounts payable account. And in most situations, a good part of the inventory increase would have to be paid for by the end of the year.

Isn't it amazing how profit ends up in so many different places?

So Where's That Profit?

As a business manager, you not only must make profit but should understand and manage the financial effects of profit. In particular, you should understand that profit does not simply mean an increase in cash. Sales revenue and expenses, the two factors of profit, affect many assets and liabilities — making sales on credit impacts accounts receivable, expenses paid in advance impact prepaid assets, and so on. You simply can't have expenses without such a smorgasbord of changes in assets and liabilities.

Knowing how much profit your business made isn't enough. You need to take another step and ask, Did the profit generate an increase in cash equal to the profit, and if not, where else is the profit?

In the example from the preceding section, where your business made $100,000 profit but the cash increase was only $35,000, the increase in cash would have been higher if the company had collected more of its accounts receivable by the end of the year, or if inventory had not increased so much. This line of discussion quickly leads into the cash-flow analysis of profit — which is explained in Chapter 7. My purpose right now is just to demonstrate that profit is a "many-splendored thing," to borrow from a song title. The following summary prepared from the balance sheet of the preceding section answers the important question of where did that $100,000 profit go:

Changes in Assets

Cash	+$35,000
Accounts receivable	+$80,000
Inventory	+$65,000
Prepaid expenses	+$15,000
Fixed assets	–$25,000
Net total increase of assets	+$170,000

Changes in Liabilities

Accounts payable	+$30,000
Accrued expenses	+$35,000
Income tax payable	+$5,000
Total increase of liabilities	+$70,000
Increase in net assets (equals net income for year)	$100,000

Note: The amounts shown in this summary are the *changes* — the increases and decreases — in the accounts caused by the sales revenue and expense transactions of your business during the year. These amounts are not the ending balances in the assets, liabilities, and owners' equity accounts because the business started the year with opening balances in these accounts, carried over from previous years.

And there you have the story of the $100,000 profit (which is equal to the increase of *net assets,* or the difference between total assets and total liabilities).

Isn't profit simpler than this? Well, no, not really. Making profit in a highly sophisticated economic system is somewhat involved, to put it mildly. The profit that a business earns drives the several changes in assets and liabilities that you see in this summary.

Other transactions also change the balance sheet of a business — such as borrowing money and buying new fixed assets. The balance sheet, in other words, is changed by all the transactions of a business. The profit-making transactions (sales and expenses) are the main transactions changing the balance sheet, but many other transactions are recorded in the asset, liability, and owners' equity accounts. Therefore, a separate summary of the profit-making transactions — limited to sales revenue and expenses — that ends with the profit for the period is a standard part of a complete financial report. This separate profit report is called the *income statement.*

The mark-to-market method of accounting

Financial statement accounting is based on the actual revenue and expense transactions and operations of a business. The basic alternative to this accounting model is the *mark-to-market* method, which goes like this: You record market values of assets and liabilities at the end of each year and compare the year-end market value of owners' equity with the value a year ago. The increase in owners' equity equals profit for the year (not counting any additional capital investment by the owners and adding back any distributions from profit to the owners).

The benefits of the mark-to-market method are that profit is simply the market value of owners' equity from start-of-year to year-end and that the balance sheet is up-to-date and not contaminated with historical costs that may be lower than assets' current market values.

The mark-to-market method is practical and appropriate for mutual funds and investments by individuals in marketable securities, and for other investment ventures for which market values of assets are readily available and which make a substantial part of their profit from the appreciation in asset values. *Caution:* This method is not practical or appropriate for businesses that sell products and services, because these businesses do not stand ready to sell their assets (other than inventory); the assets are needed for operating the business in the future. At the end of their useful lives, assets are sold for their disposable values (or traded in for new assets).

Reporting Profit: The Income Statement

At the end of each period, the accountant prepares a profit report called an *income statement.* You may think that the report would be called the *net* income statement because the bottom-line profit is called *net income,* but the word *net* is dropped off the title. Other variations of the term are also used, such as *statement of operating results* and *statement of earnings.* The income statement may also be called the *profit and loss statement,* or simply the *P&L* — although in external financial reports, very few businesses use this term for the income statement.

The income statement reports the business's sales and expense transactions for the period, with the profit result on the bottom line. These transactions are *inflows* and *outflows:* Sales revenue is an inflow, and expenses are outflows. Profit, the bottom line, is the *net* inflow.

The annual income statement included in an external financial report that circulates outside the business has two basic sections (also referred to as *layers*):

✔ The first section presents the usual, ordinary, continuing sales and expense operations of the business for the year.

✔ The second section presents any unusual, extraordinary, and nonrecurring gains and losses that the business recorded in the year.

However, a business that didn't experience any extraordinary gains or losses wouldn't include that second section in its income statement — its income statement would consist simply of the top section.

Reporting normal, ongoing profit-making operations

The top section of an income statement (or the only section of the income statement, if the business doesn't have any extraordinary gains or losses to report) typically breaks total expenses for the year into four separate, basic classes (see the sample income statement at the end of this section to see how this format looks):

✔ **Cost of goods sold expense:** The cost of the products sold to customers for which the company received the sales revenue reported on the first line of the income statement. The profit line following the deduction of this expense from sales revenue is called *gross margin* (or *gross profit*) — that's your profit before you factor in the other expenses.

Note: Companies that sell services rather than products (airlines, movie theaters, CPA firms, and so on) do not have a cost of goods sold expense line in their income statements.

✔ **Sales, administrative, and general expenses:** A broad, catch-all category for all expenses except those reported on the other lines in the income statement. This expense combines such things as legal fees, the president's salary, advertising costs, travel and entertainment costs, and much more — probably including some of the company's dirty laundry buried deep within.

The next profit line, which is generally called *operating earnings before interest and tax* and abbreviated EBIT, is the result after deducting the sales, administrative, and general expenses from gross margin.

✔ **Interest expense:** Interest paid on borrowed money (applies only to businesses that have borrowed money, obviously). This expense is usually reported on a separate line even though it may be relatively small. The profit line after deducting interest expense from earnings before interest and tax is typically called *earnings before income tax,* or something very similar. (Unfortunately, accounting terminology is not entirely uniform and standardized; you see variations from business to business.)

✔ **Income tax expense:** Income taxes paid by the business, *not* including property and employer payroll taxes, which are included in the sales, administrative, and general expenses line. Income tax expense is always reported on a separate line. The final profit line, the bottom line after you deduct income tax, is called *net income* — the bottom-line profit figure.

Note: Chapter 11 explains that a business may be organized as a *pass-through tax entity,* which means that it does not pay income tax itself but instead passes its taxable income through to its owners, who end up paying the income tax.

Here are two key points to keep in mind about income statements:

✔ The income statement format that I discuss here is what you find in external financial reports. It doesn't provide the level of detail about sales revenue and expenses that you need for management analysis. See Chapter 9 for more information about what type of information and format you should request when you want to analyze profit.

✔ The income statement does not report the financial effects of sales revenue and expenses — the increases and decreases in the assets and liabilities that revenue and expenses cause. Readers of the profit report have to look at the balance sheet to see the assets and liabilities of the business. Actually, the cash flow statement that is explained in

Chapter 7 is the connecting link between the income statement and the balance sheet. In short, the income statement is not really a stand-alone financial statement; you have to put it into the financial context of the business's other two primary financial statements (the balance sheet and the cash flow statement).

And finally, to end the business example that I've been using throughout this chapter, here is that business's income statement (if the business needs to report unusual gains and losses, its income statement has a second part as well, discussed next):

Sales revenue	$1,000,000
Cost of goods sold expense	(600,000)
Gross margin	$400,000
Sales, administrative, and general expenses	(230,000)
Operating earnings before interest and income tax	$170,000
Interest expense	(20,000)
Earnings before income tax	$150,000
Income tax expense	(50,000)
Net income	$100,000

Reporting unusual gains and losses

The road to profit is anything but smooth and straight. Every business experiences an occasional *discontinuity* — a serious disruption that comes out of the blue, doesn't happen regularly or often, and can dramatically affect bottom-line profit. In other words, a discontinuity is something that disturbs the basic continuity of business operations — the regular flow of profit-making.

Here are some examples of discontinuities:

- **Downsizing the business:** Layoffs require severance pay or early retirement costs.

- **Abandoning product lines:** When you decide to stop selling a line of products, you lose at least some of the money that you paid for obtaining or manufacturing the products, either because you sell the products for less than you paid or because you just get rid of the products you can't sell.

✔ **Settling lawsuits and other legal actions:** Damages and fines that you pay — as well as damages that you *receive* in a favorable ruling — are obviously nonrecurring extraordinary losses or gains (unless you're in the habit of being taken to court every year).

✔ **Writing down (also called *writing off*) damaged assets:** If your products become damaged and unsellable, or your fixed assets need to be replaced unexpectedly, you need to remove these items from the assets account.

✔ **Changing accounting methods:** A business may decide to use different methods for recording revenue and expenses than it did in the past, in some cases because the accounting rules (set by the Financial Accounting Standards Board, or FASB) have changed. Often, the new method requires a business to record a large expense or loss that had not been recognized in previous years.

✔ **Correcting errors from previous financial reports:** If you or your accountant discover that a past financial report had an accounting error, you can't very well revise and reissue that financial report (kind of smacks of rewriting history, don't you think?). So you do a catch-up correction in the current financial report instead, which means that you're recording a loss or gain that had nothing to do with your performance this year.

With all these extraordinary losses and gains, how can you distinguish the profit that a business earned from its normal revenue and expense activities from profit caused by other forces entirely? This is one case where accounting rules are actually working *for you,* the non-accountant reader of financial reports.

According to financial reporting standards, a business must make these one-time losses and gains very visible on the income statement. So in addition to the normal part of the income statement, which reports normal profit activities, a business with unusual, extraordinary losses or gains must add a second layer to the income statement to report on *these* activities.

If a business has no unusual gains or losses in the year, its income statement ends with the net income line. When an income statement includes a second layer, that line becomes *net income from continuing operations before unusual gains and losses* (although the text *before unusual gains and losses* is often omitted). Below this line, those unusual gains and losses appear for each significant discontinuity.

Say that a business suffered a relatively minor loss from quitting a product line and a very large loss from adopting a new accounting standard. Here's what the second layer of this business's income statement looks like:

Net income from continuing operations	$267,000,000
Discontinued operations, net of applicable income taxes	(20,000,000)
Earnings before cumulative effect of changes in accounting principles	$247,000,000
Cumulative effect of changes in accounting principles, net of applicable income taxes	(456,000,000)
Net earnings (loss)	$(209,000,000)

What new accounting standards could possibly cause a $456 million charge? A very likely scenario could be that this charge is the result of the FASB changing the way a business records medical benefits to retired employees. This business probably hadn't been recording those benefits all along, while the employees were still working (see Chapter 13 for more about recording these kinds of future expenses). For a mature business with many retired employees, the accumulated cost for those benefits could quite conceivably reach that high.

The second layer of the income statement tells you which other factors were at play in the business's profit performance. *Explaining* exactly what those other factors are is another story — the gains and losses reported in the second layer of the income statement are generally complex and not fully explained in the financial report. So where does that leave you? As I advise in Chapter 14, your best bet is to seek the counsel of expert financial report readers — financial reports are designed for an audience of stockbrokers, *The Wall Street Journal* readers, and the like, so don't feel bad that you can't understand a report without a degree in accounting-ese.

Even if you have someone else analyze a two-layer income statement for you, you should be aware of the issues that extraordinary losses or gains raise. To really get some respect from your stockbroker or from Joe in Accounting, ask these questions about an unusual loss that a business reports:

- ✔ Were the annual profits reported in prior years overstated?

- ✔ Why wasn't the loss recorded on a more piecemeal and gradual year-by-year basis instead of as a one-time charge?

- ✔ Was the loss really a surprising and sudden event that could not have been anticipated?

- ✔ Will such a loss occur again in the future?

Every company that stays in business for more than a couple of years experiences a discontinuity of one sort or another. But beware of a business that takes advantage of discontinuities in either of the following ways:

- **Discontinuities become "continuities":** This business makes an extraordinary loss or gain a regular feature on its income statement. Every year or so, the business loses a major lawsuit, or abandons product lines, or restructures its organization. It reports "nonrecurring" gains or losses from the same source every year.

- **A discontinuity becomes an opportunity to dump all sorts of write-downs and losses:** When recording an unusual loss (such as settling a lawsuit), the business opts to record other losses at the same time — everything but the kitchen sink (and sometimes that, too) gets written off. This *big-bath theory* says that you may as well take a big bath now in order to avoid taking little showers in the future.

Obviously, a business may just have the bad (or good) luck of facing certain discontinuities regularly. And if you're facing a major, unavoidable expense this year, cleaning out all your other expenses in the same year so as to start off fresh next year can be a clever, legitimate accounting method. But these accounting practices come uncomfortably close to profit manipulation and fraud. All I can advise you to do is stay alert to these potential problems. And if you have reason to believe that a business is using questionable accounting practices, remember that you have the ultimate power: Use your buy-and-sell decisions as your vote against this kind of behavior.

Putting the income statement in perspective

The income statement occupies center stage; the spotlight is on the profit report. But think of the three primary financial statements — the other two being the balance sheet and the cash flow statement — as a three-ring circus. The income statement may draw the most attention, but you have to watch what's going on in all three places. As important as profit is to the financial success of a business, the income statement is not an island unto itself. To understand and manage profit, managers have to follow through to the financial effects of revenue and expenses on the assets and liabilities of the business and pay particular attention to cash flow, as Chapter 7 discusses.

The term *financial report* is the umbrella term referring to a complete set of financial statements, which are supplemented with footnotes and other commentary from a business's managers and which may also include a short report by the CPA auditor if its financial statements have been audited. Most financial reports, even by small businesses, are bound between two covers. A financial report can be anywhere from 5 pages to more than 50 pages, and even 100 pages for very large, publicly owned business corporations. The term *financial statement* refers to one of the following three key summaries prepared periodically by every business:

- **Income statement:** Summarizes sales revenue and expenses and ends with the net income (profit) earned for the period, or the loss suffered for the period

- **Balance sheet:** Summarizes the balances in the business's assets, liabilities, and owners' equity accounts at the close of the period

- **Cash flow statement:** Summarizes the sources and uses of cash during the period

The annual financial report of a business must include all three of these financial statements. Some businesses also prepare other schedules and summaries of a more limited focus that may also be called a financial statement — but in this book, the term *financial statement* refers only to the three mandatory financial statements that I just listed.

Chapter 6

Why Assets Are Needed and Where They Come From

Suppose you're ready to retire after working for many years. Based on your lifestyle and family situation, you'd like an annual retirement income of $49,000 in addition to your social security benefits to provide for a comfortable retirement. Your retirement income has to come from *income-producing assets*. You can earn a 7 percent annual rate of income on the money you save for your retirement. At this rate, you need $700,000 of assets — 7% × $700,000 yields $49,000 annual investment income. In short, it takes money to make money. For a business, it takes assets to make profit.

This chapter explains which assets are needed to make profit — and also explains a couple of liabilities that are generated by expenses. Making profit means making sales and controlling expenses — and these profit-making activities of a business require several different kinds of assets. Assets are the first act of a two-act play. The second act looks at where the assets come from, or the sources of the assets. As Chapter 1 explains, the *balance sheet* of a business is the financial statement that reports its assets on one side and the sources of its assets on the other side.

Of course, as I drill into your head throughout this book, you need to use all three primary financial statements to paint a business's complete financial picture. The *income statement* details sales revenue and expenses, which directly determine the amounts of assets (and two or three of the liabilities) that are summarized in the *balance sheet*. The *cash flow statement* answers the important question of how much of the profit has been converted to cash.

This chapter connects sales revenue and expenses from the income statement with their corresponding assets and liabilities in the balance sheet. (Cash flow follows in Chapter 7.)

Connecting the Income Statement with the Balance Sheet

Sales revenue is the inflow of assets, and expenses are the outflow of assets. *Which specific assets?* This is the key question that this chapter answers. More than just cash (money) is involved in the sales revenue and expenses of a business. If only cash were involved in making profit, only checkbook bookkeeping would be needed. Accounting for profit involves much more than keeping track of cash inflows and outflows. Chapter 5 explains that sales and expenses cause financial effects, or increases and decreases in several different assets. (Well, there is a small complication: A business pays certain expenses sometime after the end of the profit period, which means that those expenses don't immediately decrease assets. To account for these delayed expenses in the period financial reports, accountants track them as liabilities.)

This chapter explains how the profit-making transactions reported in the income statement connect with the assets (and a couple of liabilities) reported in the balance sheet. I stress the tongue-and-groove fit between these two primary financial statements — emphasizing that a lot of assets are needed to make profit. And don't forget that business accounting also keeps track of where assets come from — to invest in its assets, a business needs to raise money by borrowing and persuading owners to put money in the business. You shouldn't look at assets without also looking at where the assets come from.

The *balance sheet,* or statement of financial condition, summarizes a business's assets, liabilities, and owners' equity (money that others have invested in the business) at a point in time and is organized according to the following equation:

```
Assets = liabilities + owners' equity
```

Figure 6-1 shows a balance sheet for a fictitious company — not from left to right as shown in the accounting equation just above, but rather from top to bottom, which is a vertical expression of the accounting equation. This balance sheet is limited to the essential assets and liabilities in the business's profit-making activities — please note that it would need a little tidying up before you'd want to show it off to the world in an external financial report (see Chapter 8).

Assets	
Cash	$2,000,000
Accounts Receivable	2,500,000
Inventory	3,575,000
Prepaid Expenses	480,000
Fixed Assets	$11,305,000
Accumulated Depreciation	(2,780,000) 8,525,000
Totals	$17,080,000

Figure 6-1:
This sample balance sheet shows a business's assets, liabilities, and owners' equity.

Liabilities and Owners' Equity	
Accounts Payable	$800,000
Accrued Liabilities	1,280,000
Debt (Interest bearing)	5,000,000
Owners' Equity	10,000,000
Totals	$17,080,000

A balance sheet doesn't have a punch line like the income statement does — the income statement's punch line being the net income line (which is rarely humorous to the business itself but can cause some snickers among analysts). You can't look at just one item on the balance sheet, murmur an appreciative "ah-hah," and rush home to watch the game. No, you have to read the whole thing (sigh) and make comparisons among the items. See Chapters 8 and 14 for more information about interpreting financial statements.

But at the most basic level, the best way to understand a balance sheet (most of it, anyway) is to focus on the assets that are generated by sales revenue and expenses and the kinds of assets that provide support for these profit-making activities — in other words, the cause-and-effect relationship between an item that's reported in the income statement and an item that's reported in the balance sheet. The following table lists the key items from an income statement and the related items in the balance sheet. The arrows indicate the direction of the cause-and-effect relationship (for example, sales revenue causes the need for accounts receivable).

Note: The following table does not illustrate the whole income statement or the whole balance sheet. Only the fundamental relationships between sales revenue and operating expenses and their corresponding assets (and liabilities) are shown. The purpose is to highlight the most important connections with those particular assets and liabilities that are tightly interwoven with sales revenue and expenses. Cash itself — an extremely important asset, of course — is not shown in the table. The purpose of the table is to call attention to the assets other than cash that are involved in the profit-making process.

Most people understand that sooner or later sales revenue increases cash and expenses decrease cash (except depreciation expense, as explained in Chapters 5 and 7). It's the "sooner or later" that gives rise to the assets and liabilities involved in making profit. After studying this table, you should have a much clearer picture of how sales revenue and expenses drive the assets and liabilities of a business. Business managers need a good grip on these connections for controlling assets and liabilities. And outside investors need to understand these connections for interpreting the financial statements of a business (see Chapter 14).

Income Statement	Balance Sheet	
Item	*Assets*	*Liabilities*
Sales revenue	→ Accounts receivable	
Cost of goods sold expense	→ Inventory	
Sales, administrative, and general expenses	→ Prepaid expenses	→ Accounts payable
		→ Accrued liabilities
Depreciation expense	← Fixed assets	
Interest expense		← Debt
Income tax expense		→ Income Tax Payable**
Income Tax		→ Deferred Payable**

** The balance sheet example in Figure 6-1 does not include these two income-tax-related liabilities.

The balance sheet assets (other than cash) and liabilities connected with sales revenue and expenses are as follows:

✔ Sales revenue derives from selling products and services to customers. Customers may pay cash at the time of sale, or they may pay sometime later (on a line of credit). The total amount of credit sales goes in the accounts receivable asset account. A business that doesn't make any sales on credit doesn't have accounts receivable.

✔ The cost of goods sold expense is what the business paid for the products that it sells to its customers. You can't charge that cost to this expense account until you actually sell the goods, so that cost goes into the inventory asset account until the goods are sold. Inventory acts like a holding account that delays letting the cost go into expense until the goods are actually sold.

✔ The sales, administrative, and general expenses (SA&G) category covers many different operating expenses (such as advertising, travel, and telephone costs). This category drives three items on the balance sheet:

 • The prepaid expenses asset account holds the total cost of cash payments for future expenses — amounts that aren't recorded as expenses until the next period (according to the accrual basis of accounting, you charge a cost to the period actually benefited by the cost, not to the period when you pay the cost; for example, you pay insurance premiums before the policy goes into effect, so you charge those premiums to the period covered by the policy).

 • The accounts payable liability account is the total amount of expenses that haven't been paid yet but that affect the current period. For example, you receive a bill for electricity that you used the month before, so you charge that bill to the month benefited by the electricity — again thanks to the accrual basis of accounting.

 • The accrued liabilities account is the opposite of the prepaid expenses asset account: Accrued liabilities holds costs that are paid before the cost should be recorded as an expense. An example is the accumulated vacation pay that the company's employees have earned by the end of the year; when the employees take their vacations next year, the company pays this liability. The company has received the benefit of their labor but hasn't yet paid the employees for their vacation pay, and the accumulated amount is recorded in the accrued liabilities account.

✔ The concept of depreciation is to spread out the cost of a fixed asset over the course of the asset's life. If you buy a truck that's going to serve you for five years, you split the cost in five and charge one-fifth to the depreciation account each of the five years. (Instead of this straight line, or level amount to each year, a business can choose an accelerated depreciation method, as explained in Chapter 13.)

Turning over assets

Assets should be *turned over,* or put to use by making sales. The higher the turnover — the more times the assets are used and then replaced — the better. The higher the sales given a certain amount of assets, the better because every sale is a profit-making opportunity. The *asset turnover ratio* compares annual sales revenue with total assets:

```
Annual  sales  revenue  ÷  total
    assets = asset turnover ratio
```

Some industries are very capital-intensive; they have low asset turnover ratios, which means that they need a lot of assets to support their sales. For example, public gas and electric utilities are capital-intensive. Many retailers, on the other hand, do not need a lot of assets to make sales. Their asset turnover ratios are relatively high; their sales are three, four, five or more times their assets. Putting it

another way, they bring in $300, $400, $500, or more in sales from every $100 of their assets.

The asset turnover ratio is interesting as far as it goes, but it unfortunately doesn't go very far. This ratio looks only at total assets as a glob, or aggregate total. And the ratio looks only at sales revenue. The expenses of the business for the year are not considered — even though expenses are responsible for most of the assets of a business.

Note: The asset turnover ratio is a quick-and-dirty test of how well a business is using its assets to generate sales. The ratio does not evaluate profitability; profit is not in the calculation. Basically, the ratio indicates how well assets are being used to generate sales and nothing more.

> ✔ Interest expense depends on the amount of money that the business borrows and the interest rate that the lender charges. *Debt* is the generic term for borrowed money; all debt bears interest. A business that hasn't borrowed any money has no interest expense and no debt.

Sizing Up Assets and Liabilities

Based on its experience and operating policies, the managers of a business can estimate what the size of each asset and liability should be — and these estimates provide very useful *control* benchmarks, or yardsticks against which the actual balances of the assets and liabilities are compared with, to spot any serious deviations. In other words, assets (and liabilities, too) can be too high or too low in relation to sales revenue and expenses that drive them, and these deviations can cause problems that managers should try to head off or correct as soon as possible.

Note: These formulas provide *estimates* only. The actual amount of accounts receivable, for example, is the sum of all the individual customers' balances at the close of business on the last day of the period. But, based on the credit terms extended to customers and the company's actual policies regarding how aggressive the business is in collecting past-due receivables, the manager can determine what the ending balance of accounts receivable should be. If the actual balance is reasonably close to this control estimate, accounts receivable is under control. If not, the manager should investigate why not.

Four assets and two liabilities of making profit

The following sections discuss the fundamental assets and liabilities in the balance sheet that result from sales and expenses. The sales and expenses are the *drivers,* or causes of the assets and liabilities. Let me put it this way: If a business earned profit simply by investing in stocks and bonds, for example, it would not need all the various assets and liabilities explained in this chapter. Such a business — a mutual fund, for example — would have just one income-producing asset: investments in securities. But this chapter focuses on a business that sells products to make profit.

Sales revenue and accounts receivable

A business that makes all its sales on credit and has fairly uniform sales over the year can estimate what its accounts receivable should be, based on its typical collection period, according to the following general formula:

```
Annual sales revenue × (x ÷ 52 weeks collection period) =
      accounts receivable
```

The *x* in this formula stands for the average collection period — for example, if customers take an average of five weeks to pay off a purchase, *x* = 5. Here's an example:

```
$26,000,000 annual sales revenue × (5 ÷ 52 weeks collection
      period) = $2,500,000 accounts receivable
```

The five weeks is based on the credit terms extended to its customers and the company's actual collection experience. The actual balance of the accounts receivable asset would probably be a few thousand dollars higher or lower than the $2,500,000 amount just calculated. A relatively small deviation is no cause for concern. But suppose that, at the end of the period, the accounts receivable is $3,000,000. This $500,000 variance from the control estimate should sound an alarm bell — the manager should look into the reasons for the abnormal accounts receivable balance. Perhaps some customers are seriously late in paying and should not be extended new credit until they pay up.

Note: The balance sheet presented in Figure 6-1 presents accounts receivable exactly equal to the $2,500,000 amount it should be — but its actual balance would be somewhat different, as just mentioned.

Cost of goods sold expense and inventory

To estimate what the balance of its inventory asset account should be, a business calculates how much inventory it carries in terms of weeks of sales and uses this formula:

```
Cost of goods sold expense × (x ÷ 52 weeks) = inventory
```

The x in this formula stands for the number of weeks that products are held in inventory on average before being sold to customers. For example, from its experience and inventory-holding policies a business may carry total inventory equal to 13 weeks of sales (which may sound like a lot of inventory to have hanging around, but a business needs to ensure that it has the products on hand and ready for immediate delivery or risk losing the sale). Here's what a business's inventory estimate may look like:

```
$14,300,000 cost of goods sold expense × (13 ÷ 52 weeks) =
                $3,575,000 inventory
```

The actual balance of its inventory asset would probably be a few thousand dollars higher or lower than the $3,575,000 balance just calculated. A relatively small deviation is no cause for concern. But suppose that at the end of the period the inventory is only $3,000,000. This $575,000 variance from the control estimate should be looked into — the manager should determine the reasons for the lower-than-normal inventory balance. Perhaps some products are out of stock and should be immediately reordered to avoid lost sales. Most customers want immediate delivery of products and are not willing to wait until later.

Note: The balance sheet presented in Figure 6-1 presents inventory exactly equal to the $3,575,000 amount it should be — but the actual balance would be somewhat different, as just mentioned.

Operating (SA&G) expenses and prepaid expenses, accounts payable, and accrued liabilities

You use a single formula to determine prepaid expenses, accounts payable, and accrued liabilities, based on the category of sales, administrative, and general (SA&G) expense:

```
SA&G expense × (x ÷ 52 weeks)
```

The *x* in this formula stands for a number of weeks. The SA&G expense total in this calculation does not include depreciation expense, for the reasons discussed in the following section. Nor does it include cost of goods sold expense, which is already explained in connection with inventory. Some SA&G costs are paid for *before* the amounts are charged to expense, and some are paid *after* the amounts are recorded to expense — which causes the following asset and liabilities.

For example, if you know from your experience that your *prepaid expenses* asset is equal to three weeks of the annual SA&G expense, you come up with this estimate:

```
$8,320,000 SA&G annual expense × (3 ÷ 52 weeks) = $480,000
                     prepaid expenses
```

Unpaid expenses at the end of the year fall into two types: accounts payable and accrued liabilities. A business receives an invoice (bill) for the liabilities categorized as accounts payable, whereas it does not receive any invoice for those liabilities categorized as accrued liabilities (for example, property taxes and accrued employee vacation pay).

Here are examples of what a business may come up with for its *accounts payable* and *accrued liabilities:*

```
$8,320,000 SA&G annual expense × (5 ÷ 52 weeks) = $800,000
              accounts payable
$8,320,000 SA&G annual expense × (8 ÷ 52 weeks) = $1,280,000
              accrued liabilities
```

These calculated amounts serve as control guidelines. If the actual balance in one of these accounts deviates more than a small percent compared with the estimated amount, you should investigate and determine the reason. For example, accounts payable may have an actual $915,000 balance at the end of the period, instead of its $800,000 estimated balance. Perhaps the business has fallen behind in paying some of its bills, which may adversely affect its credit rating and damage its ability to get favorable credit terms from its suppliers in the future.

Note: The balance sheet presented in Figure 6-1 presents balances for these three accounts that are exactly equal to the estimates just calculated. Their actual balances would be somewhat different, of course.

Fixed assets and depreciation expense

As explained in Chapter 5, depreciation is a truly unique expense — unlike any other expense — keeping in mind that all expenses are deducted from sales revenue to determine profit. Depreciation expense is not an amount of money paid out during the period; depreciation does not involve the prepaid expenses asset or accounts payable or accrued liabilities. And, of course, depreciation is not a decrease in inventory. Rather, depreciation expense for the period is that portion of the total cost of a business's fixed assets that is allocated to the period.

The higher the total cost of its fixed assets, the higher a business's depreciation expense. However, there is no standard ratio of depreciation expense to the total cost of fixed assets. The amount of depreciation expense depends on the useful lives of the company's fixed assets and which depreciation method the business selects. (The choice of depreciation methods is explained in Chapter 13.) The annual depreciation expense of a business seldom is more than ten or fifteen percent of the total cost of its fixed assets. The depreciation expense for the year is either reported as a separate expense in the income statement or the amount is disclosed in a footnote.

Because depreciation is based on the cost of fixed assets, the balance sheet reports not one but two numbers: the original cost of the fixed assets and the accumulated depreciation amount (the amount of depreciation that has been charged as an expense from the time of acquiring the fixed asset to the current balance sheet date).

The point isn't to confuse you by giving you even more numbers to deal with. Seeing both numbers gives you an idea of how old the fixed assets are and also tells you how much these fixed assets originally cost.

For example, suppose the business invested $11,305,000 in its fixed assets and had already charged off depreciation of $2 million in previous years. In this year, the business records $780,000 depreciation expense (you can't tell from the balance sheet how much depreciation was charged this year; you have to look at the income statement). The remaining undepreciated cost of this business's fixed assets at the end of the year is $8,525,000. So the fixed assets part of this year's balance sheet looks like this:

| Fixed assets | $11,305,000 | |
| Accumulated depreciation | (2,780,000) | $8,525,000 |

Overall, the collection of fixed assets must be fairly new because the company has recorded only $2,780,000 total depreciation since the assets were bought.

Note: The balance sheet presented in Figure 6-1 uses the preceding amounts for the cost of fixed assets and the accumulated depreciation. You should take note that the $8,525,000, being the undepreciated cost of the fixed assets at the end of the most recent year, is the amount included in the total assets of the business. This amount is also called the *book value* of the fixed assets.

What about cash?

A business's cash account consists of the money it has in its checking accounts plus the money that it keeps on hand to make change for its customers. Cash is the essential lubricant of business activity. Sooner or later, virtually everything passes through the cash account.

Every business needs to maintain a working cash balance as a buffer against fluctuations in day-to-day cash receipts and payments. You can't try to get by with a zero cash balance, hoping that enough customers will come in and pay cash to cover all the cash payments that you need to make that day. But just like many individuals, a business may allow its cash balance to drop to a pretty low level at certain times of the month.

How much of a cash balance should a business maintain? This question has no right answer. A business needs to determine how large a cash safety reserve it's comfortable with to meet unexpected demands on cash while keeping the following wisdom in mind:

✔ Excess cash balances are nonproductive and don't earn any profit for the business.

✔ Insufficient cash balances can cause the business to miss taking advantage of opportunities that require quick action and large amounts of cash.

The cash balance of the business whose balance sheet is presented in Figure 6-1 is $2,000,000 — which would be too large for some other businesses and too small for others. Again, what's right for a particular business is an individual thing.

Debt and interest expense

Calculating interest expense is a pretty obvious procedure — you just need to know the amount of borrowed money (debt) and the annual interest rate on that debt:

```
Debt × interest rate = interest expense
```

The business example whose balance sheet is presented in Figure 6-1 has borrowed $5 million at 8 percent interest, and thus its interest expense is determined as follows:

```
$5,000,000 debt × 8 percent = $400,000 interest expense
```

Financing a Business: Owners' Equity and Debt

To run a business, you need financial backing, otherwise known as *capital*. Capital is all incoming funds that are not derived from sales revenue (or from selling off assets). A business raises capital by borrowing money, getting owners to invest money in the business, and making profit that is retained in the business. Borrowed money is known as *debt;* invested money and retained profits are the two sources of *owners' equity* (those two sources need to be kept separate, according to the rules of accounting). See Chapters 5 and 9 for more about profit.

To determine the amount of capital that a business needs, add up the accounts payable and the accrued liabilities and then subtract this figure from total assets, as follows:

```
Total assets - (accounts payable + accrued liabilities) =
              capital needed
```

Accounts payable and accrued liabilities are short-term, non-interest-bearing liabilities that are sometimes called *spontaneous liabilities* because they arise directly from a business's expense activities — they aren't the result of borrowing money but rather are the result of buying things on credit or delaying payment of certain expenses.

Here's the business example whose balance sheet is presented in Figure 6-1:

```
$17,080,000 total assets - $2,080,000 spontaneous
         liabilities = $15,000,000 capital needed
```

This particular business has decided to finance itself one-third from debt and two-thirds from owners' equity, leaving it with the following sources of capital:

Debt	$5,000,000
Owners' equity	10,000,000
Total sources of capital	$15,000,000

Deciding how to divide your sources of capital can be tricky. In a very real sense, the debt-versus-equity question never has a final answer; it's always under review and reconsideration by most businesses. Some companies, just like some individuals, are strongly anti-debt, but even they may find that they need to take on debt eventually to keep up with changing times.

Debt is both good and bad, and in extreme situations it can get very ugly. The advantages of debt are as follows:

✔ Most businesses can't raise all the capital they need from owners' equity, and debt offers another source of capital (though, of course, many lenders may provide no more than half the capital that a business needs).

✔ Interest rates charged by lenders are lower than rates of return expected by owners. Owners expect a higher rate of return because they're taking a greater risk with their money — the business is not required to pay them back the same way that it's required to pay back a lender. For example, a business may pay 8 percent interest on its debt and have to earn a 13 percent rate of return on its owners' equity. (See Chapter 11 for more on distributing profit to owners.)

The disadvantages of debt are as follows:

✔ A business must pay the fixed rate of interest for the period even if it suffers a loss for the period.

✔ A business must be ready to pay back the debt on the specified due date, which can cause some pressure on the business to come up with the money on time. (Of course, a business may be able to *roll over* its debt, meaning that it replaces its old debt with an equivalent amount of new debt, but the lender has the right to demand that the old debt be paid and not rolled over.)

If you default on your debt contract — you don't pay the interest on time, or you don't pay back the debt on the due date — you face some major unpleasantries: In extreme cases, a lender can force you to shut down and liquidate your assets (that is, sell off everything you own for cash) to pay off the debt and unpaid interest. Just as you can lose your home if you don't pay your home mortgage, your business can be forced into involuntary bankruptcy if you don't pay your business debts.

A lender may allow the business to try to work out its financial crisis through bankruptcy procedures, but bankruptcy is a nasty business that invariably causes many problems and can really cripple a business.

Trading on the equity: taking a chance on debt

The large majority of businesses borrow money to provide part of the total capital needed for their assets. The main reason for debt, by and large, is to close the gap between how much capital the owners can come up with and what the business needs. Lenders are willing to provide the capital because they have a senior claim on the assets of the business. Debt has to be paid back before the owners can get their money out of the business. The owners' equity provides the permanent base of capital and gives the lenders a cushion of protection.

The owners use their capital invested in the business as the basis to borrow. For example, for every two bucks the owners have in the business, lenders may be willing to add another dollar (or even more). Thus, for every two bucks of owners' equity the business can get three dollars total capital to work with. Using owners' equity as the basis for borrowing is called *trading on the equity*. It is also referred to as *financial leverage*, because the equity is the lever for increasing the total capital of the business.

These terms also refer to the potential gain a business can realize from making more EBIT (earnings before interest and income tax) on

the amount borrowed than the interest on the debt. For a simple example, assume that debt supplies one-third of the total capital of a business (and owners' equity two-thirds, of course), and its EBIT for the year just ended is a nice round $3,000,000. Fair is fair, so you could argue that the lenders, who put up one-third of the money, should get one-third or $1,000,000 of the profit. This is not how its works. The lenders (investors) get only the interest amount on their loans (their investments). Suppose this total interest is $750,000. The financial leverage gain, therefore, is $250,000. The owners would get their two-thirds share of EBIT plus the $250,000 financial leverage gain.

Trading on the equity may backfire. Instead of a gain, the business may realize a financial leverage loss — one-third of its EBIT may be *less* than the interest due on its debt. That interest has to be paid no matter what amount of EBIT the business earns. Suppose the business just breaks even, which means its EBIT equals zero for the year. Nevertheless, it must pay the interest on its debt. So, the business would have a bottom-line loss for the year. The interest comes out of the hide of the owners.

Reporting Financial Condition: The Classified Balance Sheet

The assets, liabilities, and owners' equity of a business are reported in its *balance sheet*, which is prepared at the end of the income statement period.

The balance sheet is not a flow statement but a *position* statement, which reports the financial condition of a company at a precise moment in time. The balance sheet is unlike the income and cash flow statements (which report inflows and outflows). The balance sheet presents a company's assets, liabilities, and owners' equity that exist at the time the report is prepared.

An accountant can prepare a balance sheet at any time that a manager wants to know how things stand financially. However, balance sheets are usually prepared only at the end of each month, quarter, and year. A balance sheet is always prepared at the close of business on the last day of the profit period, so that the financial effects of sales and expenses (reported in the income statement) also appear in the assets, liabilities, and owners' equity sections of the balance sheet.

The balance sheet shown in Figure 6-1 is a bare-bones statement of financial condition. Yes, the basic assets, liabilities, and owners' equity accounts are presented. However, for both internal management reporting and for external reporting to investors and lenders, the balance sheet must be dressed up more than the one shown in Figure 6-1.

For internal reporting to managers, balance sheets include much more detail, either in the body of the financial statement itself, or more likely, in supporting schedules. For example, only one cash account is shown in Figure 6-1, but the chief financial officer of a business needs to see the balances in each of the business's checking accounts.

As another example, the balance sheet shown in Figure 6-1 includes just one total amount for accounts receivable, but managers need details on which customers owe money and whether any major amounts are past due. Therefore, the assets and liabilities of a business are reported to its managers in greater detail, which allows for better control, analysis, and decision-making. Management control is very detail-oriented: Internal balance sheets and their supporting schedules should provide all the detail that managers need to make good business decisions.

In contrast, balance sheets presented in *external* financial reports (which go out to investors and lenders) do not include much more detail than the balance sheet shown in Figure 6-1. However, external balance sheets must classify (or group together) short-term assets and liabilities. For this reason, external balance sheets are referred to as *classified balance sheets*. This classification is not mandatory for internal reporting to managers, although separating short-term assets and liabilities for managers is also useful.

The following shows a classified balance sheet for the same company. What's new? Not the assets, liabilities, and owners' equity accounts and their balances. The following external balance sheet shows more detail for current assets and current liabilities. (These numbers are the same ones shown in Figure 6-1.)

External Classified Balance Sheet

Assets

Cash	$2,000,000	
Accounts receivable	2,500,000	
Inventory	3,575,000	
Prepaid expenses	480,000	
Current assets		$8,555,000
Fixed assets	$11,305,000	
Accumulated depreciation	(2,780,000)	8,525,000
Total assets		$17,080,000

Liabilities and Owners' Equity

Accounts payable	$800,000	
Accrued liabilities	1,280,000	
Short-term notes payable	2,000,000	
Current liabilities		$4,080,000
Long-term notes payable		3,000,000
Owners' equity:		
Capital stock	$4,500,000	
Retained earnings	5,500,000	10,000,000
Total liabilities and owners' equity		$17,080,000

The preceding classified balance sheet includes the following new items of information:

- The first four asset accounts (cash, accounts receivable, inventory, and prepaid expenses) are added to give the $8,555,000 subtotal for *total current assets*.

- The $5,000,000 total debt of the business is divided between $2,000,000 short-term notes payable and $3,000,000 long-term notes payable.

- The first three liability accounts (accounts payable, accrued liabilities, and short-term notes payable) are added to give the $4,080,000 subtotal for *total current liabilities*.

Current (short-term) assets

Short-term, or *current,* assets are cash, marketable securities that can be immediately converted in cash, and operating assets that are converted into cash within one *operating cycle*. The operating cycle refers the process of putting cash into inventory, selling products on credit (which generates accounts receivable), and then collecting the receivables in cash. In other words, the operating cycle is the "from cash — through inventory and accounts receivable — back to cash" sequence. The term *operating* refers to those assets that are directly part of making sales and directly involved in expenses of the company.

Current (short-term) liabilities

Short-term, or *current,* liabilities are those non-interest-bearing liabilities that arise from the operating (or profit-making) activities of the business, as well as interest-bearing notes payable that have a maturity date one year or less from the balance sheet date. Current liabilities also include any other liabilities that must be paid within the upcoming financial period.

Current liabilities are generally paid out of current assets. That is, current assets are the first source of money to pay the current liabilities when those liabilities come due. Thus, total current assets are compared against total current liabilities in order to compute the *current ratio*. For the balance sheet shown in the preceding section, you can compute the current ratio as follows:

```
$8,555,000 current assets ÷ $4,080,000 current liabilities =
                2.1 current ratio
```

The rule of thumb is that a company's current ratio should be 2.0 or higher. However, business managers know that the current ratio depends a great deal on how the business's short-term operating assets are financed from current liabilities. Some businesses do quite well with a current ratio less than 2.0. Therefore, take the 2.0 current ratio rule with a grain of salt. A lower current ratio does not necessarily mean that the business won't be able to pay its short-term (current) liabilities on time. Chapters 14 and 17 explain current ratios in more detail.

Classifying assets and liabilities as either current or non-current helps managers and investors judge the *solvency* of a business. Solvency refers to the ability of a business to pay its liabilities on time. Delays in paying liabilities on time can cause very serious problems for a business. In extreme cases, a business could be thrown into *bankruptcy* — even the threat of bankruptcy can cause serious disruptions in the normal operations of a business, and profit performance is bound to suffer. If current liabilities become too high relative to current assets — which are the first line of defense for paying those current liabilities — managers should move quickly to raise additional cash to reduce one or more of the current liabilities. Otherwise, a low current ratio will raise alarms in the minds of the outside readers of its financial report.

Costs and Other Balance Sheet Values

The balance sheet summarizes the financial condition for a business at a point in time. Business managers and investors should clearly understand the values reported in this primary financial statement. In my experience, understanding balance sheet values can be a source of confusion for both business managers and investors, who tend to put all dollar amounts on the same value basis. In their minds, a dollar is a dollar, whether it's in the accounts receivable, inventory, fixed assets, or accounts payable. Assigning the same value to every account value tends to gloss over some important differences and can lead to serious misinterpretation of the balance sheet.

A balance sheet mixes together several different types of accounting values:

- **Cash:** Amounts of money on hand in coin and currency; money on deposit in bank checking accounts
- **Accounts receivable:** Amounts not yet collected from credit sales to customers (value is based on sales prices)
- **Inventory:** Amounts of purchase costs or production costs for products that haven't sold yet
- **Fixed assets:** Amounts of costs invested in long-life operating assets

✔ **Accounts payable** and **accrued liabilities:** Amounts for the costs of unpaid expenses

✔ **Notes payable:** Amounts borrowed on interest-bearing liabilities

✔ **Capital stock:** Amounts of capital invested in the business by owners (stockholders)

✔ **Retained earnings:** Amounts remaining in the owners' equity account

In short, a balance sheet represents a diversity or a rainbow of values — not just one color. This is the nature of the generally accepted accounting principles (GAAP) — the accounting methods used to prepare financial statements.

Book values are the amounts recorded in the accounting process and reported in financial statements. Do not assume that the book values reported in a balance sheet necessarily equal the current *market values*. Book values are based on the accounting methods used by a business. Generally speaking — and I really mean *generally* here because I'm sure that you can find exceptions to this rule — cash, accounts receivable, and liabilities are recorded at close to their market or settlement values. These receivables will be turned into cash (at the same amount recorded on the balance sheet), and liabilities will be paid off at the amounts reported in the balance sheet. It's the book values of inventory and fixed assets that most likely are lower than current market values, as well as any other non-operating assets in which the business invested some time ago.

A business can use alternative accounting methods to determine the cost of inventory and the cost of goods sold, and to determine how much of a fixed asset's cost is allocated to depreciation expense each year. The point here is that a business is free to use very conservative accounting methods — with the result that its inventory cost value and the undepreciated cost of its fixed assets may be much lower than the current replacement cost values of these assets. Chapter 13 explains more about choosing different accounting methods.

Chapter 7

Cash Flow: Making Money or Just Making Profit?

* *

In This Chapter

▶ Connecting the cash flow statement with the balance sheet and the income statement

▶ Understanding that cash flow does not equal profit

▶ Looking at depreciation and changes in net short-term operating assets

▶ Reporting investments in fixed assets

▶ Reporting distribution of profit to owners

▶ Evaluating managers' decisions by analyzing the cash flow statement

* *

Suppose that you bought some vacant land a few years ago for $100,000. Also suppose that you could unquestionably get $250,000 (its current market value) if you sold the land today. On the basis of the land's market-value appreciation, you *could* legitimately prepare an income statement reporting a profit of $150,000. But that's only *paper profit* — you don't have that $150,000 in cash. Although your profit is technically $150,000, your increase in cash from that profit is zero.

The moral of this story: You can't equate profit with cash flow! If a business's income statement reports a profit of $1.3 million for the period (usually a year, but financial reports can be generated for other periods, such as a month or a quarter), you can't jump to the conclusion that the business's *cash flow* increased by $1.3 million.

Profit is only one side of the coin. The other side is whether all, most, some, or none of the profit actually generated an increase in cash flow. In most situations, cash flow from profit is lower or higher than the profit number for the period, leading to three key questions that business managers and investors should ask:

✔ How much cash did profit generate for the business through the end of the period, and why is the business's cash flow different from its profit?

✔ Where else did the business get money during the period?

✔ What did the business do with its available cash?

The cash flow statement is where you turn for the answers to these questions. And this chapter is where you turn to answer the question, "Just how the heck do you read a cash flow statement?"

Positioning the Cash Flow Statement

The cash flow statement is one of the three primary financial statements that a business must report to the outside world, according to generally accepted accounting principles (or GAAP). The *income statement* summarizes sales revenue and expenses and ends with the bottom-line profit for the period. The *balance sheet* summarizes a business's financial condition by reporting its assets, liabilities, and owners' equity. (See Chapters 5 and 6 for more about these reports.) You can probably guess what the *cash flow statement* does by its name alone: This statement tells you where a business got its cash in the first place and what the business did with its cash during the period. Personally, I prefer the name given in the old days to the predecessor of the cash flow statement, the *Where Got, Where Gone* statement — this nickname goes straight to the heart of asking where the business got its money and what it did with the money.

To give you a rough idea of what a cash flow statement reports, let me ask you the following questions: How much money did you earn last year? Did you get all your income in cash (did some of your wages go straight into a retirement plan, or did you collect a couple of IOUs)? Where did you get other money (did you take out a loan, win the lottery, or receive a gift from a rich uncle)? What did you do with your money (did you buy a house, support your out-of-control Internet addiction, or lose it in Saturday night poker)?

Getting a little too personal for you? That's exactly why the cash flow statement is so important: It bares a business's financial soul to its lenders and owners. Sometimes, the cash flow statement reveals questionable judgment calls that the business's managers made. At the very least, the cash flow statement reveals how well a business handles its profit.

History lesson: the cash flow statement

The cash flow statement was not required for external financial reporting until 1987. Until then, the accounting profession had turned a deaf ear to calls from the investment community for routine cash flow statements from businesses. (Accountants had presented a *funds flow statement* prior to 1987, but that report proved to be a disaster — the term "funds" included more assets than just cash and represented a net amount after deducting short-term liabilities from assets.)

In my opinion, the reluctance to require cash flow statements came from fears that the *cash flow from profit* figure would usurp net income — people would lose confidence in the net income line.

Those fears were unfounded: Although the income statement continues to get most of the fanfare (because it shows the magic bottom-line number of net income), the cash flow statement does get its share of attention, and deservedly so.

The most important number reported on the cash flow statement is *cash flow from profit,* the amount of money generated by a business's profit-making operations, exclusive of all other sources of cash (such as borrowed money, sold-off fixed assets, and owners' investments in the business). This number indicates a business's ability to make profit and turn that profit into usable cash flow. Cash flow from profit is just as important a number as net income (the bottom-line profit number). The cash flow from profit figure is reported in the first section of the cash flow statement (see the section "Determining Cash Flow from Profit," later in this chapter).

The cash flow statement is divided into three areas, each listing the three types of cash that flow through a business:

- ✔ **Cash flow from operating (profit-making) activities:** The activities in which a business makes profit and turns the profit into cash flow (includes depreciation and changes in short-term operating assets and liabilities)

- ✔ **Cash flow from investing activities:** Investments in long-term assets needed for a business's operations; also includes money taken out of these assets from time to time (such as when a business sells its assets)

- ✔ **Cash flow from financing activities:** Capital (from debt and owners' equity) and distribution of profit to owners

The final line of the cash flow statement reports a business's net cash increase or decrease, based on these three sections of the cash flow statement. The following table shows what a cash flow statement typically looks like for a *growing* business (which means that its assets and liabilities both increase during the period).

Cash flow from operating activities:

Net income		$x,xxx,xxx
Depreciation expense		<u>xxx,xxx</u>
Net income plus depreciation		$x,xxx,xxx

Changes in short-term operating assets and liabilities:

Accounts receivable	($xxx,xxx)	
Inventory	(xxx,xxx)	
Prepaid expenses	(xxx,xxx)	
Accounts payable	xxx,xxx	
Accrued liabilities	<u>xxx,xxx</u>	<u>(x,xxx,xxx)</u>
Cash flow from operating activities	$xxx,xxx	

Cash flow from investing activities:

Purchases of fixed assets	(x,xxx,xxx)	

Cash flow from financing activities:

Increase in debt	$x,xxx,xxx	
Distribution of profit to owners	<u>(xxx,xxx)</u>	<u>xxx,xxx</u>
Net cash increase (decrease)		<u>$xxx,xxx</u>

When you were a kid, did your mother or father make you eat everything on your dinner plate? Mine did, and I don't know about you, but I always started with the things I didn't like so that I could enjoy the rest of the meal. I couldn't eat the things I liked first, knowing that I still had liver and onions to eat. In the same way, I start off this discussion of the cash flow statement with cash flow from profit, the most important (and difficult) part of the cash flow statement. The rest of the cash flow statement is a piece of cake — the dessert that rewards you for first getting through cash flow from profit.

Determining Cash Flow from Profit

At the beginning of this chapter, I warn you not to equate profit with cash flow. Why can't you? Well, actually, if you were to collect cash from your customers for all sales during the period, pay cash for all your expenses for the period, and not have any unpaid or prepaid expenses at the end of the period, your cash flow *would* equal your profit. That is, your sales revenue would be equal to your cash inflow, and your total expenses would be equal to your cash outflow for the period.

But that's not a realistic situation. In the real business world, you have to consider the following factors when determining cash flow from profit (I explain each of these items in more detail later in this chapter):

- ✔ **Depreciation expense:** This expense is included in total expenses but isn't something that you actually put out cash for in the year that you record the expense — you paid out the cash when you purchased the fixed asset some years ago.

- ✔ **Accounts receivable:** If you make sales on credit, you probably have some uncollected sales revenue at the end of the period, which is recorded in accounts receivable.

- ✔ **Inventory:** A business often buys more inventory than it sells during the period, which can be bad from the cash flow point of view. When you increase inventory and buy more products than you sell during the period, you end up having some of your cash tied up in the cost of this unsold inventory.

- ✔ **Prepaid expenses:** A business pays some expenses in advance, before the costs are charged to expense. So it pays cash for some expenses that haven't been recorded as expenses for that period.

- ✔ **Accounts payable and accrued liabilities:** A business buys some items and services on credit; it may have other expenses with delayed payments as well. So a business records expenses for which it hasn't paid cash yet.

The following steps for determining cash flow from profit take the preceding factors into consideration:

1. **Add depreciation expense to net income.**

2. **Add up the changes in accounts payable and accrued liabilities, resulting in the *net change in short-term operating liabilities*.**

3. **Add up the changes in accounts receivable, inventory, and prepaid expenses, resulting in the *net change in short-term operating assets*.**

4. **Subtract the net change in short-term operating liabilities (Step 2) from the net change in short-term operating assets (Step 3), resulting in the *net change in short-term operating assets*.**

5. **Subtract the net change in short-term operating assets (Step 4) from Step 1, resulting in *cash flow from profit*.**

In other words, the equation is as follows:

```
(Depreciation expense + net income) - net change in short-
          term operating assets = cash flow from profit
```

Cash flow generated by profit depends on these two factors: depreciation and the net change in short-term operating assets.

The trick to understanding the cash flow statement is to link it to changes in the balance sheet because changes in a business's assets and liabilities directly determine cash flow. In my experience, many business managers, lenders, and investors don't fully understand these links, but the savvy ones know to keep a close eye on balance sheet changes. Of course, the income statement also impacts the cash flow statement (depreciation and net income come from the income statement). The following sections show how to relate these three financial statements to each other in understanding depreciation and the change in net short-term operating assets.

A simple example for cash flow analysis

Here's an example of a balance sheet with an unorthodox format, customized to better illustrate the connection between the cash flow statement and the balance sheet (see Chapter 6 for more details on balance sheets). This balance sheet compares the amounts at the end of the previous period with the amounts for the period just ended — in other words, the start-of-period and end-of-period amounts are both necessary for analyzing the period's cash flow.

Item	End of Most Recent Period	One Period Ago	Increase (Decrease)
Cash	$2,000,000	$2,500,000	($500,000)

Item	End of Most Recent Period	One Period Ago	Increase (Decrease)
Accounts receivable	$2,500,000	$1,785,000	$715,000
Inventory	3,575,000	2,650,000	925,000
Prepaid expenses	480,000	355,000	125,000
Accounts payable	(800,000)	(600,000)	(200,000)
Accrued liabilities	(1,280,000)	(915,000)	(365,000)
Net short-term operating assets	$4,475,000	$3,275,000	$1,200,000
Fixed assets, at original cost	$11,305,000	$9,305,000	$2,000,000
Accumulated depreciation	(2,780,000)	(2,000,000)	(780,000)
Net of depreciation	$8,525,000	$7,305,000	$1,220,000
Assets less operating liabilities	$15,000,000	$13,080,000	$1,920,000
Debt	$5,000,000	$4,000,000	$1,000,000
Owners' equity	10,000,000	9,080,000	920,000
Total debt and owners' equity	$15,000,000	$13,080,000	$1,920,000

The following example shows what this business's income statement looks like (see Chapter 5 for more information about income statements):

Sales revenue	$26,000,000
Cost of goods sold expense	(14,300,000)
Gross margin	$11,700,000
Sales, administrative, and general (SA&G) expenses	(8,320,000)
Depreciation expense	(780,000)
Operating earnings before interest and tax (EBIT)	$2,600,000
Interest expense	(400,000)
Earnings before income tax	$2,200,000
Income tax expense	(880,000)
Net income	$1,320,000

What do the preceding figures reveal about this business's all-important cash flow over the past period? In the preceding example, this business experienced rapid sales growth over the past period. Sales revenue for the previous period was $18.5 million, compared with $26 million for the period just ended — a dramatic increase of 40 percent. However, the downside of sales growth is that short-term operating assets and liabilities also grow — the business needs more inventory at the higher sales level and also has higher accounts receivable.

The business's prepaid expenses, accounts payable, and accrued liabilities also increased. It bought new fixed assets, borrowed money, and did not distribute all its net income to its owners. These changes (caused by the rapid growth of the business) yielded higher profit but also caused quite a bit of turbulence in its operating assets and liabilities.

In the balance sheet example, notice the increases in the business's assets and liabilities — except for cash, which dropped $500,000. One of the purposes of the cash flow statement is to explain that drop.

Note the following points about the preceding balance sheet and income statement:

- ✔ Short-term operating liabilities (accounts payable and accrued liabilities) are deducted from the short-term operating assets (which are accounts receivable, inventory, and prepaid expenses). The result is *net short-term operating assets* — a key figure in explaining cash flow from profit.

- ✔ Accumulated depreciation increased $780,000 during the period, and this amount equals the depreciation expense reported in the income statement. (Depreciation expense is reported separately from the sales, administrative, and general expenses in the income statement.)

Now look at the following cash flow statement for this business example, based on the information from the preceding comparative balance sheet and income statement.

Cash flow from operating activities:

Net income	$1,320,000
Depreciation expense	780,000
Net income plus depreciation	$2,100,000

Changes in short-term operating assets and liabilities:

Accounts receivable	($715,000)	
Inventory	(925,000)	
Prepaid expenses	(125,000)	
Accounts payable	200,000	
Accrued liabilities	365,000	(1,200,000)
Cash flow from operating activities		$900,000

Cash flow from investing activities:

Purchases of fixed assets	(2,000,000)

Cash flow from financing activities:

Increase in debt	$1,000,000	
Distribution of profit to owners	(400,000)	600,000
Net cash increase (decrease)		($500,000)

Note: Where the depreciation line goes in the cash flow statement is a matter of personal preference — there's no standard location. Many businesses put it in with the changes in short-term operating assets and liabilities to avoid giving people the idea that computing cash flow from profit simply requires adding back depreciation to net income.

A very quick read through this cash flow statement goes something like this: The company generated $900,000 cash from its profit, used $2 million to buy new fixed assets, borrowed $1 million, and distributed $400,000 from profit to its owners. In summary, it had $1.9 million cash coming in and $2.4 million going out, so cash decreased by $500,000.

Adding back depreciation

The first step in determining cash flow from profit is to add depreciation (in the preceding example, $780,000, as reported as a depreciation expense on the income statement and as an increase in depreciation accumulation on the balance sheet) to net income ($1.32 million). See Chapters 5 and 6 for more about depreciation.

When you're measuring profit, you count depreciation as an expense. But from the cash flow point of view, depreciation is actually *cost recovery.* In a real sense, a business "sells" some of its fixed assets each period to its customers — it factors the cost of fixed assets into the prices that it charges its customers. For example, when you go to a supermarket, a very small slice of the price you pay for that box of cereal goes toward the cost of the building, the shelves, the refrigeration equipment, and so on (no wonder they charge so much for a box of flakes!).

So the business does recoup part of the cost invested in its fixed assets. In other words, $780,000 of its sales revenue went toward reimbursing the business for its fixed assets.

Looking at net short-term operating assets

Many people who analyze financial statements think of the net income + depreciation equation as a shortcut to cash flow from profit — but it isn't! That's just the *first* step toward determining cash flow from profit. The next step is to take the change in net short-term operating assets and either add it or deduct it from net income (depending on whether it's negative or positive).

So why isn't net income + depreciation a good shortcut?

The business in the example earned $1.32 million net income and recovered $780,000 cash flow from depreciation of its fixed assets. The sum of these two is $2.1 million. Is $2.1 million the amount of cash flow from profit for the period? The knee-jerk answer of many investors and managers is *yes*. But as they say in Iowa, "Hold 'er down, Newt!" If net income + depreciation truly equals cash flow, then *both* factors in the brackets — both net income and depreciation — must be realized in cash. That's usually not the case.

To determine the amount of cash flow from profit, you have to also consider changes in the business's short-term operating assets and liabilities. In this business's case, the increase in its net short-term operating assets and liabilities uses up $1.2 million of the $2.1 million net income plus depreciation — leaving only $900,000 cash flow from profit.

The managers did not have to go outside the business for this $900,000; this money was generated by the profit-making activities of the business. Cash flow from profit is an *internal* source of capital generated by the business itself, in contrast to *external* capital, which the business raises from lenders and stockholders.

In some situations, the cash effects caused by unfavorable changes in the short-term operating assets and liabilities wipe out all the depreciation cash recovery *and* all the net income, with the result that cash flow from profit is *negative*. A negative cash flow from profit is usually caused by very large increases in accounts receivable and inventory. Changes in these two assets deserve very close attention by managers, lenders, and investors.

In other situations, cash flow from profit is much higher than the profit. How can this be? Well, again, the place to start is net income plus depreciation. For the business example, this figure is $2.1 million. Now, suppose that the business actually reduced its net operating assets over the period — both its accounts receivable and inventory balances went down, meaning that the business ended the period with fewer credit sales (as recorded in accounts receivable) and less inventory than it started off the period with. *Warning:* Maybe accounts receivable decreased because the business became more aggressive at collecting payment on credit sales, and maybe the business had too much inventory last period and is tightening up in that area; but note that these decreases could also be signs that sales are slipping, and the business may be in financial trouble.

So how much did the net short-term operating assets of my sample business change during the period? The comparative balance sheet reports a $1.2 million increase in this key amount, which reduces cash flow from profit. Remember that the equation for net short-term operating assets is short-term operating assets – short-term operating liabilities.

✔ **Short-term operating assets:** At the start of the period, the business had $1,785,000 uncollected sales revenue (accounts receivable), $2,650,000 cost of unsold products (inventory), and $355,000 expenses paid in advance for the coming period (prepaid expenses). These numbers are good from the cash flow point of view. The accounts receivable were collected during the period, the company sold products that it had already purchased the previous period, and some of its expenses had already been paid in advance.

✔ **Short-term operating liabilities:** At the start of the period, the business had $600,000 accounts payable and $915,000 accrued liabilities. These amounts are bad from the cash flow point of view because they had to be paid during the early part of the period.

All together, the *net* short-term operating assets at the start of the period provide $3,275,000 cash flow. That's the good news. The bad news is that just the opposite happens with the period-end amounts. Looking at the end-of-period balances, the $2,500,000 accounts receivable was not collected in cash during the period. The business also had to purchase $3,575,000 in inventory and had to prepay $480,000 in expenses. True, the company did not have to pay the $800,000 accounts payable and the $1,280,000 accrued liabilities, which are the end-of-period balances of these liabilities. But it's still out $4,475,000 cash at the end of the period, equal to its net short-term operating assets at the end of the period.

In summary, the company's cash flow was helped by the $3,275,000 beginning net short-term operating assets, but cash flow was hurt by the $4,475,000 ending amount. The $1,200,000 increase in its net-short term operating assets is a drag on cash flow.

To determine cash flow from profit, you *subtract* the net short-term operating assets increase (if it were a decrease, you'd *add* it) from net income — which wipes out the depreciation recovery and reduces cash flow from profit.

These steps leave you with the following cash flow from profit:

Net income	$1,320,000
Depreciation expense	780,000
Net income plus depreciation	$2,100,000
Increase in net short-term operating assets	(1,200,000)
Cash flow from profit	$900,000

The $900,000 cash generated by profit-making activities is quite a bit less than net income for the period. The increase in this business's net short-term operating assets was more than the depreciation expense for the period. Therefore, cash flow from profit suffered. The good news is that the company did obtain $900,000 cash flow from profit, even though that's less than net income for the period.

Getting specific about those short-term operating assets and liabilities

The net short-term operating assets of the business increased by $1.2 million during the period, as explained in the preceding section. This increase reduced the company's cash flow from profit (operating activities) by $1.2 million down to only $900,000. As a business manager, you should take a close look at each of your short-term operating assets and liabilities and understand the cash flow effects of increases in each. Investors focus on the ability of the business to generate a healthy cash flow from profit, and they should be equally concerned about these changes. The following sections examine each of the five items making up the net short-term operating assets in more detail.

Accounts receivable increase

The first factor in net short-term operating assets is accounts receivable. Remember that the accounts receivable asset shows how much money customers who bought products on credit owe the business; this asset is a promise of cash that the business will receive and is *not* a record of how much cash the business has actually received. Cash does not increase until the business collects money from its customers.

But the amount in accounts receivable *is* included in the total sales revenue of the period — after all, you did make the sales, even if you haven't been paid yet. Obviously, then, you can't look at sales revenue as being equal to the amount of cash that the business received during the period.

To calculate the actual cash flow from sales, you need to subtract from sales revenue the amount of credit sales that you did not collect in cash over the period — but you add in the amount of cash that you collected during the period just ended for credit sales that you made the *previous* period. Take a look at the equation:

```
Sales revenue + (start-of-period accounts receivable - end-
     of-period accounts receivable) = cash flow from sales
```

The key point is that you need to keep an eye on the increase or decrease in accounts receivable from the beginning of the period to the end of the period:

- If the amount of sales you made on credit this period is more than what you collected during the period, your accounts receivable *increased* over the period, and you need to *subtract* from sales revenue that difference between start-of-period accounts receivable and end-of-period accounts receivable. An increase in accounts receivable hurts cash flow because the ending balance is a larger negative item than the positive beginning balance.

- If accounts receivable *decreased*, meaning that the amount of cash you collected on credit sales was more than the amount of credit sales that you made and haven't collected yet, you *add* that decrease to sales revenue to determine cash flow from profit. In this situation, you collected cash for more than just the products you sold during this period; your sales revenue figure includes just the products sold during this period, so to get a true reading on your cash flow from this period, you need to include sales from the previous period.

Remember: What you're doing is calculating how much *cash* you took in *this* period; you need to remove the complicating factor of credit sales in order to concentrate solely on cash.

In my business example, accounts receivable increased from $1,785,000 at the start of the period to $2,500,000 at the end of the period — a $715,000 increase. This increase had a negative impact on cash flow from profit for the period because cash collections from sales were $715,000 less than sales revenue. Ouch! The business increased its sales substantially over the last period, so you should expect that its accounts receivable would increase. The higher sales revenue was good for profit but bad for cash flow from profit.

That's the price of growth; managers and investors need to clearly understand this point. If the business could've increased its sales without increasing accounts receivable, that would've been a happy situation for cash flow, but in the real world, you just can't have one increase without the other.

Inventory increase

Inventory is the second component of net short-term operating assets — and usually the largest one for businesses that sell products. If the inventory account is greater at the end of the period than at the start of the period — either because unit costs increased or the quantity of products increased — what the business actually paid out in cash for inventory is more than what the business recorded as its cost of goods sold expense. Therefore, you need to deduct the inventory increase from net income to determine cash flow from profit.

In my business example, inventory increased by $925,000 from start-of-period to end-of-period. In other words, this business replaced the products that it sold during the period *and* increased its inventory by $925,000. The easiest way to understand the effect of this increase on cash flow is to pretend that the business paid for all its inventory purchases in cash immediately upon receiving them. It purchased the inventory that it started the period off with *last* period, so that cost does not affect this period's cash flow. Those products were sold during the period and involved no further cash payment by the business. But the business did pay cash *this* period for the products that were in inventory at the end of the period.

In other words, if the business had bought just enough new inventory (at the same cost that it paid out last period) to replace the inventory that it sold during the period, the actual cash outlay for its purchases would equal the cost of goods sold expense reported in its income statement. And ending inventory would exactly equal the beginning inventory. But this scenario doesn't fit the example, because the company increased its sales substantially over last period, as already mentioned. The higher sales level increased its bottom-line profit.

But to support the higher sales level, the business needed to increase its inventory level. So the business bought $925,000 more products than it sold during the period — and it had to come up with the cash to pay for this inventory increase. Basically, the business wrote checks amounting to $925,000 more than its cost of goods sold expense for the period. This course was necessary to increase profit, even though cash flow took a hit.

It's that accrual basis accounting thing again, folks: The cost that a business pays *this* period for *next* period's inventory is reflected in this period's cash flow but isn't recorded until next period's income statement. So if a business paid more *this* period for *next* period's inventory than it paid *last* period for *this* period's inventory, you can see how the additional expense would adversely affect cash flow but would not be reflected in the bottom-line net income figure. Right? Right.

Prepaid expenses increase

The third component of net short-term operating assets is prepaid expenses. A change in this account works the same way as a change in inventory and accounts receivable, though changes in prepaid expenses are usually much smaller than changes in those other two accounts.

Again, the beginning balance of prepaid expenses is recorded as an expense on this period's balance sheet, but the cash for those expenses was actually paid out last period, not this period. This period, a business pays cash for next period's prepaid expenses — which affects this period's cash flow but doesn't affect net income until next period.

So the $125,000 increase in prepaid expenses from start-of-period to end-of-period in this business example is deducted from net income to determine cash flow from profit. As a business manager, you should decide whether this $125,000 increase in prepaid expenses is consistent with the higher level of expenses this period (due to the growth of sales) compared with last period. You shouldn't just accept such an increase; you should control the increase, just like you should control the increases in accounts receivable and inventory.

Accounts payable and accrued liabilities increases

The two factors in short-term operating liabilities are accounts payable and accrued liabilities. When the beginning balance of one of these liability accounts is the same as the ending balance of the same account, the business breaks even on cash flow. When the end-of-period balance is higher than the start-of-period balance, the business did not pay out as much money as was actually recorded as an expense on the period's income statement.

In this example, the business paid $600,000 in cash for accounts payable to pay off last period's account balance (this $600,000 was reported as the accounts payable balance on last period's balance sheet). Its cash flow this period decreased by $600,000 because of that payment. But this period's balance sheet shows the amount of accounts payable that the business will need to pay off next period: $800,000. The business actually paid off $600,000 and recorded an $800,000 expense, so this time, cash flow is *richer* than what's reflected in its net income figure by $200,000. The increase in accrued liabilities works the same way. The $365,000 increase in this operating liability (see the example balance sheet presented earlier in the chapter) is added to net income to determine cash flow from profit.

Therefore, liability increases are favorable to cash flow — in a sense, the business borrowed more than it paid off. Such an increase means that the business delayed paying cash for certain things until next year. So you need to add the increases in these two liabilities to net income to determine cash flow from profit.

Taking a cash flow view of sales revenue and expenses

The following table brings together the changes in short-term operating assets and liabilities discussed in the preceding sections and presents a cash flow "X-ray" picture of the income statement. *Note:* In the example, the business has paid all interest and income tax during the year, so the interest payable and income tax payable accounts have no beginning or ending balances. Also, depreciation expense isn't a cash outflow, so it's not listed.

Cash flow from sales:

$26,000,000 sales revenue – $715,000 accounts receivable increase =	$25,285,000

Cash flow for purchase of products:

$14,300,000 cost of goods sold expense + $925,000 inventory increase =	(15,225,000)

Cash flow for SA&G expenses:

$8,320,000 SA&G expenses + $125,000 prepaid expenses increase – $200,000 accounts payable increase – $365,000 accrued liabilities increase =	(7,880,000)
Cash flow for interest expense =	(400,000)
Cash flow for income tax expense =	(880,000)
Net cash flow from net income =	$900,000

As you can see, cash flow from profit (net income) is $900,000 — the same as in the cash flow statement shown earlier in the chapter. As a matter of fact, the rule-making body of the accounting profession — the Financial Accounting Standards Board (FASB) — actually prefers that the cash flow from operating activities section of the cash flow statement appear in this manner (not the calculations, just the final amounts). But the overwhelming majority of businesses don't like this approach, and you seldom see it in external financial reports.

After you work your way through cash flow from profit, the next question is "What did the business do with that $900,000 cash flow from profit?" Did the business distribute all of it to the owners so that they could take a Caribbean cruise, or what? Time to move on to the rest of the cash flow statement — read on!

Sailing through the Rest of the Cash Flow Statement

After you get past cash flow from operating activities (profit), the rest of the cash flow statement is a breeze. The last two sections of the statement explain where the cash went and where some of the cash (the cash that didn't come from profit) came from.

Cash flow from improving profit margin versus improving sales volume

Chapter 9 discusses increasing profit margin versus increasing sales volume to improve bottom-line profit. Improving your profit margin is the better way to go, compared with increasing sales volume. Both actions increase profit, but the profit margin tactic is much better in terms of cash flow. When sales volume increases, so does inventory (and so inventory expense increases).

On the other hand, when you improve profit margin (by raising the sales price or by lowering product cost, for example), you don't have to increase inventory — in fact, reducing product cost may actually cause inventory to decrease a little. In short, increasing your profit margin yields a higher cash flow from profit than does increasing your sales volume.

Investing activities

The second section of the cash flow statement reports the investment actions that a business's managers took. Investments are like tea leaves: This information gives cash flow statement readers some idea of how the business is preparing for its future.

Certain fixed assets are required for doing business — for example, Federal Express wouldn't be terribly successful if it didn't have trucks for delivering packages and computers for tracking deliveries. When those assets wear out, the business needs to replace them. Also, to remain competitive, a business may need to upgrade its equipment to take advantage of the latest technology or provide for the business's growth. These investments in fixed assets are critical to the future of the business and are called *capital expenditures* to stress that capital is being invested for the long haul.

So the first claim on cash flow from profit — the first category explaining where the cash went — is capital expenditures.

Cash flow statements generally don't go into any detail regarding exactly which specific types of fixed assets a business purchased — how many additional square feet of space the business acquired, how many new drill presses it bought, and so on. (Some businesses do leave a clearer trail of their investments, though; for example, airlines describe how many new aircraft of each kind were purchased to replace old equipment or expand their fleets.)

Get your free cash flow here!

A new term has emerged in the lexicon of accounting and finance: *free cash flow*. Like most new words being tossed around for the first time, this one hasn't settled down into one universal meaning. However, its most common usage is for describing cash flow from profit minus *capital expenditures* (the purchases of new fixed assets, such as buildings, equipment, or vehicles).

The idea is that a business needs to make capital expenditures in order to stay in business and thrive. And to make capital expenditures, the business needs cash. Only after paying for its capital expenditures does a business have "free" cash flow that it can use as it likes.

Businesses dispose of fixed assets that have reached the end of their useful lives and will no longer be used. These discarded fixed assets are thrown away, traded in on new fixed assets, or sold for relatively small amounts of money. (The value of a fixed asset at the end of its useful life is called its *salvage value.*) The disposal proceeds from selling fixed assets are reported as a source of cash in the investments section of the cash flow statement. Usually, these amounts are fairly small. In contrast, a business may sell off fixed assets because it's downsizing the organization or abandoning a major segment of its business. These cash proceeds, on the other hand, are usually fairly large.

Other sources and uses of cash: financing activities

The third and last section of the cash flow statement summarizes the financing activities of the business over the period. *Financing activities* describe the sources of cash that are not generated by profit and any cash that was distributed to investors in the business. This section of the cash flow statement distinguishes between the two sources of capital to a business: debt (borrowed money) and owners' equity.

Most businesses have a mix of *short-term* (less than one year) debt, *medium-term* (generally two to five years) debt, and *long-term* (more than five years) debt. In general, a cash flow statement reports the following:

✔ Only the net increase or decrease of short-term debt

✔ Any new medium-term or long-term debt that the business has taken on

✔ Any medium-term or long-term debt that the business has paid off (or *retired*)

Although in my example cash flow statement I show all the business's debt in a single amount, an actual cash flow statement distinguishes between short-term and long-term debt (which Chapter 6 explains). Generally, only the net change in short-term debt is reported, but both the borrowings on new long-term debt and the payoffs of old long-term debt are reported in this section of the cash flow statement.

The financing section of the cash flow statement next turns to owners' equity, which serves both as a *source* of a business's cash (capital invested by owners) and a *use* of a business's cash (profit distributed to owners). This section of the cash flow statement reports capital raised from its owners, if any, as well as capital returned to the owners, if any.

Passing Judgment Based on the Cash Flow Statement

Analyzing a business's cash flow statement inevitably raises certain questions: What would I have done differently if I were running this business? Would I have borrowed more money? Would I have raised more money from the owners? Would I have distributed so much of the profit to the owners? Would I have let my cash balance drop so much?

One purpose of the cash flow statement is to show readers what judgment calls and financial decisions the business's managers made during the period. Of course, management decisions are always subject to second-guessing and criticizing, and passing judgment based on a financial statement isn't totally fair because it doesn't reveal the pressures faced by the managers during the period. Maybe they made the best decisions possible, given the circumstances. Maybe not.

For example, the business shown in my cash flow statement example paid $400,000 from profit to its owners — a 30 percent *pay-out ratio* (which is distribution divided by net income). In analyzing whether the pay-out ratio is too high, too low, or just about right, you need to look at the broader context of the business's sources and needs for cash.

First, look at cash flow from profit: $900,000, an amount that fell $1.1 million shy of covering the business's $2 million capital expenditures. The business did not secure any more capital from its owners, though it did increase its debt by $1 million. Even so, that's still $100,000 too little for capital expenditures. Given these circumstances, maybe the business should've hoarded its cash and not paid any cash distribution to its owners. But that's not the decision that the business's managers made. Instead, the cash balance dropped $500,000 over the period — a big drop.

So does this business have enough cash to operate with? You can't answer that question by just examining the cash flow statement, or any of the financial statements, for that matter. Every business needs a buffer of cash to protect against unexpected developments and to take advantage of unexpected opportunities, as I explain in Chapter 10 on budgeting. This particular business has a cash balance equal to four weeks of annual sales revenue for the period just ended, which may or may not be enough, depending on circumstances and the business's attitude about cash. If you were the boss of this business, how much working cash balance would you want? Not an easy question to answer! Don't forget that you need to look at all three primary financial statements — the income statement and the balance sheet as well as the cash flow statement — to get the big picture of a business's financial health. Chapters 6 and 14 show you how to analyze a business's financial statements.

Chapter 8

Getting a Financial Report Ready for Prime Time

Chapters 5, 6, and 7 explain the three financial statements of a business:

- ✔ **Income statement:** Summarizes sales revenue inflows and expense outflows for the period and ends with the bottom-line profit, which is the net inflow for the period (a loss is a net outflow)

- ✔ **Balance sheet:** Summarizes financial condition at the end of the period, consisting of assets, liabilities, and owners' equity at this time

- ✔ **Cash flow statement:** Summarizes the net cash inflow or outflow from profit for the period, plus other sources of cash and the uses of cash during the period, and ends with the net cash increase or decrease during the period

An annual financial *report* of a business contains more than just these three financial statements. In the "more," the business manager plays an important role — which outside investors and lenders should understand. The manager should do two or three critical things before the financial report is released to the outside world:

1. First, the manager should review with a critical eye the *vital connections* between the sales revenue and expenses in the income statement and their related assets and liabilities in the balance sheet, checking for out-of-control situations and possible errors.

2. Second, the manager should review carefully the *disclosures* in the financial report (all information in addition to the three financial statements) to make sure that the additional disclosures are adequate according to financial reporting standards, and that they are truthful but not damaging to the interests of the business.

3. Third, the manager should consider whether net income and balance sheet numbers need "touching up" to smooth the jagged edges off the trend of the company's year-to-year profit amounts or to improve the business's short-term solvency picture.

Certain parts of this chapter walk on thin ice. Some topics are, shall I say, rather delicate. The manager has to strike a balance between the interests of the business on the one hand and the interests of the owners (investors) and creditors of the business on the other. The best analogy I can think of is advertising done by a business. Although advertising must be truthful and sales prices must be accurate, advertisers have some leeway. So do managers in putting together their financial reports.

Reviewing the Vital Connections

Business managers and investors read financial reports because these reports give a synopsis of how the business is doing. A financial report is designed to answer certain basic financial questions:

- ✔ Is the business making a profit or suffering a loss, and how much?

- ✔ How do assets stack up against liabilities?

- ✔ Where did the business get its capital, and is it making good use of the money?

- ✔ Is profit generating cash flow?

- ✔ Did the business reinvest its profit or distribute profit to owners?

- ✔ Does the business have enough capital for future growth?

People read a financial report like a road map — to point the way and check how the trip is going. Managing and investing in a business is a financial journey. A manager is like the driver and must pay attention to all the road signs; investors are like the passengers who watch the same road signs. Some of the most important road signs are the vital connections and ratios between sales revenue and expenses and the related asset or liability in the balance sheet.

Figure 8-1 presents an overview of these vital connections, which are introduced in Chapter 5, on making profit, and explained in greater detail in Chapter 6, on why assets (and some liabilities) are needed in the process of making profit. Figure 8-1 shows five key connections. The savvy manager or investor checks these ratios to see whether everything is in order or whether some danger signals point to problems.

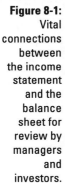

Figure 8-1: Vital connections between the income statement and the balance sheet for review by managers and investors.

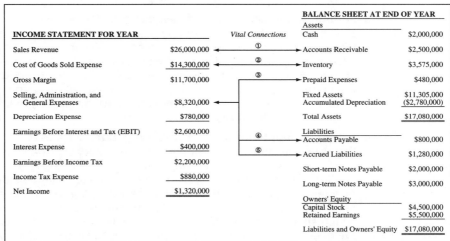

In the following list, I briefly explain these five connections from the *manager's* point of view. Chapter 14 explains how investors and lenders read a financial report and interpret these ratios. (Investors and lenders are on the outside looking in; managers are on the inside looking out.) The following numbers refer to the number of each connection in Figure 8-1.

Note: I cut right to the chase in the following brief comments, and I do not illustrate the calculations behind the comments. The purpose here is to emphasize why managers should pay attention to these important connections and ratios. Chapter 6 explains each calculation.

1. **Sales Revenue — Accounts Receivable:** This business's ending balance of accounts receivable is five weeks of its annual sales revenue. The manager should compare this ratio to the normal credit terms offered to the business's customers. If the ending balance is too high, the manager should identify which customers' accounts are past due and take actions to collect these amounts, or perhaps shut off future credit to these customers. (See the sidebar "What to do if your income isn't coming in" for more information.)

2. **Cost of Goods Sold Expense — Inventory:** This business's ending inventory is 13 weeks of annual cost of goods sold expense. The manager should compare this ratio to the company's inventory policies and objectives regarding how long inventory should be held awaiting sale. If inventory is too large, the manager should identify which products have been in stock too long; further purchases should be curtailed. Also, the manager may want to consider sales promotions or cutting sales prices to move these products out of inventory faster.

3. **Selling, Administration, and General (SA&G) Expenses — Prepaid Expenses:** This business's ending balance of prepaid expenses is three weeks of these annual operating expenses. The manager should know what the normal ratio of prepaid expenses should be relative to the annual SA&G operating expenses (excluding depreciation expense). If the ending balance is too high, the manager should investigate which costs have been paid too far in advance and take action to bring these prepaids back down to normal.

4. **Selling, Administration, and General (SA&G) Expenses — Accounts Payable:** This business's ending balance of accounts payable is five weeks of these annual operating expenses. Delaying payment of these liabilities is good from the cash flow point of view. But delaying too long may jeopardize the company's good credit rating with its key suppliers and vendors. If this ratio is too high, the manager should pinpoint which specific liabilities have not been paid and whether any of these are overdue and should be paid immediately. Or the high balance may indicate that the company is in a difficult short-term solvency situation and needs to raise more money to pay the amounts owed to suppliers and vendors.

5. **Selling, Administration, and General (SA&G) Expenses — Accrued Liabilities:** This business's ending balance of accrued liabilities is eight weeks of these annual operating expenses. This ratio may be consistent with past experience and the normal lag before paying these costs. On the other hand, the ending balance may be too high. The manager should identify which of these unpaid costs are higher than they should be. As with accounts payable, inflated amounts of accrued liabilities may signal serious short-term solvency problems.

These five key connections are the most important ones, but the manager should scan all basic connections to see whether the ratios pass the common sense test. For example, the manager should make a quick eyeball test of interest expense compared with interest-bearing debt. In Figure 8-1, interest is $400,000 compared to $5,000,000 total debt, which indicates an 8 percent interest rate. This seems okay. But if the interest expense is more than $500,000 or $600,000, the manager should investigate it to determine why it's so high.

There's always the chance of an error in the accounts of a business. Reviewing the vital connections between the income statement items and the balance sheet items is a very valuable last check before the financial statements are put into the business's financial report. After the financial report is released to the outside world, it becomes the official financial record of the business. If the financial statements are wrong, the business and its top managers are responsible.

Making Sure That Disclosure Is Adequate

The three primary financial statements are the bedrock of a financial report. In fact, a financial report is not deserving of the name if these three financial statements are not included. But, as mentioned earlier, there's more to a financial report than these three financial statements. A financial report needs *disclosures*. Of course, the financial statements provide disclosure of the most important financial information about the business. The term *disclosures,* however, usually refers to *additional* information provided in a financial report. In a nutshell, there are two basic parts of a financial report: (1) the three financial statements and (2) disclosures.

The chief officer of the business (the CEO of a large publicly owned corporation, the president of a private corporation, or the managing partner of a partnership) has the primary responsibility to make sure that the financial statements have been prepared according to generally accepted accounting principles (GAAP) and that the financial report provides *adequate disclosure*. He or she works with the chief financial officer and Controller of the business to make sure that the financial report meets the standard of adequate disclosure. (Many smaller businesses hire an independent CPA to advise them on their financial statements and disclosure in their financial reports.)

What to do if your income isn't coming in

After making credit sales, a business should closely monitor collections from customers to make sure that the money is coming in on time. In larger organizations, someone is assigned responsibility for credit and collections. This person (or department) screens first-time customers who ask for credit and keeps a close eye on actual collections of accounts receivable. When a customer does not pay on time, the business sends out a friendly reminder. If the customer doesn't respond to one or more of these requests for payment, the business follows up with a very unfriendly *dun letter*.

Eventually, the business may take legal action against *deadbeats* (customers whose accounts receivable are overdue by 60 to 90 days or longer). The business might hire a *collection agency* even though the cost is high — usually half or more of the amount collected.

Types of disclosures in financial reports

For a first look at disclosures in financial reports — in addition to the properly presented three financial statements — the following distinctions are helpful:

- ✔ **Footnotes** that give additional information about financial figures are an integral part of the statements; virtually all financial statements need footnotes.

- ✔ **Supplementary financial schedules and tables** to the financial statements provide more details than can be included in the body of financial statements.

- ✔ A wide variety of **other information** is included, some of which is required if the business is a public corporation subject to federal regulations regarding financial reporting to its stockholders, and other information that is voluntary and not strictly required legally or according to GAAP.

Footnotes: needed but nettlesome

Footnotes appear at the end of the three financial statements; usually, the financial statements specifically refer to one or more of the footnotes. At the bottom of each financial statement, you can find the following sentence (or words to this effect): "The footnotes are integral to the financial statements." You should read all footnotes for a full understanding of the financial statements.

Footnotes come in two types:

- ✔ One or more footnotes must be included to identify the **major accounting methods** that the business uses. (Chapter 13 explains that a business must choose among alternate accounting methods for certain expenses.) The business must reveal which accounting methods it uses for its major expenses. In particular, the business must identify its cost of goods sold expense (and inventory) method and its depreciation method. Other accounting methods that have a material impact on the financial statements are disclosed as well.

- ✔ Footnotes are used to provide **supplementary information and details** for many assets and liabilities. For example, during the asbestos lawsuits that went on for many years, the businesses that manufactured and sold these products included long footnotes describing the lawsuits. Details about stock option plans for key executives are the main type of footnote to the capital stock account in the owners' equity section.

Some footnotes are always required; a financial report would fall short of adequate disclosure without at least a few footnotes. Deciding whether a footnote is needed (after you get beyond the obvious one disclosing the business's accounting methods) and how to write the footnote is largely a matter of judgment and opinion. Believe it or not, there is no official codification for which specific footnotes are required — although many authoritative financial reporting standards laid down by the Financial Accounting Standards Board (FASB) and the Securities & Exchange Commission (SEC) for publicly owned corporations include provisions that require disclosure of certain information, such as the recent FASB pronouncement on stock options.

One problem that most investors face when reading footnotes — and, for that matter, many managers who should understand their own footnotes but find them a little dense — is that footnotes often deal with complex issues (such as lawsuits) and rather technical accounting matters. Let me offer you one footnote that brings out this latter point. This footnote is taken from the financial report a few years ago of a well-known manufacturer that uses the most conservative accounting method for determining its cost of goods sold expense and inventory cost value.

I know that I have not yet talked about these accounting methods; this is deliberate on my part. (Chapter 13 explains accounting methods.) I want you to read the following footnote and try to make sense of it. Other than updating the years to make the example look as current as possible, the footnote reads as it was presented in the annual financial report of the company.

Footnote 1.B. —
With minor exceptions, inventories are stated on the basis of the LIFO (last-in-first-out) method of inventory valuation. This method was first adopted for the major portion of inventories in 1950. If the FIFO (first-in-first-out) method had been in use, inventories would have been $1,634,000,000, $1,645,000,000, and $1,899,000,000 higher than reported at December 31, 1995, 1996, and 1997, respectively.

Yes, these amounts are in *billions* of dollars. This is a big, publicly owned corporation. The footnote is clear on one point: Its inventory cost value at the end of the three years would have been $1.6 to $1.9 billion higher if the FIFO method had been used. Of course, you have to have some idea of the difference between the two methods, which I explain in Chapter 13.

What is not clear concerns how much different the company's annual profits would have been for the three years if the alternate method had been in use. An investor would have to compute this amount; managers could ask the accounting department to do this analysis. Businesses disclose which accounting methods they use, but they do not have to disclose how much different annual profit would have been if alternate methods had been used — and very few do.

Other disclosures in financial reports

The following discussion includes a fairly comprehensive list of the various types of disclosures found in annual financial reports of larger, publicly owned businesses. A few caveats are in order. First, not every public corporation includes every one of the following items, although the disclosures are fairly common. Second, the level of disclosure by private businesses — after you get beyond the financial statements and footnotes to the statements — is much less than in public corporations. Third, tracking the actual disclosure practices of private businesses is difficult because their annual financial reports are issued only to their owners and lenders. A private business may include any or all of the following disclosures, but by and large it is not legally required to do so. The next section explains further the differences between private and public businesses regarding their financial report disclosure practices.

Public corporations typically include most of the following disclosures in their annual financial reports to their stockholders:

- ✔ **Cover (or transmittal) letter:** A letter from the chief executive of the business to the stockholders — which usually takes credit for good news and blames bad news on big government, unfavorable world political developments, a poor economy, or some other thing beyond management's control.

- ✔ **Highlights table:** A short table that presents key figures from the financial statements, such as sales revenue, total assets, profit, total debt, owners' equity, number of employees, and number of products sold (such as the number of vehicles sold by a car manufacturer, or the number of seat miles flown by an airline). The idea is to give the stockholder a financial thumbnail sketch of the business.

- ✔ **Management discussion and analysis (MD&A):** Deals with the major developments and changes during the year that affected the financial performance and situation of the business. The SEC requires this disclosure to be included in the annual financial reports of publicly owned corporations.

- ✔ **Supporting financial schedules and tables:** Additional financial statements, such as a statement of changes in owners' equity (beginning balances, new stock issues during the year, purchases of its own stock shares by the corporation, dividends, and ending balances).

- ✔ **Segment information:** The sales revenues and operating profits (before interest and income tax, and perhaps before certain costs that cannot be allocated among different segments) are reported for the major divisions of the organization, or for its different markets (international versus domestic, for example).

✔ **Historical summaries:** Financial history that extends back beyond the years included in the three primary financial statements.

✔ **Graphics:** Bar charts, trend charts, and pie charts representing financial conditions; pictures of key people and products.

✔ **Promotional material:** Information about the company, its products, its employees, and its managers.

✔ **Profiles:** Information about members of top management and the board of directors.

✔ **Quarterly summaries of profit performance:** Shows financial performance for all four quarters in the reporting period (required by the SEC).

✔ **Management's responsibility statement:** A short statement describing that management has the primary responsibility for the accounting methods used to prepare the financial statements, for writing the footnotes to the statements, and for providing the other required disclosures in the financial report. Usually, this statement appears on the same page of the auditor's report (see "CPA auditor's report").

✔ **CPA auditor's report:** The report from the CPA firm that performed the audit, expressing an opinion on the fairness and disclosure adequacy of the financial statements and footnotes (and any supporting financial schedules and tables). Chapter 15 discusses the nature of audits by CPAs and the audit report that they present to the board of directors of the corporation for inclusion in the annual financial report. The audit report is based on a critical review of the accounting records of the business and includes examination of evidence to support the business's assets, liabilities, owners' equity, sales revenue, and expenses. For example, the auditor makes test counts of inventory to verify the existence of the products and requests the banks in which the business has checking accounts to confirm these balances directly to the auditor.

✔ **Company contact information:** Information on how to contact the company and get copies of the reports filed with the SEC.

Managers of public corporations rely on lawyers, CPA auditors, and their financial and accounting officers to make sure that everything that should be disclosed in the business's annual financial reports is included, and that the exact wording of the disclosures is not misleading, inaccurate, or incomplete. This is a tall order. The field of financial reporting disclosure changes constantly. Both federal and state laws, as well as authoritative accounting standards, have to be observed. *Inadequate disclosure* in an annual financial report is just as serious as using wrong accounting methods for measuring profit and presenting values for assets, liabilities, and owners' equity. A financial report can be misleading because of improper accounting methods or because of inadequate or misleading disclosure. Both types of deficiencies can lead to nasty lawsuits against the business and its managers.

Financial Reporting by Private versus Public Companies

If you have the opportunity to compare 100 annual financial reports from large, publicly owned corporations with 100 annual reports from small, privately held businesses, you'd see many differences. Compared with their big brothers and sisters, privately owned businesses provide very little additional disclosures in their annual financial reports. The three financial statements and footnotes are pretty much the whole enchilada. Often, their financial reports may be typed on plain paper and stapled together. A privately held company many have very few stockholders, and typically one or more of the stockholders are also managers of the business.

The annual financial reports of publicly owned corporations include all or most all of the disclosure items listed earlier. Somewhere in the range of 10,000 corporations are publicly owned, and their stock shares are traded on the New York Stock Exchange, Nasdaq, or other stock exchanges. These publicly owned companies must file annual financial reports with the Securities & Exchange Commission (SEC), which is the federal agency that makes the rules for trading in securities and for the financial reporting requirements of publicly owned corporations.

Annual reports published by large publicly owned corporations can run 30, 40, or 50 and more pages. Generally they are very well done — the quality of the editorial work and graphics is excellent; the color scheme, layout, and design have very good eye appeal. But be warned that the volume of detail in their financial reports is overwhelming. A person needs two or more hours to read through everything included in one of these annual financial reports. Some of their footnotes are heavy going.

Both privately held and publicly owned businesses are bound by the same accounting rules for measuring profit, assets, liabilities, and owners' equity in annual financial reports to the owners of the business and that are made available to others (such as the lenders to the business). These ground rules are called *generally accepted accounting principles (GAAP)* and are mentioned many times in the book. There are not two different sets of accounting measurement rules — one for private companies and a second set for public businesses. The accounting measurement and valuation rules are the same for all businesses. However, disclosure requirements and practices differ greatly between private and public companies.

Publicly owned businesses live in a fish bowl. When a company goes public with an *IPO* (*initial public offering* of stock shares), it gives up a lot of the privacy that a closely held business enjoys. Publicly owned corporations whose stock shares are traded on national stock exchanges live in glass houses. In contrast, privately owned business corporations lock their doors regarding disclosure. They certainly have to include financial statements and footnotes. But beyond this, they have much more leeway and do not have to include the additional disclosure items listed in the preceding section.

A private business may have its financial statements audited by a CPA firm. If so, the audit report is included in the business's annual financial report. The very purpose of having an audit is to reassure stockholders and potential investors in the business that the financial statements can be trusted. But as I look up and down the preceding list, I don't see any other absolutely required disclosure item for a privately held business. The large majority of closely held businesses guard their financial information like Fort Knox.

The less information divulged in the annual financial report, the better — that's their thinking. I don't disagree. The stockholders don't have the liquidity for their stock shares that stockholders of publicly held corporation enjoy. The market prices of public corporations is everything, so information is made publicly available so that market prices are fairly determined. The stock shares of privately owned business are not traded, so there is not such an urgent need for the complete information that public markets depend on.

A private corporation could provide all the disclosures given in the preceding list — there's certainly no law against this. But usually they don't. Investors in private businesses can request confidential reports from managers at the annual stockholders' meetings; but doing so is not practical for a stockholder in a large public corporation.

Touching Up the Numbers

This section discusses two topics that business managers and investors should know about. I don't necessarily endorse either technique, but I think that you need to be aware of both of them. In some cases, the financial statement numbers don't come out exactly the way the business wants. Accountants use certain tricks of the trade to make the numbers closer to what the business prefers. One technique improves the appearance of the short-term solvency of the business, in particular the cash balance reported in the balance sheet at the end of the year. The other device shifts profit from one year to the next to make for a better-looking net income trend from year to year.

Not all businesses use these techniques, but the extent of their use is hard to pin down because no business would openly admit to using these manipulation methods. The evidence is fairly convincing, however, that many businesses use these techniques.

Fluffing up the cash balance with "window dressing"

Suppose you run a business and your accountant submits the following preliminary, first draft year-end balance sheet showing the following numbers:

Cash	$0	Accounts payable	$235,000
Accounts receivable	$486,000	Accrued operating liabilities	$187,000
Inventory	$844,000	Income tax payable	$58,000
Prepaid expenses	$72,000	Short-term notes payable	$200,000
Current assets	$1,402,000	Current liabilities	$680,000

You start scanning the numbers when something strikes you: a *zero cash balance?* How can that be? Maybe your business has been having some cash flow problems and you've intended to increase your short-term borrowing and speed up collection of accounts receivable to help the cash balance. But that plan doesn't help you right now, with this particular financial report that you must send out to your business's investors. Folks generally don't like to see a zero cash balance — it makes them kind of nervous, to put it mildly, no matter how you try to cushion it. So what do you do to avoid alarming them?

Your accountant might suggest a technique known as *window dressing,* a very simple method for making the cash balance look better. You just wait a few days past the end of your fiscal year before you officially close the books for the period; then you recalculate the numbers. After all, customers' checks are in the mail — that money is yours, as far as the customers are concerned, so your reports should reflect that cash inflow.

What impact does window dressing have? It reduces the amount in accounts receivable and increases the amount in cash by the same amount — it has absolutely no effect on the profit figure. It just makes your cash balance look a touch better.

Sounds like everybody wins, doesn't it? Your investors don't panic, and your job is safe. I have to warn you, though, that window dressing can be dangerous: You're taking away a few days from the next fiscal year, which you may end up needing to make up this time next year, and that leads you into a nasty cycle. At the very least, it's deceptive to your investors, who have every right to expect that the end of your fiscal year as stated on your financial reports is truly the *end of your fiscal year.* Think about it this way: If you've invested in a business that has fudged this date, how do you know what other numbers on the report are suspect?

Smoothing the rough edges off of profit

You should not be surprised when I tell you that business managers are under tremendous pressure to make profit every year and to keep profit on the up escalator year after year. Reporting a loss for the year, or even a dip below the profit trend line, is like a red flag that investors view with alarm. Everyone likes to see a steady upward trend line for profit; no one likes to see a profit curve that looks like a roller coaster. Most investors want a smooth journey and don't like putting on their investment life preservers.

Managers can do certain things to deflate or inflate profit (net income) recorded in the year, which are referred to as *profit smoothing* techniques. Profit smoothing is also called *income smoothing.* Profit smoothing is not nearly as serious as *cooking the books,* which refers to fraudulent accounting practices such as recording sales revenue that has not happened or not recording expenses that have happened. Cooking the books is very serious; managers can go to jail for fraudulent financial statements. Profit smoothing is more like a white lie that is told for the good of the business, and perhaps for the good of the managers as well. Managers know that there is always some noise in the accounting system. Profit smoothing muffles the noise.

Managers of publicly owned corporations whose stock shares are actively traded are under intense pressure to keep profits steadily rising. Security analysts who follow a particular company make profit forecasts for the business, and their buy-hold-sell recommendations are based largely on these earnings forecasts. If a business fails to meet its own profit forecast or falls short of stock analysts' forecast, the market price of its stock shares suffers. Stock option and bonus incentive compensation plans are also strong motivations for achieving the profit goals set for the business.

The evidence is fairly strong that publicly owned businesses engage to some degree in profit smoothing. Frankly, it's much harder to know whether private businesses do so. Private businesses don't face the public scrutiny and expectations that public corporations do. On the other hand, key managers in a private business may have incentive bonus arrangements that depend on recorded profit. In any case, business investors and managers should know about profit smoothing and how it's done.

Most profit smoothing involves pushing revenue and expenses into other years than they would normally be recorded. For example, if the president of a business wants to report more profit for the year, he or she can instruct the chief accountant to accelerate the recording of some sales revenue that normally wouldn't be recorded until next year, or to delay the recording of some expenses until next year that normally would be recorded this year. The main reason for smoothing profit is to keep it closer to a projected trend line and make the line less jagged.

Chapter 13 explains that managers choose among alternate accounting methods for several important expenses. After making these key choices, the managers should let the accountants do their jobs and let the chips fall where they may. If bottom-line profit for the year turns out to be a little short of the forecast or target for the period, so be it. This hands-off approach to profit accounting is the ideal way. However, managers often use a *hands-on* approach — they intercede (one could say interfere) and override the normal accounting for sales revenue or expenses.

Both managers who do it and investors who rely on financial statements in which profit smoothing has been done should definitely understand one thing: These techniques have "robbing Peter to pay Paul" effects. Accountants refer to these as *compensatory effects.* The effects next year offset and cancel out the effects of this year. Less expense this year is counterbalanced by more expense next year. Sales revenue recorded this year means less sales revenue recorded next year.

Two profit histories

Figure 8-2 shows the profit histories of two different companies over six years. The top chart shows a nice steady upward trend of profit. The bottom chart shows more of a roller coaster ride over the six years. Both businesses earned the same total profit for the six years — a total of $1,050,449. Their six-year profit performance is the same, down to the last dollar. Which company would you be more willing to risk your money in? I suspect that you'd prefer the top company because of the steady upward slope of its profit history.

Does Figure 8-2 really show two different companies — or are the two profit histories for the same company? The top chart could be the company's smoothed profit, and the bottom chart could be its actual profit, or the profit that would have been recorded if the smoothing techniques had not been applied.

Figure 8-3 merges the two profit histories side by side for each year. For the first year in the series, 1994, no profit smoothing occurred. Actual profit is on target. For each of the next five years, the two profit numbers differ. The under-gap or over-gap of actual profit compared to smoothed profit for the year is the amount of revenue or expense manipulation that was done in the

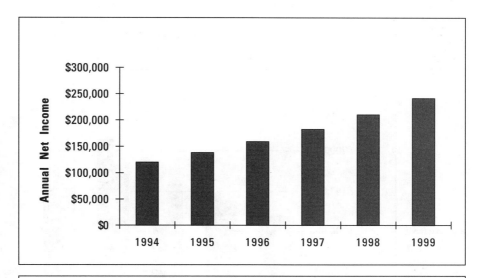

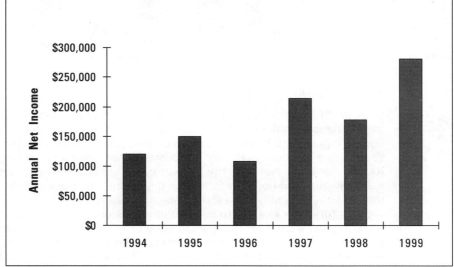

Figure 8-2:
Comparison
of two net
income
histories.

year. For example, in 1995, actual profit would have been too high, so the company moved some expenses that normally would be recorded the following year into 1995. In contrast, in 1996, actual profit was running too low, so the business took action to put off the recording of some expenses until 1997.

A business can go only so far in smoothing profit. If a business has a particularly bad year, all the profit smoothing tricks in the world would not close the gap. But several smoothing techniques are available for filling the potholes and straightening the curves on the profit highway.

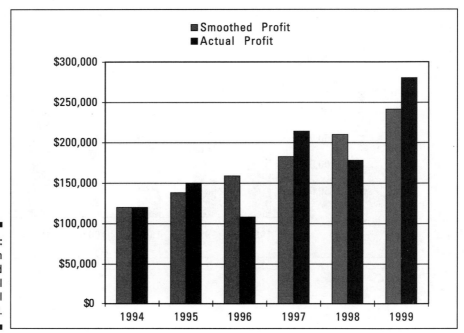

Figure 8-3:
Comparison
of smoothed
and actual
annual
profit.

Profit smoothing techniques

Most profit smoothing techniques require one essential ingredient: *management discretion* in deciding when to record a cost or when to record a sale. For example, when I was in public accounting, one of our clients was a contracting business that used the *completed contract method* for recording its sales revenue. Not until the job was complete did the company book the sales revenue and deduct all costs to determine the gross margin from the job (contract). In most cases, the company had to return a few weeks later for final touch-up work or to satisfy minor customer complaints. In the past, the company waited for this final visit before calling a job complete. But the year I was on the audit, the company was falling short of its profit goals. So the president decided to move up the point at which a job was called complete. The company decided not to wait for the final visit, which rarely involved more than a few minor expenses. Thus more jobs were completed during the year, and more sales revenue and more gross margin were recorded in the year.

One common technique of profit smoothing is *deferred maintenance*. Many routine and recurring maintenance costs of autos, trucks, machines, equipment, and buildings can be put off, or deferred until later. These costs are not recorded to expense until the actual maintenance is done, so putting off the work means that no expense is recorded for the work not done. Likewise, a business may spend a fair amount of money for employee training and development. These programs may be delayed until next year, and this expense would be lower. Or a company could cut back on its current year's outlays for market research and product development. Keep in mind that most of these expenses would be incurred next year, so the effect is to rob Peter (next year) to pay Paul (this year).

A business could ease up on its rules regarding when slow-paying customers are classified as *bad debts* (uncollectible accounts receivable). A business can put off recording some of its bad debts until next year. A *fixed asset out of active use* may have very little value to a business. Instead of writing off the undepreciated cost of the fixed asset as an expense this year, the business may delay the write-off until next year.

So a manager has control over the timing of many expenses, and he or she can use this discretion for profit smoothing. The expenses can be accelerated into this year or deferred to next year in order to make for a smoother profit trend. Of course, a business does not divulge in its external financial report the extent to which it has engaged in profit smoothing.

Into the future: online electronic financial reporting

A quick glance toward the future shows one thing for certain: Financial reporting is going digital. More and more people are using computer-based, electronic means to gain access to financial report data and information. For some time now, financial report information has been entered in computer databases and has been accessible through the information superhighway, which includes the Internet and other commercial online services. The SEC has sponsored a program called EDGAR (Electronic Data Gathering, Analysis, and Retrieval), which surely will expand and become more popular in the future. You can access the EDGAR database on the World Wide Web at the U.S. Securities and Exchange Commission Web site at www.sec.gov.

For some years, annual financial report information has been available through the LEXIS/NEXIS system. Most public corporations have established Internet sites that can be accessed for many things, including financial information.

Perhaps the traditional hard copy annual report will someday be replaced by electronic equivalents. I doubt this, but you never know. My crystal ball is no better than yours.

Part III

Accounting Tools and Techniques for Business Managers

The 5th Wave — By Rich Tennant

I'm mathematically dyslexic. But it's not that unusual - 100 out of every 15 people are.

In this part . . .

*B*usiness managers and owners depend on financial statements to know how much profit they're making, where that profit is at the end of the period, and whether the business is in good financial shape or needs improvement. They also use financial statements to keep a close watch on the lifeblood of the business: cash flows. Managers must know how to read their financial statements. Also, they should take advantage of proven accounting tools and techniques to make profit, control cash flow, and keep the business in good financial condition.

Managers need a basic accounting model for analyzing profit; they can use budgeting to plan and achieve the financial goals of the business, which is the essence of management control. Business managers and owners must decide which ownership structure to use, especially from an income tax point of view. Finally, managers should clearly understand how the costs of the business are accounted for, and they should get involved in choosing the basic accounting methods for measuring profit and the values of their assets and liabilities. This part of the book talks about the tools that managers and owners can use to help them make choices.

Chapter 9

Controlling and Improving Profit

● ●

In This Chapter

▶ Sizing up your current profit position by using the income statement

▶ Using hindsight to plan your future: What if sales had been lower or higher?

▶ Improving profit by working on the contribution profit margin

▶ Carefully considering whether a price cut will help or hurt your bottom line

● ●

*A*s a manager, you get paid to make profit happen. That's what separates you from the nonmanager employees at your business. Of course, you have to be a motivator, innovator, consensus builder, lobbyist, and maybe sometimes a baby-sitter, too, but the real purpose of your job is to control the profit of your business. No matter how much your staff loves you and those doughnuts you bring in every Monday, if you don't meet your profit goals, you're facing the unemployment line.

You have to be relentless in your search for better ways to do things. Competition in most industries is fierce, and you can never take profit performance for granted. Changes take place all the time — changes initiated by the business and changes pressured by outside forces. Maybe a new superstore down the street is causing your profit to fall off, and you figure that you'll have a huge sale to draw customers, complete with splashy ads on TV and Dimbo the clown in the store.

Whoa, not so fast. Make sure first that you can afford to cut prices and spend money on advertising and still turn a profit. Maybe price cuts and Dimbo's balloon creations will keep your cash register singing and the kiddies smiling, but you need to remember that making sales does not guarantee that you make a profit. As all you experienced business managers know, profit is a two-headed beast: Profit comes from making sales *and* controlling expenses.

So how do you determine what effect price cuts and advertising costs may have on your bottom line? By turning to your beloved accounting staff, of course, and asking for some what-if reports (like "What if we offer a 15 percent discount and hire Dimbo for two days at $45 an hour?").

This chapter shows you how to identify the key variables that determine what your profit would be if you changed certain factors (such as prices) and whether Dimbo is really worth that kind of money.

Getting the Basic Numbers to Play What If With

Chapter 5 presents the simplified profit equation: Profit = sales revenue – expenses. Now, some expenses are directly associated with making specific sales, whereas other expenses are not directly associated with making particular sales. Sales revenue minus direct expenses is called *margin,* an extraordinarily important concept and measure of profit. The more revealing version of the profit equation, which focuses on margin, is as follows:

```
(Margin × volume) - fixed expenses = profit
```

Before I explain these terms in more detail, take a look at the following *income statement* — which, as Chapter 5 discusses, is the full-blown version of the simplified profit equation, fleshed out with a business's actual numbers, that the accountant prepares at the end of each period. I use this particular income statement as the basis for the what-if profit questions throughout the rest of this chapter.

Sales revenue	$1,000,000
Cost of goods sold expense	(600,000)
Gross margin	$400,000
Sales, administrative, and general expenses	(230,000)
Operating earnings before interest and tax (EBIT)	$170,000
Interest expense	(20,000)
Earnings before income tax	$150,000
Income tax expense	(50,000)
Net income	$100,000

For more information about the income statement and all its sundry parts, see Chapter 5. Let me just point out the following here about this income statement:

✔ The business represented by this income statement sells products and therefore has a cost of goods sold expense. You need to subtract this expense from the sales revenue and then subtract operating expenses from the remaining sales revenue *before* you can use the rest of the sales revenue to provide profit. In contrast, companies that sell services (airlines, movie theaters, law firms) don't have a cost of goods sold expense; all their sales revenue goes toward meeting operating expenses and then providing profit.

✔ This income statement adheres to GAAP, but the GAAP standards lay down only the *minimum level of disclosure* for the benefit of people outside a business who are receiving the business's external financial report. (See Chapter 1 for more information about GAAP.) Your managers need more information than you would generally want to include in an external report, so don't base your profit decisions on just the income statement — you need to have a customized *profit model* drawn up, as discussed in "Doing 'What If' with Profit Models," later in this chapter.

✔ The income statement does not report the financial effects of the sales revenue and expenses — that is, the increases and decreases in the assets and liabilities caused by revenue and expenses. You need to control and improve these financial effects, for which purpose you need the complete financial picture provided by the two other primary financial statements (the balance sheet and the cash flow statement) in addition to the income statement. See Chapters 6 and 7 for more about these other statements.

Margin and volume

The *margin* is what's left over after you subtract your costs associated with a single product from the price that you charge for that product. This number is the starting point for making profit because each unit sold must contribute to the recovery of the company's total fixed expenses for the period. The more accurate name for *margin* is *contribution profit margin per unit.* The margin equation is as follows:

```
Margin = sales price - (product cost + other variable
          expenses)
```

Consider a retail hardware store that sells, say, a Toro lawnmower to a customer. The purchase cost per unit that the retailer paid to Toro, the manufacturer, when the retailer bought its shipment of these lawnmowers is the *product cost* in the margin equation. The retailer also provides one free servicing of the lawnmower after the customer has used it a few months (cleaning it and sharpening the blade) and also pays its salesperson a commission on the sale. These two additional expenses are examples of variable expenses in the margin equation.

Here are some other terms associated with the margin:

- ✔ **Gross margin, also called gross profit:** Gross margin = sales revenue – cost of goods sold expense. Gross margin is profit from sales revenue *before* deducting the other variable expenses of making the sales. So gross margin is one step short of the final margin earned on making sales. Businesses that sell products must report gross margin on their *external* income statements. However, GAAP standards do *not* require that you report other variable expenses of making sales on external income statements. In their external financial reports, very few businesses divulge other variable expenses of making sales. In other words, managers do not want the outside world and competitors to know their margins. Most businesses carefully guard information about their margins because that information is very sensitive.

- ✔ **Gross margin ratio:** One of several profit ratios calculated by outside investors in a business, who are limited to the information reported on the business's external income statement. Gross margin ratio = gross margin ÷ sales revenue. In the sample income statement for this chapter, the gross margin on sales is 40 percent. (See Chapter 14 for more about the gross margin ratio and other ratios.)

- ✔ **Markup:** Generally refers to starting with the product cost and adding a percent to determine the sales price. For example, a product that cost $60 may be marked up (based on cost) by 66 $2/3$ percent to determine its sales price of $100 — for a gross margin of $40 on the product. *Note:* The markup based on *cost* is 66$2/3$ percent ($40 markup ÷ $60 product cost). But the gross margin ratio is only 40 percent, which is based on *sales price* ($40 ÷ $100).

Fixed expenses

Fixed expenses are the many different costs that a business is obligated to pay and cannot decrease over the short run without major surgery on the human resources and the physical facilities of the business. You definitely should distinguish fixed expenses from your *variable expenses,* as detailed in the section "What if sales had been lower?", later in this chapter.

As an example of fixed expenses, consider the typical self-service car wash business — you know, the kind where you drive in, put some quarters in a box, and use the water spray to clean your car. Almost all operating costs of this business are *fixed:* Rent on the land, depreciation of the structure and the equipment, and the annual insurance premium cost don't depend on the number of cars passing through the car wash. The only variable expenses are probably the water and the soap.

If you want to decrease fixed expenses significantly, you need to downsize the business (lay off workers, sell off property, and so on). When looking at the various ways you have for improving your profit, significantly cutting down on fixed expenses is generally the last-resort option. See "How do you improve profit?", later in this chapter for the better options.

From EBIT to the bottom line

After deducting all operating expenses from sales revenue, you get to operating earnings before interest and tax (otherwise known as EBIT), which is $170,000 in the business example. *Operating* is an umbrella term that includes cost of goods sold expense and all other expenses of making sales and operating your business — but not interest and income tax. Sometimes EBIT is called *operating profit,* or *operating earnings,* to empha-size that profit comes from making sales and controlling operating expenses. This business earned $170,000 operating profit from its $1 million sales revenue — which seems satisfactory. But is its $170,000 EBIT really good enough, or perhaps not good enough? What's the reference for answering this question?

The main benchmark for judging operating profit (EBIT) is whether this amount of profit is adequate to cover the *cost of capital* of the business. Chapter 6 explains the various assets that a business needs to make sales and earn profit. A business must raise capital for the money to invest in its various assets — and this capital has a cost. A business has to pay interest on its debt capital, and it should earn enough after-tax net income (bottom-line profit) to satisfy its owners who have put their capital in the business. See the sidebar "How much net income is needed to make owners happy?", later this chapter.

Nobody — not even the most die-hard humanitarian — is in business just to break even, or to make a zero EBIT. You simply can't do this; profit is an absolutely necessary part of doing business — the cost of capital being the fundamental need for profit.

Don't treat the word *profit* as something that's whispered in the hallways. Profit builds owners' value and provides the basic stability for a business. Earning a satisfactory EBIT is the cornerstone of business. Without earning an adequate operating profit, a business could not attract capital, and you can't have a business without capital.

How much net income is needed to make owners happy?

People who invest in your business usually aren't philanthropists who don't want to make any money on the deal. No, these investors want a business to protect their capital investment, earn a good bottom-line profit for them, and enhance the value of their investment over time. They understand that a business may not earn a profit but suffer a loss — that's the risk they take as owners.

As described in Chapters 6 and 11, how much of a business's net income (bottom-line profit) is distributed to the owners depends on the business and the arrangement that it made with the owners. But regardless of how much money the owners actually receive, they still have certain expectations of how well the business does — that is, what the business's net income is. After all, they've staked their money on the business's success.

One test of whether the owners will be satisfied with the net income is to compute the *return on equity* (ROE), which is the ratio of net income to total owners' equity (net income ÷ owners' equity). In this chapter's sample income statement, the bottom-line profit is $100,000. Suppose that the total owners' equity in the business is $700,000. Thus, the ROE is 14 percent ($100,000 ÷ $700,000). Is 14 percent a good ROE? Well, that depends on how much the owners could earn from an alternative investment . But at this point, I'd say that a 14 percent ROE isn't bad.

Note: ROE does not imply that net income was distributed in cash to the owners. Usually, a business needs to retain a good part of its bottom-line net income to provide capital for growing the business. Suppose, in this example, that none of the net income is distributed in cash to its owners. The ROE is still 14 percent; ROE does not depend on how much, if any, of net income is distributed to the owners.

Doing What If with Profit Models

Managing profit is like driving a car — you need to be glancing in the rearview mirror constantly as well as looking ahead through the windshield. You have to know your profit history to see your profit future. Understanding the past is the best preparation for the future.

The *profit model* allows you to compare your actual income statement with what your income statement would've looked like if you'd done something differently — for example, raised prices. With the profit model, you can test-drive adjustments before putting them into effect. It lets you plan and map out your profit strategy for the *coming* period in addition to helping you analyze why profit went up or down from the *last* period.

The profit model focuses on the key factors and variables that drive profit. Here's what you should know about these factors:

- ✔ Even small decreases in the contribution profit margin per unit can have a drastic impact on profit because fixed expenses don't go down over the short run (and are hard to reduce even over the long run).

- ✔ Even small increases in the contribution profit margin per unit can have a dramatic impact on profit because fixed expenses won't go up over the short run — although they may have to be increased in the long run.

- ✔ Compared with changes in contribution profit margin per unit, sales volume changes have secondary profit impact; sales volume changes are not trivial, but margin changes can have a bigger effect on profit.

- ✔ You can, perhaps, reduce fixed expenses to improve profit, but you have to be very careful to cut fat and not muscle; reducing fixed expenses may lower the capacity of your business to make sales and deliver high-quality service to customers.

The following sections expand on these key points.

What if sales had been lower?

Better than anyone else, managers know that sales for the year could have been lower or higher. A natural question is how much different profit would have been at the lower or higher level of sales. If you'd sold 10 percent fewer total units during the year, what would your net income (bottom-line profit) have been? You might guess that profit would have slipped 10 percent, but that would *not* have been the case. In fact, profit would have slipped by much more than 10 percent. Are you surprised? Read on for the reasons.

Why wouldn't profit slip by the same percentage as sales? Because of the nature of fixed expenses — just because your sales are lower doesn't mean that your expenses are lower. *Fixed expenses* are the costs of doing business that, for all practical purposes, are stuck at a certain amount over the short term. Fixed expenses do not react to changes in the sales level. Here are some examples of fixed expenses:

- ✔ Interest on money that the business has borrowed
- ✔ Employees' salaries and benefits
- ✔ Property taxes
- ✔ Fire insurance

Over time, a business can downsize its assets and therefore reduce its fixed expenses to fit a lower sales level, but that can be a drastic reaction to what may be a temporary downturn.

A business also has *variable expenses,* which move up and down in direct proportion to changes in sales volume or revenue. Here are some examples of variable expenses:

- Cost of goods sold expense
- Commissions paid to salespeople based on their sales
- Discounts that a business pays to a bank when a customer uses a credit card such as Visa or American Express. (When a business deposits its copy of the credit card slip, the bank deducts a certain percentage of the amount deposited, as the bank's fee for handling the transaction.)

Okay, so in calculating the effect of lower sales volume on profit, you need to keep the fixed expenses as they are, and you need to adjust variable expenses to fit the lower sales level. The problem is that the income statement shows one lump sum for the category of sales, administrative, and general (SA&G) expenses, a category for which most of the expenses are fixed but some are variable. What you need to do is have your accountant carefully examine these expenses to determine which are fixed and which are variable. (Some expenses may have both fixed and variable components, but these technical details are beyond the scope of this book.)

Further complicating the matter is the fact that the accountant needs to divide variable expenses between those that vary with sales *volume* (total number of units sold) and those that vary with sales *revenue* (total dollars of sales revenue). That's an important distinction.

- An example of an expense driven by sales volume is the cost of shipping and packaging. This cost depends strictly on the *number* of units sold and is the same regardless of how much the item inside the box costs.
- An example of an expense driven by sales revenue is the sales commission paid to the salespersons, which is directly dependent on how much an item costs.

Suppose that the business represented in this chapter's sample income statement has just one variable expense among all the fixed expenses in the SA&G category: a 6 percent sales commission, resulting in an expense total of $60,000 ($1,000,000 sales revenue × 6%). Table 9-1 shows how an accountant can transform the external income statement into a report designed for managers that separates the variable expense from the fixed expenses and adds some further, clarifying information. This example is a bit oversimplified — the business sells only one product — to show you more clearly how the various parts of the report are calculated.

Note: A business's entire sales mix, which consists of the many different products it sells and the proportions of each, can be collapsed into one "average" product. Instead of grappling with 100 or 1,000 different products, you can condense them all into one proxy average product. Dealing with just one product in the following discussion is not that far removed from reality as it may seem.

Table 9-1	Management Income Statement with Variable Expenses Separated from Fixed Expenses	
Sales Volume	**Total (10,000 Units)**	**Per Unit**
Sales revenue	$1,000,000	$100
Cost of goods sold expense	(600,000)	(60)
Gross margin	$400,000	$40
Revenue-driven variable expenses (sales commission)	(60,000)	(6)
Contribution profit margin	$340,000	$34
Fixed sales, administrative, and general expenses	(170,000)	
EBIT	$170,000	
Interest expense	(20,000)	
Earnings before income tax	$150,000	
Income tax expense	(50,000)	
Net income	$100,000	

The management income statement shown in Table 9-1 is a much better design for managers to use in profit analysis than is the traditional income statement design (shown earlier in the "Getting the Basic Numbers to Play What If With" section). Here's what information has been added that isn't included in the external income statement:

✔ Sales volume for the year

✔ Per-unit values (The sales revenue per unit is called the *sales price* — in this example, the product has a $100 sales price.)

✔ Fixed versus variable expenses

✔ Contribution profit margin

Caution: Handle this information with care. The contribution profit margin is confidential, for your eyes only. This information is limited to you and other managers in the business. Clearly, you don't want your competitors to find out your margins. Even within a business, the information may not circulate to all managers — just those who need to know.

The contribution profit margin comes from deducting the variable expense from the gross margin. In this example, the business retains $34 per unit to pay the business's fixed expenses.

The contribution profit margin per unit is one of the three most important determinants of profit performance (along with sales volume and fixed expenses), as shown in the upcoming sections — particularly "Calculating a drop in sales price."

Calculating a drop in sales volume

With the income statement (as modified for management analysis) from the preceding section, you're ready to paint a what-if scenario. What if you had sold 10 percent fewer units during this period? In this example, that would mean a total of 9,000 units rather than 10,000. Table 9-2 shows you how much profit damage this seemingly modest drop in sales revenue would've caused. The first group of numbers shows you the results for 9,000 units, and the second group of numbers shows the original situation of 10,000 units, for comparison.

Table 9-2	Ten Percent Lower Sales Volume Compared with Actual Situation			
Sales Volume	**Totals for 9,000 Units**	**Per Unit (9,000 Units)**	**Totals for 10,000 Units**	**Per Unit (10,000 Units)**
Sales revenue	$900,000	$100	$1,000,000	$100
Cost of goods sold expense	(540,000)	(60)	600,000	(60)
Gross margin	$360,000	$40	$400,000	$40
Revenue-driven variable expenses (sales commission)	(54,000)	(6)	(60,000)	(6)
Contribution profit margin	$306,000	$34	$340,000	$34

Sales Volume	Totals for 9,000 Units	Per Unit (9,000 Units)	Totals for 10,000 Units	Per Unit (10,000 Units)
Fixed sales, administrative, and general expenses	(170,000)		(170,000)	
EBIT	$136,000		$170,000	
Interest expense	(20,000)		(20,000)	
Earnings before income tax	$116,000		$150,000	
Income tax expense	(38,667)		(50,000)	
Net income	$77,333		$100,000	

Bottom-line profit would fall from $100,000 to $77,333 — a drop of about 23 percent. Wait a minute! How can a decrease of only 10 percent in sales volume cause a 23 percent profit drop?

Notice that the total contribution profit margin is $340,000 at the 10,000-units sales level and $306,000 at the 9,000-units sales level — a drop of $34,000, or 10 percent, which is consistent with the 10 percent sales volume decrease. But the $170,000 SA&G expense remains the same, and the $20,000 interest expense remains the same — because these costs are fixed. *That* is the key issue here. See the sidebar "Breaking even, with a margin of safety and operating leverage to boot," later in this chapter for a formula that explains the percentage by which the net income decreased.

Calculating a drop in sales price

So what effect would a 10 percent decrease in the sales price have caused? Around a 23 percent drop, similar to the effect of a 10 percent decrease in sales volume? Not quite. Check out Table 9-3, in which the first group of numbers reflects a 10 percent lower price and the second group of numbers reflects the original sales price. Both groups of numbers are for the same number of units sold: 10,000.

Table 9-3	Ten Percent Lower Sales Price Compared with Original Situation			
Sales Volume	*Totals with Lower Price*	*Per Unit (Lower Price)*	*Totals with Original Price*	*Per Unit (Original Price)*
Sales revenue	$900,000.00	$90.00	$1,000,000.00	$100.00
Cost of goods sold expense	(600,000.00)	(60.00)	(600,000.00)	(60.00)
Gross margin	$300,000.00	$30.00	$400,000.00	$40.00
Revenue-driven variable expenses (sales commission)	(54,000.00)	(5.40)	(60,000.00)	(6.00)
Contribution profit margin	$246,000.00	$24.60	$340,000.00	$34.00
Fixed sales, administrative, and general expenses	(170,000.00)		(170,000.00)	
EBIT	$76,000.00		$170,000.00	
Interest expense	(20,000.00)		(20,000.00)	
Earnings before income tax	$56,000.00		$150,000.00	
Income tax expense	(18,667.00)		(50,000.00)	
Net income	$37,333.00		$100,000.00	

Whoa! Net income would drop from $100,000 at the $100 sales price to only $37,333 at the $90 sales price — a plunge of nearly 63 percent. What could cause such a drastic effect on net income?

Notice that the contribution profit margin drops from $34.00 per unit to $24.60 per unit, or a decrease of $9.40 per unit sold. Based on the 10,000 units sold, this serious decrease in the contribution profit margin per unit causes total contribution margin, operating earnings, and earnings before interest and tax (EBIT) to fall by $94,000.00. The drop in income tax absorbs some of this hit on profit, but even so, the after-tax effect is a $62,667.00 decrease in net income.

The moral of the story is to protect contribution profit margin per unit above all else. Every dollar of contribution margin per unit that is lost — due to decreased sales prices, increased product cost, or an increase in other variable costs — has a tremendously negative impact on net income. Conversely, if you can increase the contribution margin per unit without hurting sales volume, you reap the net income benefits, as described next.

Breaking even, with a margin of safety and operating leverage to boot

A common tool of profit analysis for a business with fixed costs (which includes just about all businesses) is calculating its *break-even point*. A business breaks even when its sales revenue is equal to its total expenses — that is, its sales prices are set to reclaim the cost of goods sold and pay operating expenses, with nothing left over for profit. You divide the total fixed operating costs by the contribution profit margin per unit, resulting in the number of units that you need to sell in order to break even.

The business example in this chapter has total fixed operating costs of $170,000 and fixed interest expense of $20,000 — for $190,000 total fixed expenses. Dividing its $190,000 total fixed expenses by its $34 contribution profit margin per unit gives the break-even volume of 5,588 units — this business needs to sell 5,588 units in order to earn $190,000 total contribution profit margin, just enough to cover its fixed operating expenses.

So the business needs to sell 5,588 units in order to earn exactly zero profit before income tax, as follows: Its total contribution profit margin is $190,000 ($34 contribution profit margin per unit × 5,588 units break-even

point). Its total fixed operating expenses are $190,000. That leaves a zero amount of earnings before income tax. At the break-even sales volume of 5,588 units, the company's taxable income would be zero, its income tax would be zero, and its net income would be zero. A lot of zeros!

The *margin of safety* is the difference between actual sales volume and the break-even point. This business sold 10,000 units, which is 4,412 units above its break-even sales volume — a rather large cushion against any downturn in sales. Only a major sales collapse would cause the business to fall all the way down to its break-even volume, assuming that it can maintain its $34 contribution profit margin per unit and that its fixed costs don't increase.

Another use of the break-even point is to explain the multiple effect that a change in sales volume has on net income — a 10 percent change in sales volume, for example, does *not* cause a 10 percent change in net income. This multiplier effect is known as *operating leverage*. In calculating what effect a sales-volume change would have on net income, you determine how many more or fewer units would be sold and what the relationship is between the

(continued)

(continued)

actual number of units sold and the break-even point. You plug these numbers into this formula:

```
Difference in number of units
sold ÷ current number of
units sold over the break-
even point = percentage of
difference in net income
```

In the example given in the "Calculating a drop in sales volume" section of this chapter, the sample business sold 10,000 units — 4,412 units over its break-even volume. The what-if scenario involves calculating the difference that a 10 percent decrease in sales volume would have on net profit:

```
1,000 fewer units sold ÷
4,412 units over break-even =
23% decrease in net income
```

So selling 9,000 units instead of 10,000 would have resulted in a 23 percent plunge in net profit.

Note: The term *operating leverage* is usually used to stress the positive effects of a sales volume increase, not the damage done by a sales volume decrease. In other words, if the company had sold 10 percent *more* units, with no increase in its fixed costs, its profit would have *increased* by 23 percent, reflecting the operating leverage effect.

How do you improve profit?

The preceding sections explore the downside of things — that is, what would've happened to profit if sales volume or sales prices had been lower. The upside — higher profit — is so much more pleasant to discuss and analyze, don't you think?

Profit improvement boils down to three factors, listed in order from the most effective to the least effective:

✔ Increase the contribution profit margin per unit.

✔ Increase sales volume.

✔ Reduce fixed expenses.

Say that the president wants to improve the bottom line from the $100,000 net income you earned this year to $120,000 next year. How can you pump up the profit by $20,000?

First of all, realize that to increase your net income *after taxes* by $20,000, you need to increase your before-tax profit by *$30,000* — to account for the one-third that goes to income tax. (If you increase your earnings by $30,000, you pay an extra $10,000 in income tax, leaving an increase of $20,000 in after-tax net income.)

You should also take into account the possibility that fixed costs and interest expense may rise next year, but for this example, I'm assuming that they won't. I'm also assuming that the business can't cut any of its fixed SA&G expenses without hurting its ability to maintain and support its present sales level (and a modest increase in the sales level). Of course, in real life, every business should carefully scrutinize its fixed expenses to see if some of them can be cut.

Okay, so how can you increase your business's before-tax profit by $30,000? You have two choices (well, actually three choices). Take another look at Table 9-1 and study these options:

✔ Increase the contribution profit margin per unit by $3, which would raise the total contribution profit margin by $30,000, based on a 10,000-units sales volume ($3 × 10,000 = $30,000).

✔ Sell 882 additional units at the current contribution profit margin per unit of $34, which would raise the total contribution profit margin by just about $30,000 (882 × $34 = $29,988).

✔ Use a combination of these two approaches: Increase both the margin per unit and the sales volume.

The second approach is obvious — you just need to set a sales goal of increasing the number of products sold by 882. (How you motivate your already overworked three-person sales staff to accomplish that lofty goal is up to you.) But how do you go about the first approach, increasing the contribution profit margin per unit by $3?

Table 9-4 illustrates how the first approach would work. Note that all numbers still reflect a total of 10,000 units sold. But the sales price has been raised from $100.00 to $105.00, dragging with it an increase in sales commission (which is set at 6 percent of sales revenue) from $6.00 to $6.30 per unit. In addition, the accountant who produced this report (me) expects the cost of selling these goods to rise from $60.00 to $61.70 per unit. The net effect of these three changes is to improve contribution profit margin per unit by $3.00, thus increasing the total contribution profit margin by the required amount as handed down from the gods — $30,000.00.

Table 9-4 Increasing Contribution Profit Margin per Unit by $3				
Sales Volume	Totals with Increase	Per Unit (Increase)	Current Totals	Per Unit (Currently)
Sales revenue	$1,050,000.00	$105.00	$1,000,000.00	$100.00
Cost of goods sold expense	(617,000.00)	(61.70)	(600,000.00)	(60.00)
Gross margin	$433,000.00	$43.30	$400,000.00	$40.00
Revenue-driven variable expenses (sales commission)	63,000.00	6.30	60,000.00	6.00
Contribution profit margin	$370,000.00	$37.00	$340,000.00	$34.00
Fixed sales, administrative, and general expenses	(170,000.00)		(170,000.00)	
EBIT	$200,000.00		$170,000.00	
Interest expense	(20,000.00)		(20,000.00)	
Earnings before income tax	$180,000.00		$150,000.00	
Income tax expense	(60,000.00)		(50,000.00)	
Net income	$120,000.00		$100,000.00	

What about dropping prices to increase sales volume?

A word of warning: Be sure to *run the numbers* (accountantspeak for using a profit model) before deciding to drop sales prices in an effort to gain more sales volume. Suppose, for example, you're convinced that if you decrease prices by 5 percent, volume will increase by 10 percent. Seems like an attractive trade-off, one that would increase both profit performance and market share. But are you sure that those are the results you'll get?

Table 9-5, an abbreviated version of the profit model, shows how such a change would affect sales revenue, cost of goods sold expense, and sales commission (the variable expense driven by sales revenue). The impact on profit may surprise you. (Note that the 11,000-units columns show the what-if scenario, and the 10,000-units columns show the current situation.)

Table 9-5 Lower Sales Price and Higher Sales Volume Trade-off

Sales Volume	Totals (11,000 Units)	Per Unit (11,000 Units)	Totals (10,000 Units)	Per Unit (10,000 Units)
Sales revenue	$1,045,000.00	$95.00	$1,000,000.00	$100.00
Cost of goods sold expense	(660,000.00)	(60.00)	(600,000.00)	(60.00)
Gross margin	$385,000.00	$35.00	$400,000.00	$40.00
Revenue-driven variable expenses (sales commission)	(62,700.00)	(5.70)	(60,000.00)	(6.00)
Contribution profit margin	$322,300.00	$29.30	$340,000.00	$34.00

Total contribution profit margin would not go up; instead, it would go down $17,700 — from $340,000 to $322,300. In dropping the sales price by $5, the company would give up too much of its margin per unit. The increase in sales volume would not make up for the big dent in margin per unit. The company would gain more market share but would pay for it with a noticeable drop in profit.

To keep profit the same, the business would have to increase sales volume. By how much? Divide the total contribution profit margin for the 10,000-units situation by the contribution profit margin per unit for the 11,000-units scenario:

```
$340,000.00 ÷ $29.30 = 11,604
```

In other words, the business wants to keep its total contribution margin at $340,000.00, so you start with this target number. At the lower sales price, its margin drops to only $29.30. In other words, each unit earns $29.30 margin. So how many additional units would the business need to sell? The answer is 11,604 units, as shown. In short, this business would have to increase its sales volume to 11,604 units — an increase of 1,604 units, or a whopping 16 percent. That would be quite a challenge, to say the least.

WARNING!

Caution: Contribution profit margin out of control!

What happens when you don't control the contribution profit margin per unit? Disaster, pure and simple.

You're in a constant battle to protect margins. Customers want lower prices, competition undercuts your sales prices, suppliers increase product costs, the sales staff wants aggressive sales promotions — these are some of the reasons for margin slippage.

Take the same sample income statement that I've used throughout this chapter and assume that the managers did not control the contribution margin per unit very well over the year just ended. They let the sales price slip to $92.00 and the product cost rise to $67.48 per unit. Assuming that all other factors remained the same (including the total number of units at 10,000), here's what this doomsday scenario looks like:

Sales Volume	Total (Lower Margin)	Per Unit (Lower Margin)	Total (Original Situation)	Per Unit (Original Situation)
Sales revenue	$920,000.00	$92.00	$1,000,000.00	$100.00
Cost of goods sold expense	(674,800.00)	(67.48)	(600,000.00)	(60.00)
Gross margin	$245,200.00	$24.52	$400,000.00	$40.00
Revenue-driven variable expenses (sales commission)	(55,200.00)	(5.52)	(60,000.00)	(6.00)
Contribution profit margin	$190,000.00	$19.00	$340,000.00	$34.00
Fixed sales, administrative, and general expenses	(170,000.00)		(170,000.00)	
EBIT	$20,000.00		$170,000.00	
Interest expense	(20,000.00)		(20,000.00)	
Earnings before income tax	$-0-		$150,000.00	
Income tax expense	-0-		50,000.00	
Net income	$-0-		$100,000.00	

At the $19.00 contribution profit margin per unit, the business would have earned only $190,000 total contribution profit margin for the year — just enough to cover the company's $170,000 fixed operating costs and its $20,000 interest expense for the year. The company's earnings before and after income tax would have been zero, called the *break-even point*.

Quite clearly, the business has to protect and maintain its contribution profit margin per unit — and, of course, improve this number, if possible.

Chapter 10

Budgeting: Setting Goals and Staying on Course

A business can't open its doors each day without having some idea of what to expect. And it can't close its doors at the end of the day not knowing what happened. When I was in the Boy Scouts, the motto was "Be Prepared." In the same way, a business must be prepared and plan its future and control its actual performance in order to reach its financial goals. The only question is how. *Budgeting* is one answer.

You can see a budget most easily in the final set of *budgeted financial statements* of a business — its budgeted income statement, balance sheet, and cash flow statement. Preparing these three budgeted financial statements requires a lot of time and effort; managers do detailed analysis to determine how to improve the financial performance of the business. The vigilance required in budgeting helps to maintain and improve profit performance and to plan cash flow.

Budgeting is much more than slapping together a few figures. A budget is an integrated financial plan put down on paper, or these days I should say entered in a computer spreadsheet. Planning is the key characteristic of budgeting. The budgeted financial statements encapsulate the financial plan of the business for the coming year.

The financial statements included in the annual financial report of a business are prepared *after the fact;* that is, the statements are based on actual transactions that have already taken place. Budgeted financial statements, on the other hand, are prepared *before the fact,* and are based on future transactions that you expect to take place based on the business's profit and financial strategy and goals. These forward-looking financial statements are referred to as *pro forma,* which is Latin for "provided in advance." *Note:* Budgeted financial statements are not reported outside the business; they are strictly for internal management use.

Why Bother with a Budget?

Managers don't just look out the window and come up with budget numbers. Budgeting is not pie-in-the-sky wishful thinking. Budgeting — to have real value to a business — starts with a critical analysis of the most recent actual performance and position of the business by the managers who are responsible for the results. Then the managers decide on specific and concrete goals for the coming year. (Budgets can be done for more than one year, but the key stepping-stone into the future is the budget for the coming year — see the sidebar "Taking it one game at a time.")

In short, budgeting demands a fair amount of management time and energy. Budgets have to be worth this time and effort. So why should a business go to the trouble of budgeting? You do budgeting and prepare budgeted financial statements for three quite different reasons, which are useful to distinguish.

The modeling reasons for budgeting

To construct budgeted financial statements, you need good *models* of the profit, cash flow, and financial condition of your business.

Note: Don't be intimidated by the term *model.* It simply refers to an explicit, condensed description of how profit, cash flow, and assets and liabilities behave. A model is analytical, but not all models are mathematical. In fact, none of the financial models in this book is the least bit mathematical — but you do have to look at each factor of the model and how it interacts with one or more other factors. The simple accounting equation — assets = liabilities + owners' equity — is a model of the balance sheet, for example.

Taking it one game at a time

A company generally prepares one-year bud-gets, although many businesses also develop budgets for two, three, or five or more years. However, reaching out beyond a year be-comes quite tentative and very iffy. Making forecasts and estimates for the next 12 months is tough enough. A one-year budget is much more definite and detailed in comparison to longer-term budgets. As they say in the sports world, a business should take it one game (or year) at a time.

Budgeting relies on these financial models, or blueprints that serve as the foundation for each budgeted financial statement:

- **Budgeted income statement:** Chapter 9 presents the basic profit model; refer to Table 9-1 for the critical variables that drive profit. This man-agement income statement is a model that separates variable and fixed expenses and includes the sales volume, margin, and other key factors that determine profit performance. The profit model is like a schematic that shows the path to the bottom line. It reveals the factors that must be improved upon in order to improve profit performance in the coming period.

- **Budgeted balance sheet:** The key connections and ratios between sales revenue and expenses and their related assets and liabilities are the elements of the basic model for the budgeted balance sheet. These vital connections are explained throughout Chapter 6; Chapter 8 (specifically Figure 8-1) presents a comprehensive overview of these connections.

- **Budgeted cash flow statement:** The changes in operating assets and liabilities from their actual balances at the end of the year just con-cluded and the budgeted balances at the end of the coming year determine cash flow from profit for the coming year. These changes constitute the basic model of cash flow from profit, which Chapter 7 explains. The other sources and uses of cash depend on managers' strategic decisions regarding capital expenditures that will be made during the coming year, and how much new capital will be raised by increased debt and from owners' additional investment of capital in the business.

In short, budgeting requires good working models of profit, financial condi-tion (assets and liabilities), and cash flow from profit. It's a good incentive for businesses to develop financial models that not only help in the budget-ing process but also help managers make day-to-day decisions.

Planning reasons for budgeting

One main purpose of budgeting is to develop a definite and detailed plan for the coming financial period. To do budgeting, managers have to establish explicit financial objectives for the coming year and identify exactly what has to be done to accomplish these financial objectives. Budgeted financial statements and their supporting schedules provide clear destination points — the financial flight plan for a business.

Doing budgeting directs attention to the specific things that you must do to achieve your profit objectives and to optimize your assets and capital requirements. Basically, planning pushes managers to answer the question "How are we going to get there from here?"

Budgeting also has other planning-related benefits:

- **Budgeting encourages a business to articulate its vision, strategy, and goals.** A business needs a clearly stated strategy guided by an over-arching vision, and should have definite and explicit goals. It is not enough for business managers to have strategy and goals in their heads. Developing budgeted financial statements forces managers to get explicit and definite about the objectives of the business and to formulate realistic plans for achieving the business objectives.

- **Budgeting imposes discipline and deadlines on the planning process.** Many busy managers have trouble finding enough time for lunch, let alone planning for the upcoming financial period. Budgeting pushes managers to set aside time to prepare a detailed plan that serves as a road map for the business. Good planning results in a concrete course of action that details how a company plans to achieve its financial objectives.

Management-control reasons for budgeting

Budgets can be and usually are used as a means of *management control,* which involves comparing budget against actual performance and holding individual managers responsible for keeping the business on its budget timeline. The board of directors of a corporation focus their attention on the master budget for the whole business: the budgeted management income statement, the budgeted balance sheet, and the budgeted cash flow statement for the coming year.

The chief executive officer and the president of the business focus on the master budget. They also look at how each manager in the organization is doing on his or her part of the master budget. As you move down the organization chart of a business, managers have narrower responsibilities — say, for the business's northeastern territory or for one major product line — therefore, the master budget is broken down into parts that follow the business's organizational structure. In other words, the master budget is put together from many pieces, one for each separate organizational unit of the business. So, for example, the manager of one of the company's far-flung warehouses has a separate budget for expenses and inventory levels, which also include other performance measures, such as on-time delivery of products.

By using budget targets as benchmarks against which actual performance is compared, managers can closely monitor progress toward (or departures from) the budget goals and timetable. You use a budget plan like a navigation chart to keep your business on course. Significant deviations from budget raise red flags, in which case you can determine that performance is off course or that the budget needs to be revised because of unexpected developments.

For management control, the annual budgeted management income statement is divided into months or quarters. The budgeted balance sheet and budgeted cash flow statement are also put on a monthly or quarterly basis. The business should not wait too long to compare budgeted sales revenue and expenses against actual performance (or to compare actual cash flows and asset levels against the budget timetable). You need to take prompt action when problems arise, such as a discrepancy between budgeted expenses and actual expenses. Profit is the main attention, but accounts receivable and inventory can get out of control (or become too high relative to actual sales revenue and cost of goods sold expense), causing cash flow problems. (Chapter 7 explains how increases in accounts receivable and inventory hurt cash flow from profit.) A business cannot afford to ignore its balance sheet and cash flow numbers until the end of the year.

Using budgets for detailed management control in a smaller business may not be very practical and, frankly, not worth the effort and cost. Even a relatively large business may decide not to compare actual performance against budget department by department or division by division. However, actual overall results should be compared against budget in the general year-end review of operations, and preferably quarter by quarter.

Obviously, managers should keep close tabs on what's going on throughout the business.

A business may not do any formal budgeting, and thus it would not prepare budgeted financial statements. But its managers should receive regular income statements, balance sheets, and cash flow statements — and these key internal financial statements should contain detailed management control information. Some years ago in one of my classes, I asked students for a short definition of management control. One student answered that management control means "watching everything." I can't think of a better definition. Internal financial statements and other accounting reports are essential to managers for keeping a close watch on the financial performance and position of their business.

Management control is very important, of course. But first of all, managers make *decisions,* and the first job of accounting is to give managers the information they need to make good decisions. Business managers make many decisions affecting profit — setting sales prices, buying products, determining wages and salaries, hiring independent contractors, and purchasing fixed assets are just a few that come to mind. Managers should carefully analyze how their actions would impact profit before reaching a final decision. Most of all, they need a good management income statement that is designed to serve as a useful profit model that helps them make decisions (refer to Table 9-1 for an example).

Other benefits of budgeting

Budgeting has advantages and ramifications that go beyond the financial dimension and have more to do with business management in general. These points are briefly discussed as follows:

- ✔ **Budgeting forces managers to do better forecasting.** Managers should constantly scan the business environment to identify "sea changes" that can impact the business. General impressions are not good enough for budgeting. Managers are forced to put their thoughts into more-definite forecasts.

- ✔ **Budgeting motivates managers and employees by providing useful yardsticks for evaluating performance and for setting managers' compensation when goals are achieved.** The budgeting process can have a good motivational impact on employees and managers by involving managers in the budgeting process (especially in setting goals and objectives) and by providing incentives to managers to strive for and achieve the business's goals and objectives. Budgets can be used to reward good results. Budgets provide useful information for superiors to evaluate the performance of managers. Budgets supply baseline financial information for incentive compensation plans. The profit plan (budget) for the year can be used to award year-end bonuses according to whether designated goals are achieved.

> ✔ **Budgeting is essential in writing a business plan.** New and emerging businesses must present a convincing *business plan* when raising capital. Because these businesses may have little or no history, the managers and owners of a small business must demonstrate convincingly that the company has a clear strategy and a realistic plan to make money. A coherent, realistic budget forecast is an essential component of a business plan. Venture capital sources definitely want to see the budgeted financial statements of the business.

In larger businesses, budgets are typically used to hold managers accountable for their areas of responsibility in the organization; actual results are compared against budgeted goals and timetables, and variances are highlighted. Managers do not mind taking credit for *favorable* variances, or when actual comes in better than budget. Beating the budget for the period, after all, calls attention to outstanding performance. But *unfavorable* variances are a different matter. If the manager's budgeted goals and targets are fair and reasonable, the manager should carefully analyze what went wrong and what needs to be improved. But if the manager perceives the budgeted goals and targets to be arbitrarily imposed by superiors and not realistic, serious motivational problems can arise. In reviewing the performance of their subordinates, managers should handle unfavorable variances very carefully. Stern action may be called for, but managers should recognize that the budget benchmarks may not be entirely fair and should make allowances for unexpected developments that occur after the budget goals and targets are established.

Budgeting in Action

Suppose you're the general manager of one of a company's several divisions. You have broad authority to run this division, as well as the responsibility for meeting the financial expectations for your division. To be more specific, your profit responsibility is to produce a satisfactory annual earnings before interest and tax (EBIT). (Interest and income tax expenses are handled at a higher level in the organization.)

The CEO has made clear to you that she expects your division to increase EBIT during the coming year by 10 percent. In fact, she has asked you to prepare a budgeted management income statement showing your plan for increasing your division's EBIT by 10 percent. She also has asked you to prepare a budgeted cash flow from profit based on your profit plan for the coming year.

Table 10-1 presents the management income statement of your division for the year just ended. The format of this accounting report follows the profit model introduced in Chapter 9 (specifically Table 9-1), which explains profit behavior and how to increase profit. Note that fixed expenses are separated from the two variable expenses. To simplify the discussion, I have significantly condensed the management income statement presented in Table 10-1. (Your monthly reports would include much more detailed information about sales and expenses.)

Table 10-1	Management Income Statement for Year Just Ended (Last Year)
Item	*Amount*
Sales revenue	$26,000,000
Cost of goods sold expense	(14,300,000)
Gross margin	$11,700,000
Revenue-driven expenses	(2,080,000)
Volume-driven expenses	(1,300,000)
Contribution profit margin	$8,320,000
Fixed expenses	(5,720,000)
Earnings before interest and tax (EBIT)	$2,600,000

Developing your profit strategy and budgeted management income statement for the coming year

Suppose that you and your managers, with the assistance of your accounting staff, have analyzed your fixed expenses line by line for the coming year. Some fixed expenses will actually be reduced or eliminated next year. But the large majority of these costs will continue next year, and most are subject to inflation. Based on your careful studies and estimates, you forecast your total fixed expenses for next year to be $6,005,500 (including $835,000 depreciation expense, compared with the $780,000 depreciation expense for last year).

Thus, you will need to earn $8,865,500 total contribution margin next year:

$2,860,000	EBIT goal ($2,600,000 last year plus $260,000 budgeted increase)
+ 6,005,500	Budgeted fixed expenses for next year
$8,865,500	Total contribution profit margin goal for next year

This is your main profit budget goal for next year, assuming that fixed expenses are kept in line. Fortunately, your volume-driven variable expenses will not increase next year. These are mainly transportation costs, and the shipping industry is in a very competitive, hold-the-price-down mode of operations that should last through the coming year. The cost per unit shipped will not increase, but if you sell and ship more units next year, the expense will increase in proportion.

You have decided to hold the revenue-driven expenses at 8 percent of sales revenue during the coming year, the same as for the year just ended. These are sales commissions, and you have already announced to your sales staff that their sales commission percentage will remain the same during the coming year. On the other hand, your purchasing manager has told you to plan on a 4 percent average product cost increase next year.

To make the impact of this seemingly insignificant cost increase more clear, suppose that you sell the same volume next year and that the sales mix of products remains the same. In this hypothetical scenario, your total cost of goods sold expense next year would be

```
$14,300,000 for the year just ended × 1.04 = $14,872,000, an
              increase of $572,000
```

If you do nothing next year to offset this negative impact, your profit will suffer by this amount, which translates to a 22 percent plunge. Clearly, you must plan for ways to compensate for the product cost increase next year — and to boost profit by 10 percent, as directed by your CEO.

One way to attempt to achieve your total contribution margin objective next year is to load all the needed increase on sales volume and keep sales prices the same. (I'm not suggesting that this strategy is a good one, but it's a good point of departure.) To determine how much sales volume would have to increase, you ask your accounting staff to provide a rough draft of your budgeted management income statement assuming no increase in sales prices. (The accountants take the margins for all products at the higher costs and multiply by the higher sales volumes needed to make the total contribution margin come out right on target.) Table 10-2 shows the "what-if" scenario for this strategy.

Table 10-2   Profit Plan for Next Year Assuming No Increase in Sales Prices; All Profit Improvement Comes from Higher Sales Volumes

Item	Amount
Sales revenue	$29,750,000
Cost of goods sold expense	(17,017,000)
Gross margin	$12,733,000
Revenue-driven expenses	(2,380,000)
Volume-driven expenses	(1,487,500)
Contribution profit margin	$8,865,500
Fixed expenses	(6,005,500)
Earnings before interest and tax (EBIT)	$2,860,000

As Table 10-2 shows, EBIT would increase by 10 percent, from $2,600,000 last year to $2,860,000, or $260,000 higher, next year. However, your sales volume would have to increase by more than 14 percent in this scenario:

```
$29,750,000 sales revenue next year - $26,000,000 sales
       revenue last year = $3,750,000 sales revenue
       increase
```

and

```
$3,750,000 sales revenue increase ÷ $26,000,000 sales
       revenue last year = 14.4% increase
```

After discussing this scenario with your sales manager, you conclude that sales volume cannot be increased by 14.4 percent. You'll have to raise sales prices to provide part of the needed increase in total contribution margin and to offset the increase in product cost. After much discussion, you and your sales manager decide to increase sales prices by 3 percent across the board. Again, you ask your accounting staff to run the numbers (that's why they're there) to determine how much sales volume would have to increase if sales prices were 3 percent higher for the coming year. Table 10-3 presents this budgeted profit plan based on both higher sales prices and higher sales volumes.

Table 10-3   Budgeted Management Income Statement for Next Year, Based on 3% Increase in Sales Prices and Higher Sales Volumes

Item	Amount
Sales revenue	$28,045,040
Cost of goods sold expense	(15,574,527)
Gross margin	$12,470,513
Revenue-driven expenses	(2,243,603)
Volume-driven expenses	(1,361,410)
Contribution profit margin	$8,865,500
Fixed expenses	(6,005,500)
Earnings before interest and tax (EBIT)	$2,860,000

This strategy requires that sales volume increase by only 4.7 percent. (Your accounting staff should include sales volume information with the budgeted management income statement.)

So if you do not raise sales prices, your division has to increase sales volume by 14.4 percent (as shown in Table 10-2), but if you increase sales prices by just 3 percent, the sales volume increase you need to achieve your profit goal next year is only 4.7 percent. Does this make sense?

Think of a typical product sold by your division. This "average" product serves as the proxy, or stand-in, for all products. If last year's sales price for this product was $100.00, your sales volume last year was 260,000 units ($26,000,000.00 sales revenue ÷ $100.00 sales price = 260,000 units). After you deduct the product cost and the two variable expenses, your profit margin was $32.00 per unit.

For next year, the higher $103.00 sales price minus the product cost and variable expenses will yield a slightly higher $32.56 profit margin per unit. Dividing your $8,865,500.00 total contribution margin goal by this $32.56 profit margin per unit gives the required sales volume of 272,282 units, which is 12,282 units, or 4.7 percent, higher than last year. (You can check that 272,282 units × the $103.00 sales price equals the $28,045,040.00 sales revenue shown in Table 10-3.)

You and your sales manager finally decide to adopt the 3 percent sales price increase strategy as the official budget plan. Accordingly, you forward your budgeted management income statement to the CEO. This summary-level budgeted management income statement is supplemented with appropriate schedules to provide additional detail about sales by types of customers and products and other relevant information. Also, your annual profit plan is broken down into quarters (perhaps months) to provide benchmarks for comparing actual performance during the year against your budgeted targets and timetable.

Developing your budgeted cash flow from profit for the coming year

The budgeted profit plan (refer to Table 10-3) is the main focus of attention, but the CEO also requests that all divisions present a *budgeted cash flow from profit* for the coming year. **Remember:** The profit you're responsible for as general manager of the division is earnings before interest and tax (EBIT) — not net income after interest and income tax.

Chapter 7 explains that increases in accounts receivable, inventory, and prepaid expenses *hurt* cash flow and that increases in accounts payable and accrued liabilities *help* cash flow from profit. You should compare your budgeted management income statement for the coming year to your actual statement for last year. This side-by-side comparison (not shown here) would reveal that sales revenue and all expenses are higher next year.

Therefore, these short-term operating assets will increase at the higher sales revenue and expense levels next year — unless you can implement asset-reduction improvements to prevent the increases. And your two operating liabilities should increase as well.

For example, sales revenue increases from $26,000,000 last year to the budgeted $28,045,040 for next year — an increase of $2,045,040. Your accounts receivable balance was five weeks of annual sales last year. Do you plan to tighten up the credit terms offered to customers next year — a year in which you will raise sales prices and also plan to increase sales volume? I doubt it. More likely, you will keep your accounts receivable balance at five weeks of annual sales. Assume that you decide to offer your customers the same credit terms next year. Thus the increase in sales revenue will cause accounts receivable to increase by $196,638 ($5/52 \times $2,045,040 sales revenue increase).

Last year, inventory was 13 weeks of annual cost of goods sold expense. You may be in the process of implementing inventory reduction techniques, such as *just-in-time*. If you really expect to reduce the average time inventory will be held in stock before being sold, you should inform your accounting staff so that they can include this key change in the balance sheet and cash flow models. Otherwise, they will assume that the past ratios for these vital connections will continue next year.

Table 10-4 illustrates a budgeted cash flow from profit (EBIT for your division) based on the information given for this example and using the ratios explained in Chapter 6 for short-term operating assets and liabilities. For example, accounts receivable increases by $196,638, as just explained.

Table 10-4	Budgeted Cash Flow from Profit Based on Budgeted Management Income Statement for Next Year
Item	**Amount**
Earnings before interest and tax (EBIT)	$2,860,000
Depreciation expense (given earlier)	835,000
EBIT plus depreciation expense	$3,695,000
Changes in short-term operating assets and liabilities:	
Accounts receivable	(196,638)
Inventory	(318,632)
Prepaid expenses	(29,453)
Accounts payable	49,088
Accrued liabilities	78,540
Cash flow from EBIT	$3,277,905

You submit this statement of budgeted cash flow from profit (EBIT) to top management. Top management expects you to control the increases in your short-term operating assets and liabilities so that the actual cash flow generated by your division next year comes in on target. The cash flow from profit of your division (minus the small amount needed to increase the working cash balance held by your division for operating purposes) is sent to the central treasury of the business.

Note: I am not going to discuss other aspects of the budgeting process here. For example, you would prepare a *capital expenditures request budget* for top management review, which lists the fixed assets purchases that your division needs to make during the coming year to replace and modernize old assets and to expand your division's capacity. Your division holds only a working cash balance for day-to-day operations; this is typical practice. Your division does not accumulate cash reserves for major capital expenditures. The money for these major cash outlays comes from the central treasury of the business. The chief financial officer of the business goes over your capital expenditure request budget with a fine-toothed comb.

At the company-wide level, the financial officers merge the profit and cash flow budgets of all divisions, as well as their capital expenditure request budgets. The budgets submitted by one or more of the divisions may be returned for revision before final approval is given. One main concern is whether the collective total of cash flow from all the units provides enough money for the capital expenditures that have to be made during the coming year for new fixed assets — and to meet the other demands for cash, such as for cash distributions from profit. The business may have to raise more

Business budgeting is not like government budgeting

Business and government budgeting are more different than alike. Government budgeting is preoccupied with allocating scarce resources among many competing demands. From federal agencies down to local school districts, government entities have only so much revenue available. They have to make very difficult choices regarding how to spend their limited tax revenue.

Formal budgeting is legally required for almost all government entities. First, a budget request is submitted. After money is appropriated, the budget document becomes legally binding on the government agency. Government budgets are legal straitjackets; the government entity has to stay within the amounts appropriated for each expenditure category. Any changes from the established budgets need formal approvaland are difficult to get through the system.

A business is not legally required to use budgeting. A business can use its budget as it pleases and can even abandon its budget in midstream. Unlike in government, the sales revenue of a business is not constrained; a business can do many things to increase sales revenue. In short, a business has much more flexibility in its budgeting. Both business and government should apply the general principle of cost/benefits analysis to make sure that they are getting the most bang for every buck spent. But a business can pass its costs to its customers in the sales prices it charges. In contrast, government has to raise taxes to spend more (except for federal deficit spending, of course, but efforts are being made to balance the federal budget).

capital from debt or equity sources during the coming year to close the gap between cash flow from profit and its needs for cash. This is a central topic in the field of business finance, but it extends beyond the coverage of this book.

Staying Flexible with Budgets

One thing never to lose sight of is that budgeting is a *means to an end.* It's a tool for doing something better than you could without the tool. Preparing budgeted financial statements is not the ultimate objective; a budget is not an end in itself. The budgeting process should provide definite benefits, and businesses should use their budgeted financial statements to measure progress toward their financial objectives — and not just file them away someplace.

Budgets are not the only tool for management control. Control, in my mind, means accomplishing your financial objectives. Many businesses do not use formal budgeting and do not prepare budgeted financial statements. But they do lay down goals and objectives for each period and compare actual performance against these targets. Doing at least this much is essential for all businesses.

Keep in mind that budgets are not the only means for controlling expenses. Actually, I shy away from the term *controlling* because I've found that, in the minds of most people, *controlling* expenses means minimizing them. The *cost/benefits* idea captures the better view of expenses. Spending more on advertising, for example, may have a good payoff in the additional sales volume it produces. In other words, it's easy to cut advertising to zero if you really want to minimize this expense — but the impact on sales volume may be disastrous.

Business managers should eliminate any *excessive* amount of an expense — the amount that really doesn't yield a benefit or add value to the business. For example, it's possible for a business to spend too much on quality inspection by doing unnecessary or duplicate steps, or by spending too much time testing products that have a long history of good quality. But this doesn't mean that the business should eliminate the expense entirely. Expense control means trimming the cost down to the right size. In this sense, expense control is one of the hardest jobs that business managers do, second only to managing people, in my opinion.

Chapter 11

Deciding on the Right Business Ownership Structure

. . . .

. . . .

*T*he obvious reason for investing in a business (as a partner or as a stockholder) rather than a safer kind of investment is the potential for greater rewards. As part owner of a business, you're entitled to part of the business's profit — and you're also subject to the risk that the business will go down the tubes, taking your money down with it.

But ignore the risks for a moment and look at just the rosy side of the picture: Suppose the doohickeys that this business sells become the hottest doohickeys of the year. Business is great, and you start looking at five-bedroom riverfront houses. Don't jump into that down payment just yet, though — you may not get as big a piece of the profit pie as you're expecting. First of all, profit is way down the list of what the business needs to use its sales revenue to pay for. You may not see any of that profit at all. And even if you do, the way the profit is divided among owners depends on the business's ownership structure, which can be pretty simple or extremely complex.

This chapter shows you how ownership structure affects your share of the profit — especially how changes beyond your control can make your share smaller. It also explains how the ownership structure has a dramatic impact on the income taxes paid by the business and its owners.

Divvying Up Sales Revenue

A business collects money from its customers and then redistributes that sales revenue to the many interested parties clamoring for their fair share. You may think that the second part of this process would be the easy part, but business managers sometimes have a tough time deciding what constitutes a "fair share" for each claimant. For example, in deciding how much to pay employees in regular wages and fringe benefits, business managers have to ask what value each employee adds to the business, whether to raise sales prices in order to pay higher wages, and so on.

Here's part of a typical income statement, showing where all the sales revenue goes. This particular example includes income tax expense, which not all businesses pay (as explained later in this chapter). The business in this example took in $26 million in sales revenue. (See Chapter 5 for more information about income statements.)

Income Statement Item	Amount	Claimant on Sales Revenue
Cost of goods sold expense	($14,300,000)	Suppliers from whom the business bought its products or bought the raw materials for manufacturing its products
Wages and benefits	(6,250,000)	Employees
Personal services	(875,000)	Independent contractors, such as lawyers or advertising firms
Property taxes and licenses	(367,000)	Local government
Utilities	(415,000)	Utility companies, such as gas or telephone companies
Freight	(213,000)	Transportation companies, such as trucking companies or Federal Express
Supplies and parts	(200,000)	Various vendors, such as office-supply stores
Depreciation expense	(780,000)	Money for replacing fixed assets that are being depreciated and slowly worn out
Operating earnings	$2,600,000	(Profit before the three remaining claims)

Income Statement Item	Amount	Claimant on Sales Revenue
Interest expense	(400,000)	Creditors (from whom the business borrowed money)
Income tax expense	(880,000)	Federal and state governments
Net income	$1,320,000	Owners' equity account (some of net income may be distributed to owners, which decreases the account)

Net income is the bottom-line profit that the business earned this period (or, to be more precise, the period just concluded, which often is called "this period" to mean the most recent period). This figure is the starting point for determining how much cash — if any — to distribute to the owners. Businesses are not legally required to distribute any of their profit for the period, but if they do distribute some or all of their profit, the amounts distributed to each owner depend on the business's ownership structure, as described in the following section, "What You Get for Your Money."

How can you tell whether a business is doing well for its owners? What's a good net income figure? You calculate the business's *return on equity* (ROE), which is simply net income divided by total owners' equity (you can find owners' equity listed on the business's balance sheet), and then compare the ROE with investment alternatives that have the same kinds of risks and advantages. Business managers keep a close watch on their ROE in order to judge profit performance relative to the amount of owners' equity capital being used to make that profit. Usually, managers have an ownership interest in the business — although in large public corporations, managers usually own only a small percentage of total owners' equity. For a small business, the two or three chief managers may be the only owners. But many small businesses have outside, nonmanager investors who put money in the business and share in the profit that the business earns. Chapter 14 explains more about ROE and other ways outside investors interpret the information in a business's external financial report.

What You Get for Your Money

Every business — regardless of how big it is and whether it's publicly or privately owned — has owners; no business can get all the financing it needs just by borrowing. An *owner* is someone who

- Has invested money (capital) in the business
- Expects the business to earn profit on the invested capital and expects to share in that profit

- Directly manages the business or hires others to manage the business
- Receives at least part of the proceeds if the business is sold or if the business sells off its assets

The money that owners invest in the business is known as *owners' equity capital,* which is the pool of money that the business draws on to operate. This money "belongs" to the owners, although owners don't control the account and can't withdraw funds from it. The owners' equity account has two parts:

- **Invested capital:** The money that owners have invested in the business. Owners may invest additional capital from time to time.

- **Retained earnings:** The part of a business's annual profit that is left in owners' equity after *cash distributions* to its owners. In other words, the balance in retained earnings is net of cash distributions to owners. All net income is recorded in the retained earnings account first, and then distributions are taken from the retained earnings account. Whether the profit goes to cash distributions or stays in retained earnings, though, owners still directly or indirectly benefit from the profit.

The title *retained earnings* for the profit that a business earns and does not distribute to its owners is appropriate for any type of business entity. Business corporations — the most common type of business entity — use this title. The other types of business entities discussed in this chapter can use this title, but in practice they often collapse both sources of owners' equity into just one account for each owner. Corporations are legally required to distinguish between the two sources of owners' equity: invested capital versus retained earnings. The other types of business entities are not.

A business may have just one owner or two or more owners. A one-owner business may choose to operate as a *sole proprietorship;* a multiowner business must choose to be a *corporation,* a *partnership,* or a *limited liability company.* The most common type of business is a corporation.

No ownership structure is inherently better than another; which one is right for a particular business is something that the business's managers and owners need to decide (or should consult a tax advisor about, as discussed later in this chapter). The following discussion focuses on how ownership structure affects profit distribution to owners. Later, this chapter explains how the ownership structure determines the income tax paid by the business and its owners — which is always an important consideration.

Debt's effect on profit and liability

A loan agreement (contract) between a business and its lender (creditor) may prohibit the business from distributing profit to owners during the period of the loan. Or it may at least require that the business maintain a minimum cash balance — which could mean that money the business would have distributed to owners has to go into its cash account instead.

In some situations, the business's principal officers must sign the loan agreement as individuals, meaning that the creditor can reach into the individuals' assets if the business can't pay off the debt. Even though the corporate and limited liability company forms of business organization protect the business's managers by limiting creditors' rights to reach

through to these individuals' personal assets, they give up this protection when they sign loan agreements as individuals.

If I sign a $10,000,000 note payable to the bank as "John A. Tracy, President of Bestselling Books, Inc.," then only the business (Bestselling Books, Inc.) is liable for the debt. But if I also add my personal signature, "John A. Tracy," below my signature as chief officer of the business, the bank can come after my personal assets in the event that the business can't pay the note payable. A good friend of mind once did this; only later did he learn, to his chagrin, of his legal exposure by signing as an individual. In fact, the bank made his wife sign the note as well, even though she was not an officer or manager of the business.

Corporations

The law views a *corporation* as a "person." That means that a corporation is considered to be its own entity, separate from its owners. So if a corporation doesn't pay its debts, its creditors can seize only the corporation's assets, not the assets of the corporation's owners. (This concept is known as *limited liability*.) The distinguishing features of a corporation are the one or more types of stock shares that it issues and the type of taxation to which it's subject.

Stock shares

In return for their investment in the business, a corporation's owners receive *stock shares*. A share of stock is one unit of ownership, and how much a share is worth with respect to the value of the whole business depends on the total number of shares that the business issues. If a business has issued 400,000 shares and you own 40,000, you own $1/10$ of the business. But suppose that the business issues an additional 40,000 shares; you now have 40,000 of 440,000, giving you a $1/11$ interest in the business. The more shares a business issues, the smaller the percentage of total owners' equity each share is entitled to. Issuing additional shares may or may not dilute, or decrease the value of, each share of stock.

If new shares are issued at a price equal to the going value of the stock shares, the value of the existing shares should not be adversely affected. But if new shares are issued at a discount from the going value, the value of each stock share after the additional shares are issued may decline. I bring this up because publicly owned corporations usually give their managers *stock options* as part of the total management compensation package; these allow the managers to buy stock shares below the current market price of the shares. Other employees may also be given stock purchase plans that enable them to buy shares below the going market price.

Stock shares come in various *classes,* which define the rights of the stockholders. For example, a business may offer Class A and Class B stock shares, where Class A stockholders are given the vote in elections for the board of directors and Class B stockholders do not get to vote. A business may offer just one class of stock or many classes — state laws are liberal regarding the different classes of stock shares that can be issued.

The two general types of classes are *common* and *preferred.* The common stockholders are at the top of the risk chain: A business that ends up in deep financial trouble is obligated to pay off its liabilities and its preferred stockholders first, and by the time the common stockholders get their turn, the business may have no money left to pay them. The main difference between preferred stock and common stock concerns *cash dividends* — what the business pays its owners from its profit. Here are the key points:

✔ A business pays dividends to preferred stockholders before common stockholders.

✔ Preferred stock shares usually have a fixed (limited) dividend and typically don't allow any profit beyond the stated amount of dividends. Corporations can issue *participating* preferred stock, which means that the shares can earn more than the stated amount of annual dividend. For example, net income remaining after paying the required amount of preferred dividends could continue to be used to calculate the value of common stock on a share-for-share basis. Or some other scheme can be used — such as limiting the preferred stock to a maximum of, say, a 12 percent annual dividend (based on the so-called par value of the preferred stock shares), beyond which stockholders would not participate any further.

✔ Preferred stockholders don't have voting rights unless they don't receive dividends for one period or more. In other words, preferred stock shareholders usually do not have voting rights for electing the corporation's board of directors or for participating in other critical issues facing the corporation. But to give the preferred stockholders some protection, the terms and provisions of the contract between the preferred stockholders and the corporation give the stockholders the right to vote in the event that their dividends are not paid (or are in default for more than one or two periods). Needless to say, these matters can become complex, and they vary from corporation to corporation — no wonder there are so many corporate lawyers!

Here are some things to know about stock shares in general:

- Each stock share is equal to every other stock share in its class. This way, ownership rights are standardized, and the only difference that matters is how many stock shares an owner holds.

- The only way a business has to return stockholders' invested capital is if the majority of stockholders vote to liquidate the business in part or in total. Other than that, the business's managers don't have to worry about losing the capital. Of course, stockholders are free to sell their shares at any time, as noted next.

- Whoever owns stock — individual stockholders or the business — can sell his or her shares at any time, without the approval of the other stockholders. However, stockholders of a privately owned business may have agreed to certain restrictions on this right when they invested in the business.

- Stockholders can either put themselves in key management positions or delegate the task of selecting top managers and officers to a *board of directors,* a small group elected by the stockholders to set the business's policies and represent stockholders' interests. Now don't get the impression that if you buy 100 shares of IBM, you can get yourself elected to its board of directors. On the other hand, if Warren Buffett bought 10,000,000 shares of IBM, he could very well get himself on the board. The *relative size* of your ownership interest is the key factor. If you put up more than half the money in a business, you can put yourself on the board and elect yourself president of the business. The stockholders who own 50 percent plus one share constitute the controlling group that decides who goes on the board of directors.

Note: The all-stocks-are-created-equal aspect of corporations is a nice and simple way to divide ownership, but its inflexibility can be a hindrance, too. Suppose the stockholders want to give one person extraordinary power or a share of profit out of proportion to his or her stock ownership. The business can make special compensation arrangements for key executives and ask a lawyer for advice on the best way to implement the stockholders' intentions. Nevertheless, state corporation laws require that certain voting matters be settled by a majority vote of stockholders. If enough stockholders oppose a certain arrangement, the other stockholders may have to buy them out to gain a controlling interest in the business. (One alternative for giving one owner more power than his or her ownership in the business is the limited liability company, which I talk about later in the chapter.)

If you want to sell your stock shares, how much can you get for them? You can check any daily financial newspaper — such as *The Wall Street Journal* — for the market trading prices of thousands of publicly owned corporations. But stock shares in privately owned businesses aren't publicly traded, so how can you determine the value of your stock shares in such a business? The starting point is usually to determine *book value per share,* which is based on values reported on the business's latest balance sheet:

```
Total stockholders' equity ÷ total number of shares = book
            value per share
```

However, book values are historical — based on the past transactions of the business — whereas market pricing looks to how the business is likely to do in the future and what the shares will be worth. In other words, market value depends on past and forecast profit (earnings) performance, and not directly on the balance sheet book value of the stock shares. One way of estimating the value of your stock shares in a private business corporation is the *earnings multiple* method, in which you calculate the theoretical value of a stock share by using a certain multiple of the business's earnings (net income) per share.

For example, suppose a privately owned business corporation earned $3.20 net income per share last year. You might be able to sell your shares at ten times this earnings per share, or $32.00. If someone paid $32.00 for the stock shares and the business earned $3.20 again per share next year, the new investor would earn 10 percent on his or her investment — calculated by dividing the $3.20 earnings per share by the $32.00 invested in the stock share. (Not all of the $3.20 would be paid out as a cash dividend, so part of the 10 percent earnings on the investment consists of the increase in retained earnings of the business.)

Keep in mind that the $32.00 "price" is only an estimate and just a theoretical value — although these days it would be a reasonable, and probably conservative, value for many businesses. However, you don't know the market price until you sell the stock. As a potential investor in the business, I might be willing to offer you $35.00 or $40.00 per share — or I might offer less than the book value per share.

Stockholders and managers

Stockholders (including managers who own stock shares in the business) are concerned, first and foremost, with the profit performance of their business. The dividends they receive and the value of their stock shares depend on profit. Managers, too, are concerned with profit — their jobs depend on living up to the business's profit goals. But even though stockholders and managers strive toward the common goal of making the business profitable, they have an inherent conflict of interest that revolves around money and power:

Where profit goes in a corporation

Suppose that your business earned $1.32 million net income and has issued a total of 400,000 stock shares of *capital stock* (another name for *invested capital*). Divide net income by the number of shares, and you come up with a value of $3.30 per share.

The cash flow statement reports that the business paid $400,000 cash dividends during the year, or $1.00 per share. (Cash dividends are usually paid quarterly, so the business most likely paid $0.25 dividends per share each of the four quarters.) The rest of the net income — $920,000 — remains in the retained earnings account. (***Remember:*** Net income is first entered as an increase in the retained earnings account, and distributions are taken out of this account.) The retained earnings account thus increased by $2.30 per share (the difference between the net income, or earnings per share, and the amount actually distributed).

Although stockholders don't have the cash to show for it, their investment is better off by $2.30 per share — which shows up in the balance sheet as an increase in the retained earnings account in owners' equity. They can just hope that the business will use the cash flow provided from retained earnings to make more profit in the future, which should lead to higher cash dividends.

If the business is a publicly owned business whose stock shares are actively traded, its stockholders will look to the change in the *market price* of the stock shares during the year.

The financial statements of the business report that the stockholders are better off by the $2.30 per share increase in owners' equity plus the $1.00 cash dividends paid during the year. Yet it's entirely possible that the market price of the stock shares actually *decreased* during the year, or perhaps increased much more than $2.30. Market prices are governed by market factors. Financial statements are one — but only one — of the information sources that stock investors use in making their buy-and-sell decisions. Chapter 14 explains how stock investors use the return on investment (ROI) measure to account for their investments in marketable securities.

✔ The more money that managers make in wages and benefits, the less stockholders receive as dividends. Stockholders obviously want the best managers for the job, but they don't want to pay any more than they have to. In many corporations, top-level managers, for all practical purposes, set their own salaries and compensation packages.

The best solution is often to have outside directors (with no management position in the business) set the compensation level for top-level managers instead.

✔ Who should control the business: the managers, who were hired for their competence and are intimately familiar with the business, or the stockholders, who probably have no experience relevant to running this particular business but who put up the money that the business is running on? In ideal situations, the two sides respect each other's importance to the business and use this tension constructively. Of course, the real world is far from ideal, and you have situations in which tyrannical stockholders are corrupting a business or managers are controlling the board of directors rather than the other way around. But this book isn't the proper place to get into all that.

As an investor, be aware of these issues and how they affect your profit. *Remember:* If you don't like the way your business is being run, you have the right to sell your shares and invest your money elsewhere.

In particular, watch out for actions that cause a *dilution effect* on your stock shares — that is, cause each stock share to drop in value. Now, the dilution effect may be the result of a good business decision, so even though your share of the business has decreased, the overall health of the business (and, therefore, your investment) may benefit. But you need to watch these decisions closely. The following situations cause a dilution effect:

- A business issues additional stock shares but doesn't really need the additional capital — the business is in no better profit-making position than it was before issuing the new stock shares. For example, a business may issue new stock shares in order to let a newly hired chief executive officer buy them.

- A business issues new stock shares at a discount below its stock shares' current value. For example, the business may issue a new batch of stock shares at a lower price for its employees to take advantage of in an employee stock-purchase plan.

Partnerships and limited liability companies (LLCs)

If you're starting a business and don't want it to be a corporation, you may instead choose to form a *partnership* or a *limited liability company* (or a *sole proprietorship,* if the business has just one owner — see "Sole proprietorships," later in this chapter). These ownership structures allow the division of management authority, profit sharing, and capital rights among the owners to be very flexible. Here are the key features of these two ownership structures:

- **Partnerships:** Partnerships avoid the double-taxation feature that corporations are subject to (see "Choosing the Right Legal Structure for Income Tax," later in this chapter, for details). Partnerships also differ from corporations with respect to liability. A partnership's owners fall into two categories:

  - **General partners:** Subject to unlimited liability. If a business can't pay its debts, its creditors can reach into general partners' personal assets. General partners have the authority and responsibility to manage the business. They are roughly equivalent to the president and other high-level managers of a business corporation. The general partners usually divide authority and responsibility among themselves, and often they elect one member of their group as the senior general partner or elect a small executive committee to make major decisions.

- **Limited partners:** Subject to limited liability. Limited partners have ownership rights to the business's profit, but they don't participate in the management of the business. A partnership must have one or more general partners; not all partners can be limited partners.

Many large partnerships copy some of the management features of the corporate form — for example, a senior partner who serves as chair of the general partners' executive committee acts in much the same way as a corporation's board of directors.

If a partner dies or leaves the firm, the partnership is technically dissolved, although the formation of the new partnership may be transparent to outsiders. As far as outsiders can tell, the business continues as before. Generally, a partner can't sell his or her interest to an outsider without the consent of all the other partners. You can't just buy your way into a partnership; the other partners have to approve your joining the partnership. In contrast, you can buy stock shares and thereby become part owner of a corporation; you don't need the approval of the other stockholders.

✔ **Limited liability company (LLC):** The LLC is a relatively new type of business creature. In fact, not all states recognize LLCs yet. An LLC is like a corporation regarding limited liability, and it's like a partnership regarding the flexibility of dividing profit among the owners. The IRS treats an LLC like a partnership for income tax purposes (which means that an LLC is not subject to the potential double taxation on corporations, which is discussed later in this chapter). An LLC's key advantage is flexibility — especially regarding how profit and management authority are determined. For example, an LLC permits the founders of the business to put up, say, only 10 or 20 percent of the money to start a business venture, but to keep all management authority in their hands. The other investors share in profit, but not necessarily in proportion to their invested capital.

LLCs have a lot more flexibility than corporations, but flexibility is not all good. The owners must enter into a very detailed agreement that spells out the division of profit, the division of management authority and responsibility, their rights to withdraw capital, and their responsibilities to contribute new capital as needed. These schemes can get very complicated and difficult to understand, and they may end up requiring a lawyer to untangle them. If the ownership structure of an LLC is too complicated and too far off the beaten path, the business may have difficulty explaining itself to a lender when applying for a loan, and it may have difficulty convincing new shareholders to put capital into the business.

A partnership or LLC owner who participates in running the business — that is, an owner who contributes more than just money — may receive a salary in addition to a share of the profit. The bottom-line profit accounts for all expenses *except* salaries to owners; these salaries are not deducted as expenses from bottom-line profit. The salaries are viewed as distributions from profit. I should warn you that the accounting for compensation and services provided by owners in an LLC and partners in a partnership gets rather technical and is beyond the scope of this book. *Caution:* I would advise you as a partner or as an owner in an LLC to get up to speed on the special accounting practices of the business regarding how salaries and other payments for services to owners and partners are accounted for. Don't take anything for granted; investigate first.

Professional partnerships — physicians, CPAs, lawyers, and so on — may choose to become *professional corporations (PCs),* which are a special type of legal structure that states offer to professionals who otherwise would have to operate under the specter of unlimited partnership liability. States also permit *limited liability partnerships (LLPs)* for qualified professionals (such as doctors, lawyers, CPAs, and dentists), in which all the partners have limited liability. These types of unusual legal entities were created mainly as the result of large damage awards in lawsuits against professional partnerships during the last two or three decades. The professionals pleaded for protection from the unlimited liability of the partnership form of organization, which they traditionally had used over several generations. Until these new types of professional legal entities came along, the code of professional ethics of the various professions required that practitioners operate as a partnership (or as sole practitioners). Today, almost all professional associations are organized as PCs or LLPs. They function very much as a partnership does, but without the unlimited liability feature of the partnership form of business organization.

The partnership or LLC agreement specifies how to divide profit among the owners. Whereas owners of a corporation receive a profit share that's directly proportional to the number of shares they own and, therefore, how much they invested, a partnership or LLC does not have to divide profit according to how much each owner invested. Invested capital is only one of three factors that generally play into profit allocation in partnerships and LLCs:

✔ **Treasure:** Owners may be rewarded according to how much of the "treasure" — invested capital — they contributed; they get back a certain percentage (return) on their investment. So if Joe invested twice as much as Jane did, his cut of the profit is twice as much as Jane's.

✔ **Time:** Owners who invest more time in the business may receive more of the profit. In some businesses, a partner may not contribute much more than capital and his or her name, whereas other partners work long hours. This way of allocating profit works like a salary.

✔ **Talent:** Regardless of capital or time, some partners bring more to the business than others. Maybe they have better business contacts, or they have a knack for making deals happen, or their celebrity status makes their names alone worth a special share of the profit. Whatever it is that they do for the business, they do it brilliantly and contribute much more to the business's success than their capital or time suggests.

The business needs to maintain a separate capital account for each owner. All the profit is deposited into these capital accounts, as spelled out in the partnership or LLC agreement. The agreement also specifies how much money owners can withdraw from their capital accounts — for example, owners may not be allowed to withdraw 100 percent of their anticipated share of profit for the coming year, or they may be allowed to withdraw only a certain amount until they've built up their capital accounts.

Sole proprietorships

A *sole proprietorship* is a one-owner business whose owner has elected *not* to become a corporation, a partnership, or a limited liability company — it's kind of a default option. This type of business is not considered a separate entity; it's an extension of the owner (the business *is* the owner). As the sole owner, you have *unlimited liability,* meaning that if the business can't pay all its liabilities, the creditors to whom the business owes money can come after your personal assets. Many part-time entrepreneurs may not know this or may put it out of their minds, but this is a big risk to take. I have friends who are part-time business consultants, and most operate their consulting businesses as sole proprietorships. If they are sued for giving bad advice, all their personal assets are at risk — though they may be able to buy malpractice insurance to cover these losses.

Obviously, a sole proprietorship has no other owners to prepare financial statements for — although the proprietor should still prepare these statements as a check on how his or her business is doing. (Also, banks require financial statements of proprietors who apply for loans.)

One other piece of advice for sole proprietors: Although you don't have to separate invested capital from retained earnings like corporations do, you should still keep these two separate accounts for owners' equity — not only for the purpose of tracking the business but for any future buyers of the business as well.

Spreading the joy of profit to your customers: business cooperatives

A business that shares its profit with its customers? Nobody can be *that* generous!

Actually, one type of business does just that: A *cooperative* pays its customers *patronage dividends* based on its profit for the year — each customer receives a year-end refund based on his or her purchases from the business over the year. Imagine that.

Oh, did I mention that in a cooperative, the customers are the owners? To shop in the cooperative, a customer must invest a certain amount of money in the business. (You knew there had to be a catch somewhere!)

Business cooperatives deduct patronage dividends in determining their taxable income for the year. If the business returns all profit to customers as patronage dividends, taxable income is zero.

Choosing the Right Legal Structure for Income Tax

In deciding which type of ownership structure is best for securing capital and managing their business, owners should also consider the income tax factor. They should know the key differences between two basic types of business entities from the income tax point of view:

- ✔ **Taxable-entity C corporations:** These corporations pay income tax on their annual taxable income amounts. Their stockholders pay a *second* income tax on cash dividends that the business distributes to them from profit, making C corporations subject to *double taxation*. The owners (stockholders) of a C corporation include in their individual income tax returns only cash distributions from profit paid to them by the business.

  Note: Most LLCs opt to be treated as a partnership for income tax purposes, although under the tax law they can choose to be taxed as a C corporation and pay income tax on their taxable income for the year, with their individual owners paying a second tax on cash distributions of profit from the LLC.

- ✔ **Pass-through entities — sole proprietorships, partnerships, S corporations, and most LLCs:** This type of tax entity does not pay income tax on its annual taxable income; instead, it hands off its taxable income to its owners, who pick up their shares of the taxable income on their individual tax returns. Pass-through entities still have to file tax returns with the IRS, even though they don't pay income tax on their taxable income. In their tax returns, they also inform the IRS how much taxable income is allocated to each owner and send each owner a copy of this information to include with his or her individual income tax return.

The following sections illustrate the differences between the two types of tax entities for structuring a business. In these examples, I assume that the business uses the same accounting methods in preparing its income statement that it uses for determining its taxable income — a realistic assumption. To keep it simple, I use just the federal income tax, which is much larger than any state income tax that might apply.

C corporations

The regular type of corporation is called a C corporation in the tax law (no, not an R corporation for "regular" corporation). That is, unless you qualify as a small, or S, corporation (I explain the rules later in the chapter) and elect to be taxed this way, your business corporation is assumed to be type C, which means that it pays income tax on its taxable income for the year.

Suppose you have a C corporation with the following abbreviated income statement (see Chapter 5 for details on income statements):

Sales revenue	$26,000,000
Expenses, except income tax	(23,800,000)
Earnings before income tax	$2,200,000
Income tax	(748,000)
Net income	$1,452,000

The $748,000 in income tax is determined by the fact that this business's $2.2 million taxable income puts it in the 34 percent income tax bracket (based on corporate taxable income rates effective in 1997, which have been stable for several years):

```
$2,200,000 taxable income × 34% income tax rate = $748,000
                 income tax
```

That's a big chunk of its hard-earned profit. You must also consider the so-called *double taxation* of corporate profit — a most unpleasant topic if you're a stockholder in a regular (C) corporation. Not only does the C corporation have to pay $748,000 income tax on its profit (as I just calculated), but when the business distributes some of its after-tax profit to its stockholders as their just rewards for investing capital in the business, the stockholders include these cash dividends as income in their individual income tax returns and pay a second tax.

For a rather dramatic example, suppose that this business distributed its entire after-tax net income as cash dividends to its stockholders. (Most businesses don't pay 100 percent cash dividends from their net incomes.) Its stockholders must include the cash dividends in their individual income tax returns. How much income tax would the stockholders as a group pay on their dividend income? How much each individual pays depends on his or her total taxable income for the year, but let me make an arbitrary (but reasonable) assumption that the stockholders are, on average, in the 31 percent tax bracket. In this example, the stockholders would pay $450,120 total individual income tax on their dividend income:

```
$1,452,000 dividends × 31% income tax rate = $450,120 total
             individual income tax paid by its stockholders
```

You can calculate the total tax paid by both the corporation and its stockholders as follows:

$748,000	paid by the corporation on its $2,200,000 taxable income
450,120	paid by its stockholders on $1,452,000 in cash dividends
$1,198,120	total income tax paid by both the corporation and its stockholders

Compare this to the corporation's $2,200,000 of taxable income. Out of the $2,200,000 profit that the business earned, $1,198,120 is quite a bit of total income tax to pay — more than half. On the other hand, if the corporation had retained all of its after-tax profit and paid no cash dividends, then at least for now the individual stockholders would not have to pay the second tax. Distributing no cash dividends may not go down well with all the stockholders, however. If you had persuaded your Aunt Hilda to invest some of her money in your business, but you don't pay any cash dividends, she may be very upset. Most corporations — but by no means all corporations — pay part of their after-tax net income as cash dividends to their stockholders.

S corporations

A business that meets the following criteria can file Form 2553 to be treated as an S corporation:

✔ It has issued only one class of stock.

✔ It has 75 or fewer people holding its stock shares.

✔ It has received approval for becoming an S corporation from the majority of its stockholders.

Suppose that an S corporation has allocated its $2.2 million of taxable income among its owners (stockholders) in proportion to how much stock each owner holds. The business's total number of stock shares is 400,000, so a stockholder is allocated $5.50 taxable income for each share:

```
$2,200,000 taxable income ÷ 400,000 shares = $5.50 taxable
          income per share
```

So if you own 10,000 shares, you pick up $55,000 of the business's taxable income and include this amount in your individual income tax return for the year. *Caution:* I haven't yet said anything about how much cash dividends the corporation has paid. With $2,200,000 pretax profit, the business probably has enough cash flow from profit to make a distribution to its stockholders (Chapter 7 explains cash flow from profit.) But the point is that, as a stockholder, you have to pay income tax on your share of the taxable income *whether or not* the business distributes any of its profit to its stockholders.

Assume again that the stockholders pay an average of 31 percent income tax rate. Thus, as a group, they pay $682,000 total income tax:

```
$2,200,000 taxable income × 31% income tax rate = $682,000
          total income tax
```

Compare this total income tax paid by the stockholders of an S corporation with the two-tax total paid by the C corporation and its stockholders, in which all its after-tax net income is distributed to its stockholders. In that scenario, the total income tax bill is $1,198,120 — which is a lot more than what the stockholders of the S corporation with the same taxable income would pay. Shouldn't the business therefore elect to be an S corporation? Not necessarily — don't jump the gun.

Note: I would need to know a lot more about the individual tax situations of every major stockholder — as well as other factors — before I would even consider giving tax advice in this situation. This discussion is limited to a simple comparison of a C corporation example and an S corporation example regarding who pays income tax on the business's taxable income and how the cash dividends paid by the corporation are taxed. I would urge you to consult a tax professional for advice on this important issue.

Partnerships and limited liability companies

Partnerships and limited liability companies (LLCs) are equivalent from the income tax point of view. In brief, these types of legal entities are a hybrid of the corporation form and the partnership form.

✔ A partnership is a pass-through tax entity, just like an S corporation. *Note:* When two or more owners join together and invest money to start a business and do not incorporate and do not file legal papers to form an LLC, the tax law treats the business as a de facto partnership. Most partnerships are based on written agreements among the owners — but even without a formal, written agreement, a partnership exists in the eyes of the income tax law.

✔ After an LLC has been organized as a legal entity, it can elect to be treated as a regular C corporation or, more likely, as a pass-through partnership. All you need to do is check off a box on your tax return to make the choice. (It's hard to believe that anything related to taxes and the IRS is as simple as that!) Most businesses that organize as LLCs do so because they want to be pass-through tax entities.

The partners in a partnership and the shareholders of an LLC pick up their shares of the business's taxable income in the same manner as the stockholders of an S corporation. They include their shares of the entity's taxable income in their individual income tax returns for the year. For example, suppose your share of the annual profit as a partner, or as one of the LLC's shareholders, is $150,000. You include this amount in your personal income tax return. So what's the difference between these two types of business entities and an S corporation?

In a word, flexibility. Whereas an S corporation must allocate profit based on one factor — the number of shares owned by each stockholder — partnerships and LLCs can use a number of factors in allocating profit among its owners. In an S corporation, if you own 10 percent of the stock, you pick up 10 percent of the business's total taxable income. But in a partnership or LLC, you might get 5 percent of the taxable income, or maybe 60 percent, or whatever.

Partners are owners and don't get paid actual salaries; they're treated not as employees, but rather as owners whose compensation consists of sharing in profit. A "salary" may be one of the factors used in determining a partner's share of profit. But the amount paid out as "salary" is really a withdrawal of profit by the partner. A partnership's general partners and an LLC's owners who actively manage the LLC are covered under the social security and Medicare law. That's the good news. The bad news is that they have to pay a *self-employment tax* for their social security and Medicare coverage.

To further complicate matters (what did you expect, simplicity?), partners and active managers of LLCs can deduct one-half of the self-employment tax paid each year in their personal income tax returns. The idea here is that the matching half of the tax paid by employers is not taxed as income to employees, so these self-employed partners and LLC managers are allowed to deduct half their social security and Medicare tax to keep them on a consistent basis with employees.

Once more, I must mention that choosing the best ownership structure for a business is a complicated affair that goes beyond the income tax factor. You need to consider many other factors. After you select a particular ownership structure, changing it later is not easy. Asking the advice of a qualified professional is well worth the money and can prevent costly mistakes.

Sometimes the search for the ideal ownership structure that minimizes income tax and maximizes other benefits is like the search for the Holy Grail. Business owners should not expect to find the perfect answer — they have to make compromises and choose among advantages and disadvantages.

Chapter 12

Cost Conundrums

● ●

In This Chapter

▶ Determining cost: the second most important thing accountants do

▶ Seeing how complex cost can be

▶ Understanding the various types of costs

▶ Computing costs for retailers and for manufacturers

● ●

*H*ow complicated can measuring costs be? You just take the numbers off your purchase invoices and call it a day, right? Actually, determining cost involves a lot more than just keeping track of details; it requires careful analysis and the use of arbitrary methods. In fact, measuring cost is the second most important thing that accountants do, right after measuring profit. If you're running your business based on inaccurate cost figures, you likely have inadequate sales prices, misleading profit figures, and under-stated asset values — not to mention that you're more vulnerable to law-suits.

In my experience, managers too often are inclined to take cost numbers for granted. The phrase *actual cost* gets tossed around too loosely, without a clear definition.

What business managers need to know is that putting a number on a cost is an accounting problem without an obvious answer. There's no one-size-fits-all definition of cost, and there's no one correct method of measuring cost. The conundrum is that, in spite of this ambiguity, you need precise defini-tions of costs. In order to understand the financial statements (particularly the income statement and balance sheet) that your accountants churn out for you to base business decisions on, you need to understand a little bit about the choices an accountant has for measuring cost.

This chapter covers concepts and methods that are used by both retail and manufacturing businesses, along with additional stuff for manufacturers to worry about. I also discuss how having a good handle on cost issues can help you recognize when a business is deliberately manipulating its profit figure. Service businesses — which sell a service such as transportation or entertainment — have a break here. They do not encounter the cost-accounting problems that I discuss in this chapter.

What Makes Cost So Important?

Without good cost information, a business operates in the dark. Cost affects many areas of business management, including the following ones:

✔ **Setting sales prices:** The common method for setting sales prices (known as *cost-plus* or *markup on cost*) is to start with cost and then add a certain percentage. If you don't know exactly how much a product costs, you can't be as shrewd and competitive in your pricing as you need to be.

✔ **Formulating a legal defense against charges of predatory pricing practices:** Many states have laws prohibiting businesses from selling below cost except in certain circumstances. And a business can be sued under federal law for charging artificially low prices intended to drive the competition out of business. Be prepared to prove that your pricing is based on lower costs and not some illegitimate purpose.

✔ **Measuring gross margin:** Outsiders (and many insiders) judge your business by the bottom-line profit figure that you report. As described in Chapters 5 and 14, this profit figure depends on the gross margin figure you get when you subtract your cost of goods sold expense from your sales revenue. The cost of goods sold expense depends on correct product costs — which are tricky costs for manufacturers in particular to compute (see "Calculating product cost," later in this chapter).

✔ **Valuing assets:** The balance sheet reports the cost values of many assets, and these values are, of course, included in the overall financial position of your business. See Chapter 6 for more about assets and how they are reported in the balance sheet (also called the *statement of financial condition*).

✔ **Making the right choices:** You often must choose one alternative over others in making business decisions. The best alternative depends heavily on cost factors, and you have to be careful to distinguish *relevant* costs from *irrelevant* costs, as described in the section "Relevant versus irrelevant (sunk) costs," later in this chapter.

An irrelevant cost, for example, is the book value of a fixed asset. Say book value is $35,000 for a machine used in the manufacturing operations of the business. This is the amount of original cost that has not yet been charged to depreciation, and it may seem quite relevant. However, in deciding between keeping the old machine or replacing it with a newer, more efficient machine, the *disposable value* of the old machine is the relevant cost. Suppose the old machine has a $5,000 salvage value at this time; this is the relevant cost of keeping it in the future — not the $35,000 that hasn't been depreciated yet. Making decisions involves looking at the future cash flow of each alternative — not historical-based cost values.

JARGON ALERT

Theorizing about economic cost concepts

Concepts of cost generally fall into two camps: *theoretical economic cost concepts* and *practical accounting cost methods.* No, you don't have to become an economic theorist to understand cost, but you should at least feel comfortable with the following economic concepts. (Obviously, you should understand practical accounting cost methods — the *practical* part of the name gives that away — which are discussed in the "Comprehending All Those Confounding Costs" section of this chapter.)

✔ **Opportunity cost:** The amount of income given up when you follow a better course of action. For example, say that you quit your $50,000 job, invest $200,000 to start a new business, and end up netting $80,000 in your new business for the year. Suppose also that you would have earned 7 percent on the $200,000 (a total of $14,000) if you'd kept the money in whatever investment you took it from. So you gave up a $50,000 salary and $14,000 in investment income with your course of action; your opportunity cost is $64,000. Subtract that figure from what your actual course of action netted you — $80,000 — and you end up with a "true" economic profit of $16,000.

✔ **Marginal cost:** The *incremental,* or additional, cost involved in taking a particular course of action. Generally speaking, it's the same thing as a *variable* cost (see "Fixed versus variable costs," later in this chapter). To maximize profit, you should keep moving in one direction until marginal cost equals marginal revenue. But this concept gets a little too technical for the scope of this book.

✔ **Replacement cost:** The amount for which a business can sell off its specific assets. Economists are oriented toward (*obsessed with* seems more accurate, but who am I to promote animosity toward economists?) current replacement cost because they assume that these costs are very relevant in making rational economic decisions. For a good time, those fun-lovin' economists compute the *opportunity cost* of the profit netted by the business versus the amount for which the business could have sold its assets. And you thought accountants were dull.

✔ **Imputed cost:** A variation of *opportunity cost.* The prime example of imputed cost is calculating how much a business's investors would have earned if they had invested their money elsewhere and deducting this amount from the profit earned by the business. The difference is the true profit that the business earned for the investors; that is, only the amount over and above what the investors could have earned elsewhere.

For the most part, these concepts aren't reflected in accounting reports. I've included them here just to make the practical accounting methods in this chapter more enticing by comparison — and also to familiarize you with the terms you're likely to hear at your next economist-accountant powwow. (A little closer to home, you also see these terms in the financial press and hear them on financial talk shows.)

Comprehending All Those Confounding Costs

Accountants look at costs in a binary way — a cost may be either direct or indirect, fixed or variable, relevant or irrelevant, and so on. Understanding how costs are categorized helps you better understand the balance sheet (see Chapter 6 for more about balance sheets) and expenses reported in income statements (see Chapter 5 for more about income statements). Looking at the values reported in the balance sheet and income statement, you may think that a dollar is a dollar is a dollar, but that is *not* the case. The following explanations of the different kinds of costs should help you grasp the important differences between, for example, the values reported in accounts receivable and the values reported in inventory, and the amounts reported in the depreciation and cost of goods sold expenses.

The following discussion focuses on understanding costs in your management decision-making analysis. It also considers how accounting for these costs affects the end product of the accounting process — the profit figure reported in the income statement and the financial condition reported in the balance sheet. (See also the "Puzzling Over Product Cost for Manufacturers" section of this chapter for further discussion of certain issues as they relate to manufacturer businesses.)

Direct versus indirect costs

- ✔ **Direct costs:** Can be clearly attributed to one product or product line, or one source of sales revenue, or one organizational unit of the business, or one specific operation in the process. An example of a direct cost in the book publishing industry is the cost of the paper that a book is printed on; this cost can be squarely attached to one particular phase of the book production process.

- ✔ **Indirect costs:** Are far removed from and cannot be obviously attributed to specific products, organizational units, or activities. A book publisher's phone bill is a cost of doing business but can't be tied down to just one part of the book production process.

 As another example, the cost of filling the gas tank in driving a car from Denver to San Francisco and back is a direct cost of making the trip. The annual license plate that Colorado charges you for is an indirect cost of the trip, although it is a direct cost of having the car available during the year.

Fixed versus variable costs

- **Fixed costs:** Remain the same over a relatively broad range of sales volume or production output. For example, the cost of renting office space doesn't change regardless of how much a business's sales increase or decrease, until the increase or decrease reaches the point where the business needs to either hire more people and obtain more office space or lay off employees and reduce its office space. Fixed costs are like a dead weight on the business. Its total fixed costs is the obstacle that the business must overcome by selling enough units at high enough profit margins per unit in order to move into the profit zone. (Chapter 9 explains the break-even point, which is the level of sales needed to cover fixed costs for the period.)

- **Variable costs:** Increase and decrease in proportion to changes in sales or production level. If you increase the number of books that your business produces, the cost of buying paper also goes up.

Relevant versus irrelevant (sunk) costs

- **Relevant costs:** Costs that should be considered when deciding on a future course of action. Relevant costs are _future_ costs — costs that you may need to make in the future depending on which course of action you take. For example, say that you want to increase the number of books that your business produces next year in order to increase your sales revenue, but the cost of paper has just shot up. Should you take the cost of paper into consideration? Absolutely; that cost will affect your bottom-line profit and may negate any increases in sales that you experience.

- **Irrelevant (or sunk) costs:** Costs that should be disregarded when deciding on a future course of action; if brought into the analysis, these costs could cause you to make the wrong decision. An irrelevant cost is a vestige of the past; that money is gone, so get over it. For example, suppose that your supervisor tells you to expect a slew of new hires next week. All your staff members use computers now, but you have a bunch of typewriters gathering dust in the supply room. Should you consider the cost paid for those typewriters in your decision to buy computers for all the new hires? Absolutely not; that cost should have been written off and is no match for the cost you'd pay in productivity (and morale) for new employees who are forced to use typewriters.

As a rough rule of thumb, fixed costs are irrelevant, assuming that they're truly fixed and can't be increased or decreased over the short term. Most variable costs are relevant because they depend on which alternative is decided on.

Note: Even though fixed costs are often irrelevant, meaning that the cost will be the same no matter which course of action you decide upon, they may factor into your decision with respect to the percentage of fixed-asset resources you're using. See "Determining and optimizing your production capacity," later in this chapter, for more details.

Actual (historical) versus budgeted (future) versus standard (engineered) costs

- ✔ **Actual costs:** Historical costs, based on actual transactions and operations for the period just ended, or going back to previous periods. Financial statement accounting is based on a business's actual transactions and operations; the basic approach to determining annual profit is to record the financial effects of actual transactions and allocate actual costs to the period benefited by the costs (*accrual basis accounting,* which is also discussed briefly in Chapter 6).

- ✔ **Budgeted costs:** Future costs, for transactions and operations expected to take place over the coming period, based on forecasts and predictions. Note that fixed costs are budgeted differently than variable costs — for example, if sales volume is forecast to increase by 10 percent, variable costs will definitely increase accordingly, but fixed costs may or may not need to be increased to accommodate the volume increase (see "Fixed versus variable costs," earlier in this chapter). Chapter 10 explains the budgeting process and budgeted financial statements, including the comparison of actual costs and budgeted costs for management control.

- ✔ **Standard costs:** Costs, primarily in manufacturing, that are carefully planned and controlled (engineered) based on detailed analysis of operations and budgeted costs for each component or step in an operation. Think of an assembly line: The same process is repeated again and again, with the same cost each time. Developing standard costs for variable production costs is relatively straightforward because these are direct costs, whereas most fixed costs are indirect, and standard costs for fixed costs are necessarily based on more arbitrary methods (see "Direct versus indirect costs," earlier in this chapter).

Product versus period costs

- ✔ **Product costs:** Costs that are clearly attached to particular products. The cost is recorded in the inventory asset account until the product is sold, at which time the cost goes into the cost of goods sold expense account (see Chapters 5 and 6 for more about these accounts). The product cost is deferred until the product is sold.

For example, the cost of a new Ford sitting on a car dealer's showroom floor is a product cost. The dealer keeps the cost in the inventory asset account until you buy the car, at which point the dealer charges the cost to the cost of goods sold expense.

✔ **Period costs:** Costs that are not clearly attached to particular products. These costs are recorded as expenses immediately; unlike product costs, period costs don't pass through the inventory account first. Monthly telephone and water bills are examples of period costs.

Product costs and period costs are particularly relevant to manufacturing businesses, as you find out in the following section.

Puzzling Over Product Cost for Manufacturers

Manufacturer businesses have an additional set of cost issues to deal with. I use the term *manufacturer* in the broadest sense: Automobile makers assemble cars, beer companies brew beer, gas companies pump oil, DuPont makes products through chemical synthesis, and so on. *Retailers* (or *merchandisers*), on the other hand, buy products in a condition ready for resale to the end consumer. For example, Levi Strauss manufactures clothing, and the Gap is a retailer that buys from Levi Strauss and sells the clothes to the public.

The following sections describe costs that are unique to manufacturers and address the issue of determining product cost in manufacturing.

Minding manufacturing costs

Manufacturing costs consist of four basic types:

✔ **Raw materials:** What a manufacturer buys from other companies to use in the production of its own products. For example, General Motors buys tires from Goodyear that then become part of GM's cars.

✔ **Direct labor:** The employees who work on the production line.

✔ **Variable overhead:** Indirect production costs that increase or decrease as the quantity produced increases or decreases. An example is the cost of electricity that runs the production equipment: You pay for the electricity for the whole plant, not machine by machine, so you can't attach this cost to one particular part of the process. But if you increase or decrease the use of those machines, the electricity cost increases or decreases accordingly.

✔ **Fixed overhead:** Indirect production costs that do *not* increase or decrease as the quantity produced increases or decreases. These fixed costs remain the same for a certain range of production output levels (see "Fixed versus variable costs," earlier in this chapter). Three significant fixed manufacturing costs are

- Salaries for certain production employees, such as the vice president, safety inspectors, and security guards

- Depreciation of production buildings, equipment, and other manufacturing fixed assets

- Occupancy costs, such as building insurance, property taxes, and heating and lighting charges

Figure 12-1 shows a sample management income statement for a manufacturer, including supplementary information about its manufacturing costs. Notice that the cost of goods sold expense depends directly on the product cost from the manufacturing cost summary that appears below the income statement. Retailers keep track of their purchase costs to determine their product costs. When they buy products, they enter the cost in the inventory asset account; when they sell the products, they retrieve the cost from the inventory file to determine cost of goods sold expense — although they have to choose which sequence of costs to use for the expenses, as Chapter 13 explains.

In stark contrast, a manufacturer does not *purchase* products but begins by buying the raw materials needed in the production process. Then the manufacturer pays workers to operate the machines and equipment and to move the products into warehouses after they have been produced. All this is done in a sprawling plant that has many indirect overhead costs. All these different production costs have to be funneled into the product cost so that the product cost can be entered in the inventory account, and then to cost of goods sold expense when the product is sold.

Allocating costs properly: not easy!

Two vexing issues come up in determining product cost for a manufacturer:

✔ **Drawing a very clear line of separation between manufacturing costs and nonmanufacturing operating costs:** The key difference here is that manufacturing costs are categorized as product costs, and operating costs are categorized as period costs (see "Product versus period costs," earlier in this chapter). The significance is that when calculating product cost, you factor in manufacturing costs but not operating costs.

Wages paid to production line workers are a clear-cut example of a manufacturing cost. Salaries paid to salespeople is a marketing cost, which is charged to expense in the period. Depreciation on production equipment is a manufacturing cost, but depreciation on the warehouse in which products are stored after being manufactured is a period cost.

Management Income Statement for Year

	Per Unit	Totals
Sales Volume	110,000 Units	
Sales Revenue	$1,400	$154,000,000
Cost of Goods Sold Expense	(760)	(83,600,000)
Gross Profit Margin	$640	$70,400,000
Variable Operating Expenses	(300)	(33,000,000)
Contribution Profit Margin	$340	$37,400,000
Fixed Operating Expenses	(195)	(21,450,000)
Earnings Before Interest and Tax (EBIT)	$145	$15,950,000
Interest Expense		(2,750,000)
Earnings Before Income Tax		$13,200,000
Income Tax Expense		(4,488,000)
Net Income		$8,712,000

Manufacturing Cost Summary for Year

	Per Unit	Totals
Annual Production Capacity	150,000 Units	
Actual Output	120,000 Units	
Production Cost Components	**Per Unit**	**Totals**
Raw Materials	$215	$25,800,000
Direct Labor	125	15,000,000
Variable Overhead	70	8,400,000
Total Variable Manufacturing Costs	$410	$49,200,000
Fixed Overhead	350	42,000,000
Total Manufacturing Costs	$760	$91,200,000
To 10,000 Units Inventory Increase		(7,600,000)
To 110,000 Units Sold		$83,600,000

Figure 12-2:
Example of product costing for a manu-facturer.

Moving the raw materials and work-in-progress through the production process is a manufacturing cost, but transporting the products from the warehouse to customers is a period cost. In short, product soct stops at the end of the production line — but every cost up to that point should be included as a manufacturing cost.

If you misclasssify some of the manufacturing cost as operating cost, your product cost calculation will be too low (see "Calculating product cost," later in this chapter).

✔ **Allocating indirect costs among different products, or organizational units, or assets:** See "Direct versus indirect costs," earlier in this chapter.

The first question you should always ask is whether cost allocation is really necessary. For manufacturing costs, the answer is yes; you need to include both direct and indirect manufacturing costs when calculating product cost (see "Calculating product cost," coming up). For nonmanufacturing costs, the basic test of whether to allocate is to see how allocating may help managers make better decisions and exercise better control. In any case, you should understand how indirect costs are allocated and appreciate that all allocation methods are arbitrary and open to question.

Allocating indirect costs is as simple as ABC — not!

Accountants for manufacturers have developed loads of different methods and schemes for allocating indirect overhead costs, many based on some common denominator of production activity, such as direct labor hours. The latest method is known as *activity-based costing* (ABC).

With the ABC method, you identify each necessary, supporting activity in the production process and collect costs into a separate pool for each identified activity. Then you develop a *measure* for each activity — for example, the measure for the engineering department may be hours, and the measure for the maintenance department may be square feet. You use the activity measures as *cost drivers* to allocate cost to products. So if Product A needs 200 hours of the engineering department's time and Product B is a simple product that needs only 20 hours of engineering, you allocate ten times as much cost to Product A.

The idea is that the engineering department doesn't come cheap — including the cost of their slide rules and pocket protectors as well as their salaries and benefits, the total cost per hour for those engineers could be $100 to

$200. The logic of the ABC cost-allocation method is that the engineering cost per hour should be allocated on the basis of the number of hours (the driver) required by each product. In similar fashion, suppose the cost of the maintenance department is $10 per square foot per year. If Product C uses twice as much floor space as Product D, it would be charged with twice as much maintenance cost.

The ABC method has received much praise for being better than other allocation methods, especially for management decision making, but keep in mind that it still requires rather arbitrary definitions of cost drivers — and having too many different cost drivers, each with its own pool of costs, is not too practical. Cost allocation always involves arbitrary methods. Managers should be aware of which methods are being used and should challenge a method if they think that it's misleading and should be replaced with a better (though still somewhat arbitrary) method. I don't mean to put too fine a point on this, but to a large extent, cost allocation boils down to a "my arbitrary method is better than your arbitrary method" argument.

Calculating product cost

The basic equation for calculating product cost is

```
Total manufacturing costs ÷ production output = product
            cost per unit
```

Looks pretty straightforward, doesn't it? Well, the equation itself may be simple, but the accuracy of the results depends directly on the accuracy of your manufacturing cost numbers. And because manufacturing processes are fairly complex, with many steps and operations, your accounting systems must be very complex and detailed to keep accurate track of all the manufacturing costs.

For an example, refer to Figure 12-1, which shows a business that produced slightly more units than it sold during the year, thus increasing its inventory by 10,000 units. Just to keep things simple, assume that this business manufactures just one product and calculates its product cost yearly (rather than monthly or quarterly, which is done in actual practice).

The first rule of accounting is that the inventory increase has to absorb its fair share of the total manufacturing costs for the year. The 110,000 units sold during the year do not get hit with the cost of producing 120,000 units. The cost of goods sold expense is based on the 110,000 units sold, and inventory is charged (increased) for the additional 10,000 units. In Figure 12-1, notice that the product cost per unit ($760, computed by dividing the $91.2 million total manufacturing costs by the 120,000 production output) is applied both to the 110,000 units sold and to the 10,000 units added to inventory.

Note: A business may determine its product cost monthly or quarterly rather than once a year, in which case its product cost likely varies from period to period. In these cases, the product costs charged to the cost of goods sold expense may differ from the product costs put in the inventory account.

Determining and optimizing your production capacity

Another product cost component is the *burden rate,* which is the average fixed manufacturing cost per unit produced during the period. The equation for determining the burden rate is

```
Total fixed manufacturing costs for year ÷ production
        output for year = burden rate
```

Note that the burden rate depends not just on fixed manufacturing costs but also on the number it's divided by; that is, the production output for the period. For example, suppose the company had not increased its inventory and manufactured just what it sold during the year. In this case, the burden rate would have been $381.82 per unit (computed by dividing the $91.2 million total manufacturing costs by the 110,000 units production output). Each unit sold, therefore, would have cost $31.82 more than the $350 burden rate shown in Figure 12-1 — simply because the company manufactured fewer units. The total fixed manufacturing costs would have been spread over fewer units, and the amount allocated to each unit would have been higher. The variable manufacturing costs are not subject to this problem; they would be the same, or very close to the same, as the per unit costs shown in Figure 12-1.

Fixed manufacturing costs are needed to provide *production capacity* — the people and physical resources needed to manufacture products — for the year. Once the business has the production plant and people in place for the year, its fixed manufacturing costs cannot be scaled down easily. The business is stuck with these costs over the short run. It has to make the best use it can from its production capacity.

Production capacity is a critical concept for business managers to grasp. You need to plan your production capacity well ahead of time because you naturally need plenty of lead time to assemble trained people, appropriate equipment, land, and buildings. Then when you have the necessary production capacity in place, you want to make sure that you're making optimal use of that capacity. As explained in the "Fixed versus variable costs" section of this chapter, fixed costs remain the same even as production output increases or decreases, so you may as well make optimal use of the capacity provided by those fixed costs. For example, you're recording the same depreciation amount on your machinery regardless of how much you actually use those machines, so you should be sure to optimize the use of those machines (within limits, of course — overworking the machines to the point where they break down won't do you much good).

For the example illustrated in Figure 12-1, the business's production capacity for the year is 150,000 units. This business produced 120,000 units during the year, which is 30,000 units fewer than it could have. In other words, it operated at 80 percent of production capacity, or at 20 percent *idle capacity* (which isn't unusual — the average U.S. manufacturing plant normally operates at 80 to 85 percent of its production capacity):

```
120,000 units output ÷ 150,000 units capacity =
           80 percent utilization
```

This business's burden rate for the year is $350 per unit ($42 million total fixed manufacturing costs ÷ 120,000 units output). As explained earlier, the burden rate would have been higher if the company had produced, say, only 110,000 units during the year (which is its sales volume for the year). The burden rate, in other words, is sensitive to the number of units produced.

Excessive production output and puffed-up profit

Whenever your production output is higher than sales volume, be on guard about the accounting. That kind of excessive production can puff up your profit figure. How? Until a product is sold, the product cost goes in the inventory asset account rather than the cost of goods sold expense account, meaning that the product cost is counted as a *positive* number (an asset) rather than a *negative* number (an expense). And the burden rate is included in product cost, which means that this cost component goes into inventory and is held there until the products are sold later. In short, when you overproduce, more of your fixed manufacturing costs for the period are moved to the inventory asset account and less are moved to the cost of goods sold expense, which is based on the number of units sold. (I assume that you would not do this deliberately as a means of puffing up profit, of course.)

The actual costs/actual output method and when not to use it

To determine its product cost, the business in the Figure 12-1 example uses the *actual cost/actual output method,* in which you take your actual costs — which may have been higher or lower than the budgeted costs for the year — and divide by the actual output for the year.

The actual costs/actual output method is appropriate in most situations. However, this method is not appropriate and would have to be modified in two extreme situations:

✔ **Manufacturing costs are grossly excessive or wasteful due to inefficient production operations:** For example, suppose that the business represented in Figure 12-1 had to throw away $1.2 million of raw materials during the year. The $1.2 million is included in the total raw materials cost, but you should remove that sum from the calculation of the raw material cost per unit. Instead, you treat it as a period cost — meaning that you take it directly

into expense. Then the cost of goods sold expense would be based on $750 per unit instead of $760, which lowers this expense by $1.1 million (based on the 110,000 units sold). But you still have to record the $1.2 million expense for wasted raw materials, so EBIT would be $100,000 lower.

✔ **Production output is significantly less than normal capacity utilization:** Suppose that the Figure 12-1 business produced only 75,000 units during the year but still sold 110,000 units because it was working off a large inventory carryover from the year before. Then its production capacity would be 50 percent instead of 80 percent. In a sense, the business wasted half of its production capacity, and you can argue that half of its fixed manufacturing costs should be charged directly to expense on the income statement and not included in the calculation of product cost.

You need to judge whether the inventory increase is justified. Be aware that an unjustified increase may be evidence of profit manipulation or just good old-fashioned management bungling. Either way, the day of reckoning will come when the products are sold and the cost of inventory becomes the cost of goods sold expense — at which point the cost becomes a *real* cost and subtracts from the bottom line.

As an example, check out Figure 12-1 again. This business manufactured 10,000 more units than it sold during the year. With variable manufacturing costs at $410 per unit, the business took on $4.1 million more in manufacturing costs than it would have if it had produced only the 110,000 units needed for its sales volume. In other words, if the business had produced 10,000 fewer units, its variable manufacturing costs would have been $4.1 million less. That's the nature of variable costs. In contrast, if the company had manufactured 10,000 fewer units, its *fixed* manufacturing costs would not have been any less — that's the nature of fixed costs.

Of its $42 million total fixed manufacturing costs for the year, only $38.5 million ended up in the cost of goods sold expense for the year ($350 burden rate × 110,000 units sold). The other $3.5 million ended up in the inventory asset account ($350 burden rate × 10,000 units inventory increase).

In other words, $^{11}/_{12}$ of the fixed manufacturing cost went to expense, and $^{1}/_{12}$ went to the inventory asset increase. Let me be very clear here: I'm not suggesting any hanky-panky. But the business did help its pretax profit to the amount of $3.5 million by producing 10,000 more units than it sold. If the business had produced only 110,000 units, equal to its sales volume for the year, then all the fixed manufacturing costs would have gone into cost of goods sold expense. The expense would have been $3.5 million higher, and EBIT would have been that much lower.

Now suppose that the business manufactured 150,000 units during the year and increased its inventory by 40,000 units — which may be a legitimate move if the business is anticipating a big jump in sales next year. On the other hand, an inventory increase of 40,000 units in a year in which only 110,000 units were sold may be the result of a serious overproduction mistake, and the larger inventory may not be needed next year. In any case, Figure 12-2 shows what happens to production costs and — more important — what happens to profit at the higher production output level.

The additional 30,000 units (over and above the 120,000 units manufactured by the business in the original example) cost $410 per unit. (The precise cost might have been a little higher than $410 because as you start crowding your production capacity, some variable costs may increase a little.) In any case, the business would have needed about $12 million more for the additional 30,000 units of production output:

```
$410 variable manufacturing cost per unit x 30,000
       additional units produced = $12,300,000
       additional variable manufacturing costs invested
       in inventory
```

Again, its fixed manufacturing costs would not have increased, given the nature of fixed costs. Fixed costs stay put until capacity is increased. Sales volume, in this scenario, also remains the same.

But check out the business's EBIT in Figure 12-2: $23.65 million, compared with $15.95 million in Figure 12-1 — a $7.70 million increase, even though sales volume, sales prices, and operating costs all remain the same. Whoa! What's going on here? The simple answer is that the cost of goods sold expense is $7.70 million less than before.

Management Income Statement for Year

Sales Volume		110,000 Units
	Per Unit	**Totals**
Sales Revenue	$1,400	$154,000,000
Cost of Goods Sold Expense	(690)	(75,900,000)
Gross Profit Margin	$710	$78,100,000
Variable Operating Expenses	(300)	(33,000,000)
Contribution Profit Margin	$410	$45,100,000
Fixed Operating Expenses	(195)	(21,450,000)
Earnings Before Interest and Tax (EBIT)	$215	$23,650,000
Interest Expense		(2,750,000)
Earnings Before Income Tax		$20,900,000
Income Tax Expense		(7,106,000)
Net Income		$13,794,000

Manufacturing Cost Summary for Year

Annual Production Capacity		150,000 Units
Actual Output		150,000 Units
Production Cost Components	**Per Unit**	**Totals**
Raw Materials	$215	$32,250,000
Direct Labor	125	18,750,000
Variable Overhead	70	10,500,000
Total Variable Manufacturing Costs	$410	$61,500,000
Fixed Overhead	280	42,000,000
Total Manufacturing Costs	$690	$103,500,000
To 40,000 Units Inventory Increase		(27,600,000)
To 110,000 Units Sold		$75,900,000

Figure 12-2:
Hypothetical example where production output substantially exceeds sales volume for the year — which may be good or bad, depending on how you look at it.

In the original Figure 12-1 example, $1/12$ of the company's total fixed manufacturing costs is assigned to the inventory increase (and not to cost of goods sold expense) because 10,000 of the 120,000 units produced go to the inventory increase. In other words, $3.5 million of the fixed overhead went to inventory instead of cost of goods sold expense. In the Figure 12-2 example, $4/15$ (40,000 of the 150,000 units produced) of the total fixed manufacturing costs go to inventory — which is $11.2 million, or $7.7 million more than in the original example.

The company "manufactured" $7.7 million additional before-tax profit by increasing inventory — that is, by manufacturing more units than it sold. Now *that* may arouse some suspicion. Who was responsible for the decision to go full blast and produce up to production capacity? Do you really expect sales to jump up enough next period to justify the much larger inventory level? If you prove to be right, you'll look brilliant. But if the output level was a mistake and sales do not go up next year . . . you'll have you-know-what to pay next year, even though profit looks good this year. An experienced business manager knows to be on guard when inventory takes such a big jump.

Not quite full-cost

The best way to measure product cost is to use a *full-cost* measure — that is, include every cost component and factor involved in buying a product, manufacturing a product, getting a product ready for sale, and selling a product. And the best way to measure operating expense is to use a *full-cost* measure that captures all cost elements. Furthermore, the best way to measure asset cost value is to use a *full-cost* value. Do you sense a pattern here?

But that's in the ideal world (you know, the world where you don't even have to think about any of this accounting stuff). By and large, full costs are *not* recorded. Direct and immediate costs are included in the total cost, but the indirect and incidental costs are not.

In the real world, you have time constraints and other practical problems that keep you from tracking every single element to determine full cost. Here are some categories of costs with lists of what elements of the cost should be (and in some cases, probably could be) included but generally aren't, or at least aren't included in the appropriate categories:

✔ **Product cost:** Inventory storage, fire insurance, cost of capital invested in inventory, transportation, relocation of products from shipping boxes to their appropriate location (on a sales shelf, for example), special retailer rebates from manufacturers based on yearly total purchases

✔ **Fixed assets:** Adaptation of fixed assets to suit the business's needs (such as painting a logo on a truck)

✔ **Operating expenses:** Indirect costs, such as employees' pay for their time in buying ad space (even though the cost of the ad space itself is generally included), employees' fringe benefits, and shoplifting losses

Tip: What you need to remember is that the costs you see in accounting reports are often a little short of a full-cost measure for products, fixed assets, and expenses. Full-cost accounting really isn't a practical option — unless, of course, you have an unusual need, such as defending yourself in a lawsuit.

Chapter 13

Choosing Accounting Methods

· ·

In This Chapter

▶ Choosing the right accounting method for key expenses

▶ Surveying the landscape: uniform versus elective accounting methods

▶ Understanding the methods for cost of goods sold and cost of inventory

▶ Dealing with depreciation

▶ Writing down inventory and accounts receivable

▶ Reconciling income tax

· ·

Some people put a great deal of faith in numbers: 2 + 2 = 4, and that's the end of the story. They see a number reported to the last digit on an accounting report, and they get the impression of exactitude. But accounting isn't just a matter of adding up numbers; it's not an exact science. Some even argue that accounting is more like an art, though I wouldn't go that far (and I certainly wouldn't trust any numbers that Picasso came up with — would you?). Accounting involves a whole lot more judgment and choice than most people think, especially in measuring expenses. Conscientious accountants round off their numbers as fair warning of this impreciseness.

Accountants *do* have plenty of rules that they must follow, however. The official rule book of generally accepted accounting principles (GAAP) laid down by the Financial Accounting Standards Board (and its predecessors) is more than 1,000 pages long, to say nothing of the rules and regulations issued by the chief federal regulatory agency governing financial reporting and accounting methods by publicly owned corporations: the Securities & Exchange Commission (SEC).

Perhaps the most surprising thing — considering that this rule-making activity has been going on for more than 60 years — is that a business still has options for choosing among alternative accounting methods for several key expenses. For some expenses, two or more methods are equally acceptable, even though they give different results. You can compare choosing among expense accounting methods to choosing a side of the road to drive on. In traffic, the wrong choices lead to accidents; in accounting, the wrong choices lead to inconsistent profit measures from company to company.

In addition, accounting methods change over the years, as the political environment and the business world in general change.

Because the choice of accounting methods directly affects the profit figure for the year and the values reported in the ending balance sheet, business managers need to know about accounting methods. You don't need to probe into these accounting methods in excruciating technical detail, but you should at least know whether one method over another yields higher or lower profit measures and higher or lower asset numbers in your financial statements. This chapter explains your accounting choices for measuring cost of goods sold, depreciation, and other expenses. Get involved in making these important accounting decisions — it's your business, after all.

Decision-Making behind the Scenes in Income Statements

Chapter 5 introduces the standard format for income statements included in external financial reports. Figure 13-1, in contrast, presents an income statement example that includes specific expenses under the sales, administrative, and general expenses category; it includes more expenses than you find in the typical income statement reported externally. This chapter discusses the specific expenses listed in Figure 13-1. Other than the cost of goods sold expense, don't expect to see these expenses in external income statements (although many businesses report depreciation expense). Here's a quick overview of the accounting matters and choices relating to each item:

- ✔ **Sales revenue:** How to time the recording of sales. Timing is usually not a major problem, but businesses should be consistent from one year to the next.

- ✔ **Cost of goods sold expense:** Whether to use the first-in-first-out (FIFO) method, or the last-in-first-out (LIFO) method, or the average cost method, each of which is explained in the section "Calculating Cost of Goods Sold and Cost of Inventory," later in this chapter. Cost of goods sold is a big expense for companies that sell products, naturally; the choice of method can have a real impact.

- ✔ **Gross margin:** Can be dramatically affected by the choice of method used for cost of goods sold.

Income Statement for Year		
Sales Revenue		$26,000,000
Cost of Goods Sold Expense		14,300,000
Gross Margin		$11,700,000
Sales, Administrative, and General Expenses:		
Inventory Shrinkage and Write-Downs	$378,750	
Bad Debts	385,000	
Asset Write-Downs	287,000	
Depreciation	780,000	
Warranty and Guarantee Expenses	967,250	
Other Expenses	6,302,000	
Total Expenses		9,100,000
Earnings before Interest and Tax (EBIT)		$2,600,000
Interest Expense		400,000
Earnings before Income Tax		$2,200,000
Income Tax Expense		880,000
Net Income		$1,320,000

Figure 13-1:
An income statement listing specific expenses that require accounting method choices.

✔ **Inventory shrinkage and write-downs (shrinkage caused by shoplifting and employee theft and write-downs caused by loss of sales value due to the product being outdated or available at cheaper than cost):** Whether to count and inspect inventory very carefully to determine shrinkage, and whether to apply the lower-of-cost-or-market (LCM) method strictly or loosely. See "Identifying Inventory Losses: Lower of Cost or Market (LCM)" in this chapter. Scrutinize inventory carefully because it is a high-risk asset that's subject to loss of value.

✔ **Bad debts expense:** When to assume that the debts owed to you by customers who bought on credit (accounts receivable) are not going to be paid back — the question is really when to *write down* these debts (that is, remove the amounts from your asset column). You can wait until after you've made a substantial effort at collecting the debts, or you can make your decision before that time. But the income tax law allows only the first option, so that's the method that most businesses use for their financial statements. (See "Collecting or Writing Off Bad Debts," later in this chapter.)

✔ **Asset write-downs:** Whether (and when) to *write down* or *write off* an asset — that is, remove it from the asset column. Inventory shrinkage, bad debts, and depreciation by their very nature are asset write-downs. An asset write-down reduces the book (recorded) value of an asset (and at the same time records an expense of the same amount), whereas a write-off reduces the asset's book value to zero and removes it from the accounts.

For example, your delivery truck driver had an accident. The repair of the truck was covered by insurance, so no write-down is necessary. But the products being delivered had to be thrown away and were not insured while in transit. You write off the cost of the inventory lost in the accident.

✔ **Depreciation expense:** Whether to use a short-life method and load most of the expense over the first few years or a longer-life method and spread the expense out over more years. See "Appreciating Depreciation Methods," later in this chapter. Depreciation is a big expense for some businesses, making the choice of method even more important.

✔ **Warranty and guarantee (post-sales expenses):** Whether to record the cost of warranties and guarantees that a business sells with a product now, along with the cost of goods sold, or later, when a customer returns the product for repair or replacement.

✔ **Earnings before interest and tax (EBIT):** Earnings before interest and tax may vary by 10 or even 20 percent, depending on the choices made for the preceding items on the income statement. (I caution you that this variance is an educated guess on my part.)

✔ **Interest expense:** Usually a cut-and-dried calculation, with no accounting problems. (Well, I can think of some really hairy interest accounting problems, but I won't go into them here.)

✔ **Income tax expense:** You can use different accounting methods for one or more of the expenses reported in the income statement than you use for calculating taxable income on which you base the income tax owed. Oh, boy! The income tax expense in the income statement should be on the same basis as the rest of the income statement. You use a rather technical accounting technique to reconcile the statement; see "Reconciling Income Tax," later in this chapter.

✔ **Net income:** Like EBIT, can vary considerably depending on which accounting methods you use for measuring expenses. (See also Chapter 8 on profit smoothing.)

Whereas bad debts, post-sales expenses, and asset write-downs vary in importance from business to business, inventory and depreciation methods are so important that a business must disclose which methods it uses in the footnotes to its financial statements. (Chapter 8 explains where footnotes go in a financial report and what a business must disclose in these important annotations.) And the Internal Revenue Code requires that companies record in their accounts the cost of goods sold method they use to determine taxable income — a rare requirement in the income tax law.

You'd think that with the importance given to the bottom-line profit number and the impact of the methods chosen on that number, accountants by now would have developed a clear-cut way of analyzing situations to decide on a method. As I mentioned earlier, no such luck. The final choice boils down to an arbitrary decision, made by top-level accountants with the advice and consent of managers. If you own a business or are a manager in a business, I strongly encourage you to get involved in choosing which accounting methods to use for measuring your profit and for presenting your balance sheet. Chapter 17 explains that a manager has to answer questions about financial reports on many occasions.

Accounting methods vary from business to business more than you'd probably suspect, and methods may even vary within an organization, although most larger businesses prefer to have consistency across the board.

The rest of this chapter expands on the methods available for measuring expenses. Sales revenue accounting can be a challenge as well, but profit accounting problems lie mostly on the expense side of the ledger.

Calculating Cost of Goods Sold and Cost of Inventory

One main accounting problem of companies that sell products is how to measure the *cost of goods sold expense,* which is the sum of the costs of the products sold to customers during the period. You deduct cost of goods sold from sales revenue to determine *gross margin* — the first profit line on the income statement (see Chapter 5 for more about income statements). Cost of goods sold is therefore a very important figure, because if gross margin is wrong, bottom-line profit (net income) is wrong.

First a business acquires products, either by buying them (retailers) or by producing them (manufacturers). Chapter 12 explains how manufacturers determine product cost; for retailers, product cost is simply the purchase cost. Product cost is entered in the inventory asset account and is held there until the products are sold. Then, but not before, product cost is taken out of inventory and recorded in cost of goods sold expense. You must be absolutely clear on this point. Suppose that you clear $500 from your salary for the week and deposit this amount in your checking account. The money stays in your bank account and is an asset until you spend it. Not until you write a check do you have an expense.

Likewise, not until the business sells products does it have a cost of goods sold expense. When you write a check, you know how much it's for — you have no doubt about the amount of the expense. But when a business withdraws products from its inventory and has to record cost of goods sold expense, the expense amount is in some doubt. The amount of expense depends on which accounting method the business uses.

The remaining product cost left in the inventory asset account after taking out the cost of the products sold depends on the method you choose for measuring cost of goods sold expense. In short, the method affects both the expense in the income statement and the asset value in the ending balance sheet.

The essence of this issue is that you have to divide the total cost you paid for your inventory between the units sold (cost of goods sold expense, in the income statement) and the units that remain in inventory at the end of the period (inventory asset, in the balance sheet).

You have three methods to choose from: You can follow a first-in-first-out (FIFO) cost sequence, follow a last-in-first-out cost sequence (LIFO), or compromise between the two methods and take the average costs for the period. Other methods are acceptable, but these three are the primary options. **Caution:** Product costs are entered in the inventory asset account in the order acquired, but they are not necessarily taken out of the inventory asset account in the order acquired. The different methods refer to the order in which product costs are *taken out* of the inventory asset account. You may think that only one method is appropriate — that order in should be order out. However, generally accepted accounting principles (GAAP) permit other methods.

In reality, the choice boils down to FIFO versus LIFO; the average cost method runs a distant third in popularity. If you want my opinion, FIFO is better than LIFO, for reasons that I explain in the next two sections. You may not agree, and that's your right. For your business, you make the call.

The FIFO method

With the FIFO method, you charge out product costs to cost of goods sold expense in the order in which you acquire the goods. The procedure is that simple. It's like the first people in line to see a movie get in the theater first. The ticket-taker collects the tickets in the order in which they were bought.

I think that FIFO is the best method for both the expense and the asset amounts. I hope that you like this method, but also look at the LIFO method before making up your mind. You should make up your mind, you know. Don't just sit on the sidelines. Take a stand.

Suppose that you acquire four units of a product during a period, one unit at a time, with unit costs as follows (in the order in which you acquire the items): $100, $102, $104, and $106. By the end of the period, you sell three of those units. Using FIFO, you calculate the cost of goods sold expense as follows:

```
$100 + $102 + $104 = $306
```

In short, you use the first three units in performing the calculation. (You can see the benefit of having such a standard method if you sell hundreds or thousands of different products.)

The cost of ending inventory, then, is $106, or the cost of the most recent acquisition. You divide the $412 total cost of the four units between the $306 cost of goods sold expense and the $106 cost of ending inventory. The books are in balance; nothing fell between the cracks.

FIFO works well for two reasons:

✔ The actual physical movement of most products is on a first-in-first-out basis: Businesses deliver older products to customers first, and the most recently purchased products are the ones in ending inventory. This way, the inventory asset reported on the balance sheet at the end of the period reflects the most recent purchase cost and therefore is close to the current *replacement* cost of the product.

✔ When product costs are steadily increasing, many (but not all) businesses follow a first-in-first-out sales price strategy and hold off on raising sales prices as long as possible. They delay raising sales prices until they have sold all lower-cost products. Only when they start selling from the next batch of products, acquired at a higher cost, do they raise sales prices. I strongly favor using the FIFO cost of goods sold expense method when the business follows this basic sales pricing strategy, because both the expense and the sales revenue are better matched for determining gross margin. I realize that sales pricing is complex and may not follow such a simple process, but the main point is that many businesses do use a FIFO-based sales pricing strategy. If your business is one of them, I urge you to use the FIFO expense method to be consistent with your sales pricing.

The LIFO method

Remember the movie ticket-taker I mentioned earlier? Think about that ticket-taker going to the *back* of the line of people waiting to get into the next showing and letting them in from the rear of the line first. In other words, the later you bought your ticket, the sooner you get into the theater.

This is the LIFO method, which stands for *last-in-first-out*. The people in the front of a movie line wouldn't stand for it, of course, but the LIFO method is quite acceptable for determining the cost of goods sold expense for products sold during the period.

The main feature of the LIFO method is that it selects the *last* item you purchased first and then works backward until you have the total cost for the total number of units sold during the period. What about the ending inventory, the products you haven't sold by the end of the year? Using the LIFO method, you never get back to the cost of the first products acquired; the earliest cost remains in the inventory asset account.

Using the same example from the preceding section, assume that the business uses the LIFO method instead of FIFO. The four units, in order of acquisition, had costs of $100, $102, $104, and $106. If you sell three units during the period, LIFO gives you the following cost of goods sold expense:

```
$106 + $104 + $102 = $312
```

The ending inventory cost of the one unit not sold is $100, which is the oldest cost. Or the $412 total cost for the four units acquired less the $312 cost of goods sold expense gives the $100 cost still in the inventory asset account. Determining which units you actually delivered to customers is irrelevant; when you use the LIFO method, you always count backward from the last unit you acquired.

If you really want to argue in favor of using LIFO — and I gotta tell you that I won't back you up on this one — here's what you can say:

- ✔ Assigning the most recent costs of products purchased to the cost of goods sold expense *first* makes sense because you have to replace your products to stay in business, and the most recent costs are closest to the amount you will have to pay to replace your products. Ideally, you should base your sales prices not on original cost but on the cost of replacing the units sold.

- ✔ During times of rising costs, the most recent purchase cost maximizes the cost of goods sold expense deduction for determining taxable income, and thus minimizes the taxable income. In fact, LIFO was invented for income tax purposes. True, the cost of inventory on the ending balance sheet is lower than recent acquisition costs, but the income statement effect is more important than the balance sheet effect.

The more product cost you take out of the inventory asset to charge to cost of goods sold expense, the less product cost you have in the ending inventory. In maximizing cost of goods sold expense, you minimize the inventory cost value.

But here are the reasons why LIFO, in my view, is usually the wrong choice (the following sections of this chapter go into more details about these issues):

- ✔ Unless you base your sales prices on the most recent purchase costs or you raise sales prices as soon as replacement costs increase — and most businesses don't follow either of these pricing policies — using LIFO depresses your gross margin and, therefore, your bottom-line net income.

- ✔ The LIFO method can result in an ending inventory cost value that's seriously out of date, especially if the business sells products that have very long lives.

- ✔ Unscrupulous managers can use the LIFO method to manipulate their profit figures if business isn't going well.

Note: In periods of rising costs, FIFO results in higher taxable income than LIFO does — something you probably want to avoid, I'm sure. Nevertheless, even though LIFO may be preferable in some circumstances, I still say that FIFO is the better choice in the majority of situations, for the reasons discussed earlier and in the following sections.

The graying of LIFO inventory cost

If you sell products that have long lives and for which your product costs rise steadily over the years, using the LIFO method has a serious impact on the ending inventory cost value reported on the balance sheet and can cause the balance sheet to look misleading. Over time, the cost of replacing products becomes further and further removed from the LIFO-based inventory costs. Your 1997 balance sheet may very well report inventory based on 1987, 1977, or 1967 product costs. As a matter of fact, the product costs used to value inventory can go back even further.

Suppose that a major manufacturing business has been using LIFO for more than 45 years. The products that this business manufactures and sells have very long lives — in fact, the business has been making and selling many of the same products for many years. Believe it or not, the difference between its LIFO and FIFO cost value for its ending inventory last year was about $2 *billion,* because some of the products are based on costs going back to the 1950s, when the company first started using the LIFO method. The FIFO cost value of its ending inventory is disclosed in a footnote to its financial statements; this disclosure is how you can tell the difference between a business's LIFO and FIFO cost values. (Chapter 8 discusses footnotes.) The gross margin (before income tax) over the business's 45 years would have been $2 billion higher if the business had used the FIFO method.

Of course, the business's income taxes over the years would have been correspondingly higher as well. That's the trade-off.

Note: A business must disclose the difference between its inventory cost value according to LIFO and its inventory cost value according to FIFO in a footnote on its financial statements — but of course, not too many people outside of stock analysts and professional investment managers read footnotes. Business managers get involved in reviewing footnotes in the final steps of getting annual financial reports ready for release (see Chapter 8). If your business uses FIFO, your ending inventory is stated at recent acquisition costs, and you do not have to determine what the LIFO value might have been. Annual financial reports do not disclose the estimated LIFO cost value for a FIFO-based inventory.

Many products and raw materials have very short lives; they're regularly replaced by new models (you know, with those "New and Improved!" labels) because of the latest technology or marketing wisdom. These products aren't around long enough to develop a wide gap between LIFO and FIFO, so the accounting choice between the two methods doesn't make as much difference as with long-lived products.

Manipulating LIFO to manufacture an artificial profit boon

The LIFO method opens the door to manipulation of profit — not that you would think of doing this, of course. Certainly, most of the businesses that choose LIFO do so to minimize current taxable income and delay paying income taxes as long as possible — a legitimate (though perhaps misguided in some cases) goal. However, some unscrupulous managers know that they can use the LIFO method to gin up some profit when business isn't going well.

How can LIFO impact profit? As I explain more fully in Chapter 5, bottom-line profit (net income) is basically the difference between sales revenue and expenses, and the biggest expense for a business that sells products is its cost of goods sold. When a business purchases or manufactures a product, that product cost is held in the inventory asset account until the business sells the product, at which time the cost is then transferred to the cost of goods sold expense account. (I know that this is the umpteenth time I've made this statement, but it's a very crucial point about which you should be very clear.) So if a business that uses LIFO sells more products than it purchased during the period, it has to reach back into its inventory account and pull out older costs to transfer to the cost of goods sold expense. These costs are much lower than current replacement costs would be, leading to an artificially low cost of goods sold expense, which in turn leads to an artificially high gross margin figure. This dipping into old cost layers of LIFO-based inventory is called a *LIFO liquidation gain.*

This unethical manipulation of profit is possible for businesses that have been using LIFO for many years and have inventory cost values far less than the current replacement costs; by not replacing all the quantities sold, they let inventory fall below normal levels.

Suppose that such a business sold 100,000 units during the year and normally would have replaced all units sold. Instead, it bought only 90,000 replacement units. Therefore, the other 10,000 units were taken out of inventory, and the accountant had to reach back into the old cost layers of inventory to record some of the cost of goods sold. To see the impact of LIFO liquidation gain on the gross margin, check out what the gross margin would look like if this business had replaced all 100,000 units versus the gross margin for replacing only 90,000. In this example, the old units in inventory cost only $30, and the current replacement cost is $65. Assume that the units have a $100 price tag for the customer.

Gross margin if the business replaced all 100,000 units:

Sales revenue	(100,000 units at $100 per unit)	$10,000,000
Cost of goods sold expense:	(100,000 units at $65 per unit)	(6,500,000)
Gross margin		$3,500,000

Gross margin if the business replaced only 90,000 units:

Sales revenue	(100,000 units at $100 per unit)	$10,000,000
Cost of goods sold expense:		
Units replaced	(90,000 units at $65 per unit)	(5,850,000)
Units from inventory	(10,000 units at $30 per unit)	(300,000)
		(6,150,000)
Gross margin		$3,850,000

The LIFO liquidation gain (the difference between the two gross margins) in this example is $350,000 — the $35 difference between unit costs multiplied by 10,000 units. Just by ordering fewer replacement products, this business added some nice padding to its bottom line — but in a very questionable way.

Of course, this business may have a good, legitimate reason for trimming inventory by 10,000 units — to reduce the capital invested in that asset, for example, or to anticipate lower sales demand in the year ahead. LIFO liquidation gains may also occur when a business stops selling a product and that inventory drops to zero. Still, I have to warn investors that when you see a financial statement reporting a dramatic decrease in inventory and the business uses the LIFO method, you should be aware of the possible illegitimate reasons behind the decrease.

Note: A business must disclose in the footnotes to its financial statements any substantial LIFO liquidation gains that occurred during the year. The outside CPA auditor should make sure that the company includes this disclosure. (Chapter 15 discusses audits of financial statements by CPAs.)

Average cost method

Although not nearly as popular as the FIFO and LIFO methods, the average cost method seems to offer the best of both worlds. The costs of many things in the business world fluctuate; business managers focus on the average product cost over a time period. Also, the averaging of product costs over a period of time has a desirable smoothing effect that prevents cost of goods sold from being overly dependent on wild swings of one or two purchases.

To many businesses, the compromise aspect of the method is its *worst* feature. Businesses may want to go one way or the other and avoid the middle ground. If they want to minimize taxable income, LIFO gives the best effect during times of rising prices. Why go only halfway with the average cost method? Or if the business wants its ending inventory to be as near to current replacement costs as possible, FIFO is better than the average cost method. Even using computers to keep track of averages, which change every time product costs change, is a nuisance. No wonder the average cost method is not popular! But it *is* an acceptable method under GAAP and for income tax purposes.

Identifying Inventory Losses: Lower of Cost or Market (LCM)

Regardless of which method you use to determine inventory cost, you should make sure that your accountants apply the *lower-of-cost-or-market* (LCM) test to inventory. A business should go through the LCM routine at least once a year, usually near or at year-end. The process consists of comparing the cost of every product in inventory — meaning the cost that's recorded for each product in the inventory asset account according to the FIFO or LIFO method (or whichever method the company uses) — with two benchmark values:

- ✔ The product's *current replacement cost* (how much the business would pay to obtain the same product or raw materials right now)

- ✔ The product's *net realizable value* (how much the business can sell the product for)

If the product cost is higher than either of these two benchmark values, your accountants should decrease product cost to the lower of the two. Why? So that you recognize inventory losses *now* rather than *later* when the products are sold. The drop in the replacement cost or sales value of the product should be recognized on the theory that it's better to take your medicine now than to put it off. Also, the purpose is to avoid overstating the inventory cost value on the balance sheet.

Buying and holding inventory involves certain unavoidable risks. Asset write-downs, explained in the "Decision-Making behind the Scenes in Income Statements" section of this chapter, record the consequences of two of those risks — inventory shrinkage and losses to natural disasters not fully covered by insurance. LCM records the losses from two other risks of holding inventory:

- ✔ **Replacement cost risk:** After you purchase or manufacture a product, its replacement cost may drop permanently below the amount you paid (which usually also affects the amount you can charge customers for the products because competitors will drop their prices).

- ✔ **Sales demand risk:** Demand for a product may drop off permanently, forcing you to sell the products below cost just to get rid of them.

Determining current replacement cost values for every product in ending inventory isn't easy! When I worked for a big-six CPA firm many years ago, we tested the ways clients applied the LCM method to their ending inventories. I was surprised by how hard market values were to pin down — vendors wouldn't quote current prices or had gone out of business, prices bounced around from day to day, suppliers offered special promotions that confused matters, and on and on. Applying the LCM test leaves much room for interpretation. ***Remember:*** Keeping accurate track of your inventory costs is important to your bottom line, both now and in the future, so don't fall into the trap of doing a quick LCM scan and making a snap judgment that you don't need an inventory write-down.

Some shady characters use LCM to cheat on their income tax returns. They *knock down* their ending inventory cost value — decrease ending inventory cost more than can be justified by the LCM test — to increase the deductible expenses on their income tax returns and thus decrease taxable income. A product may have proper cost value of $100, for example, but a shady character might invent some reason to lower it to $75 and thus record a $25 expense this period for each unit — which is not justified by the facts. But this evil deed will catch up: The person can deduct more this year, but he or she will have a lower inventory cost to deduct in the future. Also, if the person is selected for an IRS audit and the Feds discover inventory knockdown, the person may end up with a felony conviction for income tax evasion.

Appreciating Depreciation Methods

In theory, depreciation is straightforward enough: You divide the cost of a fixed asset among the number of years that the asset is expected to last. In other words, instead of having a huge lump-sum expense in the year that you make the purchase, you charge a fraction of the cost to expense for each year of the asset's lifetime. Using this method is much easier on your bottom line in the year of purchase, of course.

But theories are rarely as simple in real life as they are on paper, and this one is no exception. Do you divide the cost evenly across the asset's lifetime, or do you charge more to certain years than others? And how do you estimate how long an asset will last in the first place? Do you consult an accountant psychic hot line?

As it turns out, the IRS runs its own little psychic business on the side, with a crystal ball known as the Internal Revenue Code. Okay, so the IRS can't tell you that your truck is going to conk out in another five years, seven months, and two days. The Internal Revenue Code doesn't give you predictions of how long your fixed assets will *last;* it only tells you what kind of time line to use for income tax purposes, as well as how to divide the cost along that time line.

Hundreds of books have been written on depreciation, but the only book that counts is the Internal Revenue Code. Most businesses adopt the useful lives allowed in the income tax law and limit their depreciation methods to those allowed in the income tax law in their financial statements, not just their tax returns. Why complicate things if you don't have to?

Note: The tax law may change at any time and can get extremely technical. Please use the following information for a basic understanding of the procedures (as they exist in early 1997) and *not* as tax advice.

The part of the federal income tax law that regulates the rules of depreciation is known as the *modified accelerated cost recovery system* (MACRS). These regulations specify the depreciation time line to use for specific assets and the percentage of the cost to charge as depreciation expense each year of the time line.

For the depreciation time line, the regulations tell you which of two depreciation methods to use for particular types of assets:

> ✔ **Straight-line depreciation method:** With this method, you divide the cost evenly among the years of the asset's estimated lifetime. So if a new building costs $390,000 and its useful life — according to the appropriate section of MACRS — is 39 years, the depreciation expense

is $10,000 ($^1/_{39}$ of the cost) for each of the 39 years. You must use straight-line depreciation for buildings and may choose to use it for other types of assets, but once you start using this method for a particular asset, you can't change your mind and switch to another method later.

✔ **Accelerated depreciation method:** Actually, this term is a generic catch-all for several different kinds of methods. What they all have in common is that they're *front-loading* methods, meaning that you charge a greater amount of depreciation expense in the early years and less in the later years. *Accelerated depreciation method* also refers to adopting useful lives that are shorter than realistic estimates (very few automobiles are useless after five years, for example, but they can be fully depreciated over five years for income tax purposes).

One popular accelerated method is the *double-declining balance* (DDB) depreciation method. With this method, you calculate the straight-line depreciation rate and then you double that percentage. You apply that doubled percentage to the declining balance over the course of the asset's depreciation time line. After a certain number of years, you switch back to the straight-line method for the remainder of the asset's depreciation time line to ensure that you depreciate the full cost by the end of the predetermined number of years. See the sidebar "The double-declining balance depreciation method" for an example.

The straight-line method has strong advantages: It's easy to understand, and it stabilizes the expense from year to year. But many business managers and accountants favor faster depreciation in order to minimize the size of the checks they have to write to the IRS and thus conserve cash so that they can invest in new fixed assets sooner. Keep in mind, however, that the depreciation expense in the annual income statement is higher in the early years when you use an accelerated depreciation method, and so bottom-line profit is lower until later years. But minimizing taxable income and income tax in the early years to hang on to as much cash as possible is very important to many businesses, and they pay the price of lower net income in order to defer paying income tax as long as possible. (Or they may use the straight-line method in their financial statements even though they use an accelerated method in their annual income tax returns, which complicates matters. See the section "Reconciling Income Tax" for more information.)

Collecting or Writing Off Bad Debts

A business that allows customers to pay on credit granted by the business is always subject to *bad debts* — debts that some customers never pay off.

The double-declining balance depreciation method

Suppose that a business pays $100,000 for a fixed asset that has a five-year useful life (according to its MACRS classification) and that falls under the double-declining balance depreciation method. The annual depreciation expense by the straight-line method is $\frac{1}{5}$, or 20 percent, of cost per year — which in this example would be $20,000 per year. With the DDB method, you double that percentage to 40 percent and apply the percentage to the declining balance from year to year; depreciation each year decreases the balance on which depreciation is based the following year.

You then use the straight-line method for the last couple of years (the exact number of years depends on the number of years in the asset's depreciation time line), meaning that you divide the remaining balance by the number of remaining years. In this example, you need to use the straight-line method after the third year because if you applied the 40 percent rate to the $21,600 balance at the start of the fourth year and again in the following year on the declining balance, the fixed asset's cost would not be completely depreciated by the end of five years. The Depreciation Amount column adds up to the original cost of the asset ($100,000).

Got that? Good, because things get even more technical and complicated in income tax law. For example, businesses that buy fixed assets in the later part of a year to get a large depreciation deduction for the year must follow the *half-year* convention, which requires that the business use a midpoint date in the year that an asset is acquired and placed in service. I don't want to get into all the details here; suffice it to say that you need a good tax-law accountant to get the most out of your depreciation expense.

Year	Undepreciated Cost Balance	Depreciation Percent	Depreciation Amount
1	$100,000	40	$40,000
2	60,000	40	24,000
3	36,000	40	14,400
4	21,600	straight-line	10,800
5	10,800	straight-line	10,800

You may have heard of the *allowance method*, which a business would use to estimate how much of its accounts receivable (that is, the amounts owed to the business by customers who paid on credit) at year-end would turn out to be uncollectible. Based on this estimate, the business could record a bad debts expense. However, the IRS no longer allows anyone but certain financial institutions (such as banks with big loans) to use the allowance method. Although the allowance method was based on solid accounting theory — recording an expense in the same period as the sales revenue that generated the uncollectible accounts receivable — it was too easy to abuse: Estimating how much of your accounts receivable will turn out to be uncollectible is difficult and arbitrary, to put it mildly.

Businesses now must use the *direct write-off method* for bad debts. Under this method, you can't record a bad debts expense until you put serious effort into collecting on the debt and then actually write off the debt (that is, record in your books that the debt will not be paid). No later than the end of the year, though preferably at regular times throughout the year, businesses should take a hard look at their overdue accounts receivable, identify the ones they have no hope of collecting, and make a write-off entry decreasing accounts receivable and recording a bad debts expense. But look at the bright side: The expense is deductible for income tax. Most businesses adopt certain guidelines for pulling the plug and writing off a customer's account receivable, such as more than 90 days overdue and after two serious efforts of collecting the debt.

Note: You may still see the allowance method used on financial statements (which is perfectly legitimate and in accordance with GAAP), but because a business can't use that method for income tax purposes, many businesses have given up on it altogether.

Reconciling Income Tax

Income tax is a heavy influence on a business's choice of expense accounting methods. To hang on to cash as long as possible, a business minimizes its current taxable income by recording the maximum amounts of deductible expenses. Using these expense accounting methods lays a heavy hand on bottom-line profit, so you may ask whether you can use one method for income tax but an alternate method for your financial statements.

The answer is yes, you can — except for cost of goods sold expense. If you use LIFO for income tax, you must use LIFO in your financial statements. But you can use an accelerated depreciation method in your tax returns and use the straight-line method in your financial statements. You may decide that using two different accounting methods is not worth the time and effort. Then again, you may very well use the straight-line method if it weren't for income tax. You may, therefore, want your financial statements to be pre-pared using the straight-line depreciation method. In other areas of accounting for profit, businesses use one method for income tax and an alternate method in the financial statements (but I don't want to go into the details here).

If the income tax accounting method is different than the financial statement accounting method, GAAP requires that the income tax expense amount reported in the income statement be consistent with the expense methods used to prepare that income statement. So the income tax amount owed to the IRS (based on taxable income for the year) is not the correct amount of expense to report in the income statement for that year. The income tax return amount has to be adjusted to make the income tax expense consistent with the accounting methods used to prepare the income statement.

Illustrating how accountants reconcile the two income tax amounts — the tax return amount for the year and the amount of income tax expense to put in the annual income statement — gets rather technical. Instead, I'll keep it simple. Refer to the double-declining balance depreciation method example presented earlier (see the sidebar "The double-declining balance depreciation method"). Your business uses the depreciation schedule shown there, but, for your financial statements, you decide to use the straight-line method over seven years (which is longer than the five-year accelerated method useful life).

Assume that your business is a regular (C) corporation — Chapter 11 explains the income tax on this type of ownership structure — and that your income tax rate is 34 percent.

In the first year, you deduct $40,000 depreciation to determine your taxable income. In your income statement for the first year, however, you include only $1/7$ of the fixed asset's cost, or $14,286 depreciation expense. Thus your earnings before income tax (see Figure 13-1 for an example) is $25,714 higher than taxable income because of the difference in the two depreciation methods. So the amount owed to the IRS is $8,743 lower ($25,714 additional depreciation × 34% tax rate = $8,743). Starting with the amount owed to the IRS, the accountant records an $8,743 increase in the income tax expense to raise it to the amount that it would have been had the straight-line method been used for income tax.

Recall that in recording expenses, either an asset is decreased or a liability is increased. In this example, a special type of liability is increased to record the full amount of income tax expense: *deferred income tax payable*. This unique account recognizes the future liability that the business must pay when the annual depreciation amounts according to the accelerated depreciation method fall below the straight-line annual amounts in future years. This amount is a non-interest-bearing liability. Be warned that the accounting for this liability can get very complicated. The business provides information about this liability in the footnotes to its financial statements.

Part IV
Financial Reporting to the Outside World

The 5th Wave   By Rich Tennant

"COOKED BOOKS? LET ME JUST SAY YOU COULD SERVE THIS PROFIT AND LOSS STATEMENT WITH A FRUITY ZINFANDEL AND NOT BE OUT OF PLACE."

In this part . . .

*T*his part looks at accounting and financial reporting from an investor's point of view. Outside investors in a business — the owners who are not *managers* of the business — depend on the financial reports from the business as their main source of information about the business. Investors should know how to read and interpret the financial statements and what to look for in the footnotes to the statements. Their main concerns are the business's profit performance and financial health. Key ratios are calculated to test the success of the business in making profit and keeping its financial affairs in order.

Investors should also read the independent CPA auditor's report, which provides additional assurance that the financial statements have been prepared properly. The auditor's report reveals serious shortcomings in the statements (if there are any) and warns investors in the event that the business is standing on thin financial ice and may not be able to continue as a going concern.

Chapter 14

How Investors Read a Financial Report

In This Chapter

▶ Looking after your investments

▶ Understanding how financial reports differ for public and private businesses

▶ Using ratios to interpret profit performance

▶ Using ratios to interpret financial condition and cash flow

▶ Paying attention to what the auditor has to say

A few years ago, I invested some money in a private business that needed additional capital to continue its rapid growth. The existing investors needed fresh capital that they could not provide, and they invited several people to buy stock in the company. The business accepted my money and issued me new shares of stock. I understood that there was no trading in the stock shares of the business. But I thought that the profit prospects of the business looked good and that I would receive cash dividends on my investment. And maybe the business would be bought out by a bigger business someday, and I would make a capital gain on my investment. In fact, this did happen a few years later; I doubled my money, plus earned dividends along the way. (Not all investment stories have a happy ending, of course.)

You may not have an opportunity like I did to invest in a private business. But you can turn to the public markets in *securities*, those stocks and bonds listed every day in *The Wall Street Journal*. Your broker would be delighted to execute a buy order for 100 shares of, say, General Motors (GM) for you. Keep in mind that your money does not go to GM; General Motors already has all the money it needs to operate. Your money goes to the seller of the 100 shares. You're investing in the *secondary capital market* — the trading in stocks after the shares were issued some time ago — whereas I invested in the *primary capital market,* in which the money goes directly to the business.

You don't exactly have money to burn, so you want to make sure that you're investing your money wisely. Where do you look to find out whether a business is worthy of your investment? The business's financial report.

So you get a copy of the financial report. You wade through page after page of numbers, looking to your well-worn copy of *Accounting For Dummies* for help in decoding all those numbers. Even though you end up with a fair understanding of what most of the numbers mean, you still aren't sure that this business is the best one to invest in. What do you do? You take the time-honored, all-American path of having someone else do the work for you.

No, I'm not being facetious. Most individual stock investors in public companies don't have the time or expertise to study a financial report thoroughly enough to make decisions based on the report, so they rely on stockbrokers, investment managers, and publishers of credit ratings (like *Standard & Poor's*) for an interpretation of the report. The fact is that the folks who prepare financial reports have this kind of expert audience in mind; they don't include explanations or mark passages with icons to help *you,* the non-accountant, understand the report.

Then why should you bother reading this chapter if you have to rely on others to interpret financial reports anyway? Investors in private businesses have no choice in most situations; they study the financial reports of the companies they invest in. When you invest in stocks of public businesses, you should analyze their financial statements. Why? To level out the playing field a bit.

The more you understand about the factors that go into interpreting a financial report, the better prepared you are to evaluate the experts' interpretations. If you can at least nod intelligently while your stockbroker talks about a business's ROE and EPS, you'll look like a savvy investor — and therefore get more favorable treatment. (ROE and EPS, by the way, are *ratios,* which are the primary tools for interpreting financial reports, as this chapter explains.)

This chapter gives you the basics on comparing companies' financial reports, including the points of difference between private and public companies, the important ratios that you should know about, and the warning signs to look out for on audit reports. Part II of the book explains the three primary financial statements that are the core of every financial report: the income statement, the balance sheet, and the cash flow statement.

Although I don't specifically address footnotes in this chapter (they're too broad to cover here, but I do talk about them in Chapter 8), don't forget how important these notes on financial statements can be. Serious investors should read through footnotes carefully. Believe me, the pros read the footnotes with a keen eye.

Reporting by Private versus Public Businesses

When interpreting and comparing financial reports, publicly owned businesses must comply with an additional layer of reporting rules that don't apply to privately owned businesses. These rules are issued by the Securities & Exchange Commission (SEC), the federal agency that regulates financial reporting and trading in stocks and bonds of publicly owned businesses. The SEC has no jurisdiction over private businesses; those businesses need only worry about GAAP (generally accepted accounting principles), which don't have many hard-and-fast rules about financial report formats. Public businesses have to file financial reports and other forms that are made available to the public with the SEC. The best known is the 10-K, which includes the business's annual financial statements in the formats and with all the supporting schedules and detailed disclosures that the SEC requires.

Here are some key financial reporting requirements that publicly owned businesses must adhere to (private businesses may include these items as well if they want, but they generally don't):

- **Management discussion and analysis (MD&A) section:** Presents the top managers' interpretation and analysis of a business's profit performance and other important financial developments over the year.

- **Earnings per share (EPS):** The only ratio that a public business is *required* to report, though most public businesses do report a few other ratios as well. See "Earnings per share (EPS)," later in this chapter. Note that private businesses' reports generally don't include any ratios at all (but you can, of course, compute the ratios yourself).

- **Three-year comparative income statement:** See Chapter 5 for more information about income statements.

Note: A publicly owned business can make the required filings with the SEC and then prepare a different annual financial report for its stockholders, thus preparing two sets of financial reports. This is common practice. The financial information in the two documents can't differ in any material way.

Most public corporations solicit their stockholders' votes in the annual election of persons to the board of directors (whom the business has nominated) and on other matters that must be put to a vote at the annual stockholders' meeting. The method of communication for doing so is called a *proxy statement* — the reason being that the stockholders give their votes to a *proxy,* or designated person who actually casts the votes at the annual meeting. The SEC requires many types of disclosures in proxy statements that are not found in annual financial reports issued to stockholders or in the business's annual 10-K. For example, compensation paid to the top-level officers of the business must be disclosed, as well as their stockholdings. If you own stock in a public corporation, take the time to read through the annual proxy statement you receive.

One difference you're sure to notice between the financial reports issued by private and public companies concerns the graphics — such as pictures of products, colorful charts, and even photos of top executives (unless the business had a bad year, in which case those photos might be mysteriously misplaced and omitted).

You may think, then, that the financial reports of private businesses tend to be a bit on the dull and dry side. To be honest, I haven't seen enough private business financial reports to make a fair judgment — they're not easy to come by — but I think I can get away with saying that these reports are much *skinnier* than public businesses' (which isn't necessarily a bad thing!).

Analyzing Financial Reports with Ratios

The fundamental way to interpret financial reports is to compute *ratios* — that is, to divide a particular number by another. The reason that ratios are so useful is that they allow you to compare a business's current performance with its past performance or with another business's performance, regardless of whether sales revenue or net income was bigger or smaller for the other years or the other business. In other words, using ratios cancels out size differences.

You don't see too many ratios included on financial reports. Publicly owned businesses are required to report just one ratio (earnings per share, or EPS), and privately owned businesses generally don't report any ratios at all. Generally accepted accounting principles (GAAP) don't demand that ratios be reported. However, you still see and hear about ratios all the time, especially from stockbrokers and other expert financial report readers, so you should know what the ratios mean, even if you never go to the trouble of computing them yourself.

Ratios do not provide final answers — they're helpful indicators, and that's it. For example, if you're in the market for a house, you may consider cost per square foot (the total cost divided by the total number of square feet) as a way of comparing the prices of the houses you're looking at. But you have to put that ratio in context: Maybe one neighborhood is nicer than another, and maybe one house will be needing more repairs than another. In short, the ratio isn't the only factor in your decision — and the same should hold true for financial report ratios.

The following sections explain the top-ten basic ratios that you're most likely to run into. Here's what these ratios are helpful for measuring:

- ✓ **Profit ratio and gross margin ratio:** You use these ratios to measure a business's profit performance in general, with respect to sales revenue and net income.

- ✓ **Earnings per share (EPS), price/earnings (P/E) ratio, and dividend yield:** These ratios revolve around the market price of stock shares, and anyone who invests in publicly owned businesses should be intimately familiar with these three. As an investor, your main concern is the return you receive on your invested capital. Return on capital consists of two elements:

   - Periodic **cash dividends** distributed by the business

   - Increase (or decrease) in the **market price** of the stock shares

   Dividends and market prices depend on earnings — and there you have the relationship among these three ratios and why they're so important to you, the investor. Major newspapers report dividend yields and P/E ratios in their stock market activity tables; stockbrokers' investment reports focus mainly on EPS forecasts.

- ✓ **Book value per share and return on equity (ROE):** Stock shares for private businesses have no ready market price, so investors in these businesses use book value per share and ROE to measure investment return instead of EPS and P/E.

- ✓ **Current ratio and acid-test ratio:** These ratios indicate whether a business has enough cash to pay off its debts.

- ✓ **Return on assets (ROA):** This ratio is the first step in determining how well a business is using its capital and whether it is earning more than the interest rate on its debt.

Note: After dividing the numbers shown in the mathematical expressions, you multiply the result by 100 and express the ratio as a percentage or as a dollar amount, depending on the ratio (unless otherwise noted).

Hold on — it's a bumpy ride!

If you selected, say, 100 annual financial reports and read all their income statements, you might be surprised to find that so many report an extraordinary gain or loss for the year. These big numbers are out-of-the-ordinary bumps and detours along the profit highway, but they're far from uncommon. Not too many businesses have the luxury of a smooth, even performance year after year.

These kinds of discontinuities certainly make analysis of profit performance hard. A business that has reported good annual profits for five or ten years suddenly gets clobbered with some huge loss — how should you interpret that loss? By itself, or in the context of the business's historical performance? What does it mean for the coming year? You'll find none of these questions answered in a business's financial report; you have to look elsewhere. See Chapter 5 for more about the reporting of nonrecurring gains and losses.

Profit ratio

Business is motivated by profit, so the *profit ratio* is the logical place to start. The profit ratio indicates how much net income was earned on each $100.00 of sales revenue:

```
Net income ÷ sales revenue = profit ratio
```

For example, a business with $1.32 million net income and $26 million sales revenue has a 5.1 percent profit ratio, meaning that the business earned $5.10 net income for each $100.00 of sales revenue.

A seemingly small change in the profit ratio can actually have a big impact on the bottom line. Suppose that this business had a profit ratio of 5.1 percent one year and then 5.5 percent the next year. That small increase translates into a $104,000 increase of bottom-line profit (net income) on the same sales revenue.

Profit ratios vary widely from industry to industry. A 5 to 10 percent profit ratio is common in most industries, though some high-volume retailers, such as supermarkets, are satisfied with profit ratios around 1 percent.

You can turn any ratio upside down and come up with a new way of looking at the same information. If you flip the profit ratio to be sales revenue divided by net income, the result is the amount of sales revenue needed to make $1.00 profit. Using the same example, $26 million sales revenue ÷ $1.32 million net income = 18.1 to 1 upside-down profit ratio, which means that this business needs $18.10 in sales to make $1.00 profit. So you can say that net income is 5.1 percent of sales revenue, or you can say that sales revenue is 18.1 times net income — but the standard profit ratio is expressed as net income divided by sales revenue.

Gross margin ratio

Making bottom-line profit begins with making sales and earning enough gross margin from those sales, as explained in Chapters 5 and 9. In other words, a business must set its sales prices high enough over product costs to yield satisfactory gross margins on the products, because the business has to worry about many more expenses of making sales and running the business, plus interest expense and income tax expense. You calculate the _gross margin ratio_ as follows:

```
Gross margin ÷ sales revenue = gross margin ratio
```

So a business with an $11.7 million gross margin and $26 million in sales revenue ends up with a 45 percent gross margin ratio. Now, if the business had only been able to earn a 46.0 percent gross margin, that would have caused a _big_ jump in gross margin.

Outside investors know only the information disclosed in the financial report. They can't do much more than compare the gross margin for the two years. Although publicly owned businesses are required to include a management discussion and analysis (MD&A) section that should comment on any significant change in the gross margin ratio, corporate managers have wide latitude in deciding what exactly to discuss and how much detail to go into. You definitely should read the MD&A section, but it may not provide all the answers you're looking for. You have to search further in stockbroker releases, in articles in the financial press, or at the next professional business meeting you attend.

Earnings per share (EPS)

Publicly owned businesses, according to financial reporting standards, must report the _earnings per share (EPS)_ on their financial reports — giving EPS a certain distinction among the ratios. Why is EPS considered so important? Because it gives investors a means of determining the amount the business earned on their stock share investment: EPS tells you how much net income the business earned for each stock share you own. The equation for EPS is as follows:

```
Net income ÷ total number of shares held by stockholders
            = EPS
```

A business with \$132 million net income and 40 million stock shares has an EPS of \$3.30. The \$3.30 per share is either paid out in cash dividends or reinvested by the business to build a base for earning more profit in the future. For this reason, the EPS of stock shares determines market value. At the time of this writing, the stock market, on average, was putting a value of about 18 times EPS on stock shares. So the stock shares in this example might have been trading for \$59 per share (18 × \$3.30 EPS). You can find out more about the ratio of market price to EPS a little later in this chapter.

EPS is the main focus of stock market investors and is always reported in news stories about businesses' latest earnings reports. This ratio appears at the end of the income statement, below the net income line.

Calculating EPS isn't always simple. An accountant would have to adjust the EPS equation for the following complicating things that a business may do:

✔ Issue additional stock shares during the year and buy back some of its stock shares.

✔ Issue more than one class of stock.

✔ Grant its top executives stock options with below-market prices that end up diluting the value of the stock shares.

Price/earnings (P/E) ratio

The *price/earnings (P/E) ratio* is another ratio that's of particular interest to investors in public businesses. The P/E ratio gives you an idea of how much you're paying in the current price for the stock shares for each dollar of earnings, or net income being earned by the business. Remember that earnings prop up the market value of stock shares, not the book value of the stock shares that's reported in the balance sheet. (Read on for the book-value-per-share discussion.)

The P/E ratio is, in one sense, a reality check on just how high the current market price is in relation to the underlying profit that the business is earning. Extraordinarily high P/E ratios are justified only when investors think that the company's EPS has a lot of upside potential in the future.

The P/E ratio is calculated as follows:

```
Current market price of stock ÷ most recent 12 months EPS =
             P/E ratio
```

Assume that the stock shares of a business with a \$3.65 EPS are selling at \$54.75 in the stock market. The actual share price bounces around day to day and is subject to change on short notice. To illustrate the P/E ratio, I use this price, which is the closing price on the latest trading day in the stock market. This market price means that investors trading in the stock think that the shares are worth 15 times EPS ($54.75 market price ÷ 3.65 EPS = 15). This value may be below the broad market average that values stocks at, say, 18 times EPS. The outlook for future growth in its EPS is probably not too good.

In recent years, average stock market P/E ratios have been in the 15 to 20 range, though they vary quite a bit from business to business, industry to industry, and year to year. One dollar of EPS may command only a $12 market value for a mature business in a non-growth industry, whereas a dollar of EPS for dynamic businesses in growth industries may be rewarded with a $35 market value or more.

Dividend yield

The *dividend yield* tells investors how much *cash flow income* they're receiving on their investment. (The dividend is the cash flow income part of an investment return; the other part is the gain or loss in the market value of the investment over the year.)

Suppose that a stock that is selling for $54.75 paid $1.25 cash dividends per share over the last year. You calculate dividend yield as follows:

```
$1.25 annual cash dividend per share ÷ $54.75 current
          market price of stock = 2.3% dividend yield
```

You use dividend yield to compare how your stock investment is doing with how it would be doing if you'd put that money in corporate or U.S. Treasury bonds and notes or other debt securities that pay interest. The average interest rate of high-grade debt securities has recently been much higher than dividend yields on most public corporations; in theory, market price appreciation of the stock shares over time makes up for that gap. Of course, stockholders take the risk that the market value will not increase enough to make their dividend yield higher than the interest rate.

Assume that long-term U.S. Treasury bonds are currently paying 7.3 percent annual interest, which is 5 percent higher than the business's 2.3 percent dividend yield in the example just discussed. If this business's stock shares don't increase in value by at least 5 percent over the year, its investors would have been better off investing in the debt securities instead. (Of course, then they wouldn't have gotten all the perks of a stock investment, like those heartfelt letters from the president and those glossy financial reports.) The market price of publicly traded debt securities can fall or rise, so things get a little tricky in this sort of investment analysis.

Book value per share

Book value per share is one measure, but it's certainly not the only amount used for determining the value of a privately owned business's stock shares. As discussed in Chapter 6, book value is not the same thing as market value. The asset values that a business records in its books (its ledgers, or records) are *not* the amounts that a business could get if it put those assets up for sale. Book values are usually less than what the cost would be for replacing all those assets if a disaster (such as a flood or a fire) wiped out the business's inventory or machines and equipment. Recording actual market values in the books is really not a practical option. Until a seller and a buyer meet and haggle over price, trying to determine the market price for a privately owned business's stock shares is awfully hard.

You can calculate book value per share for publicly owned businesses, too. However, market value is readily available, so stockholders (and investment advisors and managers) do not put much weight on book value per share. *EPS* is the main factor that affects the market prices of stock shares of public corporations — not their book value per share. I should add that some investing strategies, known as *value investing,* search out companies that have a higher book value per share than their going market prices. But, by and large, book value per share plays a secondary role in the market values of stock shares issued by public corporations.

Although book value per share is not generally a good indicator of the market value of a private business's stock shares, you do run into this ratio, at least as a starting point for haggling over a selling price. Here's how to calculate book value per share:

```
Total owners' equity ÷ total number of stock shares = book
                 value per share
```

Here's an example of what book value per share may look like: A business with $12,600,000 total owners' equity and 450,000 stock shares has a book value per share of $28. If the business sold off its assets at their book values and paid all its liabilities, it would end up with $12,600,000 left for the stockholders, and it could therefore distribute $28 per share. But the business will not stop and liquidate its assets and pay off its liabilities. So book value per share is a theoretical, or hypothetical, value. It's not totally irrelevant, but it's not all that definitive, either.

Return on equity (ROE) ratio

The *return on equity (ROE) ratio* tells you how much profit a business earned in comparison with the book value of stockholders' equity. This ratio is useful for privately owned businesses, which have no way of determining the current value of owners' equity (at least not until the business is actually sold). ROE is also calculated for public corporations, but, just like book value per share, it plays a secondary role and is not the dominant factor driving market prices. (Earnings are.) Here's how you calculate this key ratio:

```
Net income ÷ owners' equity = ROE
```

The owners' equity figure is at book value, which is reported in the company's balance sheet. Chapter 6 explains owners' equity and the difference between invested capital and retained earnings, which are the two components of owners' equity.

Say a business with $1.32 million net income and $10 million owners' equity has a ROE of 13.2 percent ($1.32 million net income ÷ $10 million owners' equity = 13.2%). ROE is net income expressed as percentage of the amount of total owners' equity of the business, which is one of the two sources of capital to the business, the other being borrowed money, or interest-bearing debt. The cost of debt capital (interest) is deducted as an expense to determine net income. So net income "belongs" to the owners; it increases their equity in the business, so it makes sense to express net income as the percentage of improvement in the owners' equity.

Current ratio

The *current ratio* is a test of a business's *short-term solvency* — its capability to pay off debts right now and in the near future (up to one year). The ratio is a rough indicator of whether cash on hand plus the cash flow from collecting accounts receivable and selling inventory will be enough to pay off the liabilities that will come due in the next period.

As you can imagine, lenders are particularly keen on punching in the numbers to calculate the current ratio. Here's how they do it:

```
Current assets ÷ current liabilities = current ratio
```

Note: Unlike with most of the other ratios, you don't multiply the result of this equation by 100 and represent it as a percentage.

Businesses are often required to maintain a minimum current ratio (2.0, meaning a 2-to-1 ratio, is the general rule), as stipulated in their contracts with lenders. So a business with $8.5 million in current assets and $4.1 million in current liabilities would have a current ratio of 2.1 and wouldn't have to worry about lenders coming by in the middle of the night to break its legs. Chapter 6 (about the balance sheet) also discusses the current ratio.

Acid-test ratio

Most serious investors don't stop with the current ratio for an indication of the short-term solvency of the business — its capability to pay the liabilities that will come due in the short term. Investors also calculate the *acid-test ratio* (also known as the *quick ratio* or the *pounce ratio*), which is a more severe test of a business's solvency than the current ratio: The acid-test ratio excludes inventory and prepaid expenses, which the current ratio includes, and limits assets to cash and items that the business can quickly convert to cash. This limited category of assets is known as *quick* or *liquid* assets.

You calculate the acid-test ratio as follows:

```
Liquid assets ÷ total current liabilities = acid-test ratio
```

Note: Unlike most of the other ratios, you don't multiply the result of this equation by 100 and represent it as a percentage.

Here's an example of a business's liquid assets and what its acid-test ratio would be:

Cash	$2,000,000
Marketable securities	none
Accounts receivable	2,500,000
Total liquid assets	$4,500,000
Total current liabilities	$4,080,000
Acid-test ratio	1.1

What a 1.1 acid-test ratio means is that the business would be able to pay off its short-term debts and still have a little bit of assets left over. The general rule is that the acid-test ratio should be at least 1.0, which means that liquid assets equal current liabilities. Of course, falling below 1.0 doesn't mean that the business is on the verge of bankruptcy, but if the ratio falls as low as 0.5, that would be cause for alarm.

This ratio is also known as the *pounce ratio* to emphasize that you're calculating for a worst-case scenario, where a pack of wolves (more politely known as *creditors*) has pounced on the business and is demanding quick payment of the business's debts. But don't panic. Short-term creditors do not have the right to demand immediate payment, except under unusual circumstances. This is a conservative way to look at a business's capability to pay its short-term liabilities — too conservative in most cases.

Return on assets (ROA) ratio

As discussed in Chapter 6, one key factor in analyzing a business's performance is determining its *financial leverage gain* — whether it earned more profit on the money it borrowed than it paid for the use of that borrowed money in interest — to sort out how much of net income comes from the business's financial leverage. The first step in determining financial leverage gain is to calculate a business's *return on assets (ROA) ratio,* which is the ratio of EBIT (earnings before interest and tax) compared with the total capital invested in operating assets.

Here's how to calculate ROA:

```
EBIT ÷ net operating assets = ROA
```

Note: This equation calls for *net operating assets,* not *total assets.* Actually, many stock analysts and investors use the total assets figure because deducting all the non-interest-bearing operating liabilities from total assets to determine net operating assets is, quite frankly, a nuisance. But I strongly recommend using net operating assets because that's the total amount of capital raised from debt and equity.

Compare ROA with the interest rate: If a business's ROA is 14 percent and the interest rate on its debt is 10 percent, for example, the business's profit is 4 percent more than what it's paying back in interest. (Flip to Chapter 6 for further discussion of financial leverage.)

ROA is a useful earnings ratio, aside from using it to determine financial leverage gain (or loss) for the period. ROA is a *capital utilization* test — how much profit before interest and income tax was earned on the total capital used to make the profit. The basic idea is that it takes money (assets) to make money (profit); the final test is how much profit was made on the assets. If, for example, a business earns only $1 million EBIT on $20 million assets, its ROA is only 5 percent. Such a low ROA signals that the business is making very poor use of its assets and will have to improve its ROA or face serious problems in the future.

The temptation to compute cash flow per share: Don't give in!

Now that you've gotten a taste of ratios, you can't get enough — you're devouring all the numbers on the financial report, sandwiching any two numbers that look good together to make a ratio. You start eyeing the cash flow statement, licking your lips over cash flow from profit (from *operating activities,* as it's called in the cash flow statement). You chew on that number and then reach for the total number of capital stock shares. . . .

Stop right there! Businesses are prohibited from reporting a *cash flow per share* number on their financial reports. The accounting rule book (the standards set by the Financial Accounting Standards Board, or FASB) specifically prohibits very few things, and cash flow per share is on this small list of contraband. Why? Because — and this is somewhat speculative on my part — the FASB was worried that the cash flow number would usurp net income as the main measure for profit performance. Indeed, many writers in the financial press were talking up the importance of cash flow from profit, so I see the FASB's concern on this matter. Knowing how impor-

tant is EPS for market value of stocks, the FASB declared a similar per share amount for cash flow out of bounds and prohibited it from being included in a financial report. Of course, you could compute it quite easily — the FASB's rule doesn't apply to how financial statements are interpreted, only to how they are reported.

Actually, none of the common ratios involves the cash flow statement, probably because that statement has been a required part of financial reports since only 1987, making it a baby compared with the much older balance sheet and income statement. Some technical reference books mention a few cash flow ratios, but these ratios really haven't gained any foothold in the investment and credit communities.

But the temptation is just too great! Should I dare give you an example of cash flow per share? Here goes: A business with $1.9 million cash flow from profit and 450,000 total capital stock shares would end up with $4.22 cash flow per share. Shhh. . . .

Checking for Ominous Skies on the Audit Report

The value of analyzing a financial report depends directly and entirely on the accuracy of the report's numbers. How can you know whether to trust the report and take it at face value? By checking the audit report included with the financial report. Publicly owned businesses are required to have their reports audited by independent CPA firms, and many privately owned businesses have audits done, too, because they know that an audit report adds credibility to the financial report.

If a private business's financial report doesn't include an audit report, you have to trust that the business prepared accurate financial statements that follow generally accepted accounting principles.

Unfortunately, the audit report gets short shrift in financial statement analysis, maybe because it's so full of technical terminology and accountant doublespeak. But even though audit reports are a tough read, anyone who reads and analyzes financial reports should definitely read the audit report. Chapter 15 provides a lot more about audits and the auditor's report.

The auditor judges whether the business used accounting methods and procedures in accordance with generally accepted accounting principles (GAAP). In most cases, the auditor's report confirms that everything is hunky-dory, and you can rely on the financial report. However, sometimes an auditor waves a yellow flag — and in extreme cases, a red flag. Here are the two most important warnings to watch out for in an audit report:

- ✔ The business's capability to continue operating is in doubt because of what are known as *financial exigencies,* which may mean a low cash balance, unpaid overdue liabilities, or major lawsuits that the business doesn't have the cash to cover.

- ✔ One or more of the methods used in the report are not in complete agreement with GAAP, leading the auditor to conclude that the numbers reported are inadequate or misleading.

Although auditor warnings don't necessarily mean that a business is going down the tubes, they should turn on that light bulb in your head and make you more cautious and skeptical about the financial report. The auditor is questioning the very information on which the business's value is based, and you can't take that kind of thing lightly.

Auditors are human just like everyone else (though some indicators may point otherwise). Just because a business has a clean audit report doesn't mean that the financial report is completely accurate and above board. As discussed in Chapter 15, auditors don't necessarily catch everything. And the rules of GAAP are pretty flexible, leaving accountants with some room for interpretation and creativity that's just short of *cooking the books* (deliberately defrauding and misleading readers of the financial report). Some massaging of the numbers is tolerated, which may mean that what you see on the financial report isn't exactly the whole picture of the business. Window dressing and profit smoothing — two common examples of massaging the numbers — are explained in Chapter 8.

Looking beyond financial statements

Investors can't rely on just the financial report when making investment decisions. Analysis of a business's financial statements is just one part of the process. Look at these additional factors that you may need to consider, depending on the business you want to invest in:

- Industry trends and problems

- National economic and political developments

- Possible mergers, friendly acquisitions, and hostile takeovers

- Turnover of key executives

- Labor problems

- International markets and currency exchange ratios

- Supply shortages

- Product surpluses

Whew! This kind of stuff goes way beyond accounting, obviously, and is just as significant as financial statement analysis when you're picking stocks and managing investment portfolios. A good book for new investors to read is *Investing For Dummies* by Eric Tyson (and I'm not just saying that because IDG Books Worldwide, Inc., publishes that book, too).

Chapter 15

CPA Auditors: The Referees of Financial Reporting

. . . .

In This Chapter
▶ Why audits are needed
▶ Knowing what auditors catch and don't catch
▶ Interpreting an auditor's report

. . . .

*I*f a business is deliberately deceiving you with false or misleading numbers, its financial report is far from "What You See Is What You Get." That's where audits come in.

Audits are the best practical means for keeping fraudulent and misleading financial reporting to a minimum. In a sense, CPA auditors are like highway patrol officers who enforce traffic laws and issue tickets to keep speeding to a minimum. A business having an independent accounting professional come in once a year to check up on its accounting system is like your getting a physical exam once a year — it's good insurance.

An audit by an independent CPA provides additional assurance (but not an ironclad guarantee) that the business's financial statements follow accepted accounting methods and provide adequate disclosure. This is the main reason why CPA firms do annual audits of financial reports. *Note:* I'd like to stress here that the CPA auditor must be *independent* of the business being audited. The CPA can have no financial stake in the business or any other relationship with the client that might compromise his or her objectivity.

The essence and core of a business's financial report are its three primary financial statements — the income statement, the cash flow statement, and the balance sheet — and the footnotes to these statements. A financial report may consist of just these statements and footnotes and nothing else. Usually, however, there's more — in some cases, a lot more. Chapter 8 explains the additional content of financial reports, such as the transmittal letter to the owners from the chief executive of the business, historical summaries, supporting schedules, and listings of directors and top-level managers — especially of those reports issued by publicly owned corporations.

The CPA auditor's opinion covers only the financial statements and the footnotes. The auditor, therefore, does not express an opinion of whether the president's letter to the stockholders is a good letter — although if the president's claims contradicted the financial statements, the auditor would comment on the inconsistency. In short, CPAs audit the financial statements and their footnotes but do not ignore the additional disclosures included in annual financial reports.

Caution: Although the large majority of audited financial statements are reliable, a few slip through the audit net. Auditor approval is not a 100 percent guarantee that the financial statements contain no erroneous or fraudulent numbers or that the statements and their footnotes provide adequate disclosure.

Chapter 1 explains that to be licensed as a CPA, a person has to pass a rigorous national exam, have audit experience, and satisfy continuing education requirements.

The Whos and Whys of Audits

The basic purpose of an annual financial statement audit is to make sure that a business has followed the accounting methods and disclosure requirements of generally accepted accounting principles (GAAP) — in other words, to make sure that the business has stayed within the boundaries of accounting rules. After completing an audit examination, the CPA prepares a short auditor's report stating that the business has prepared its financial statements according to GAAP — or has not, as the case may be. In short, audits are the means of enforcing accounting rules.

All businesses whose ownership shares (stock shares) are traded in the public markets in the United States are required to have annual audits by independent CPAs. Every stock you see listed on the NYSE (New York Stock Exchange), Nasdaq (National Association of Securities Dealers Quotation), and other smaller stock-trading markets must be audited by an outside CPA firm.

The Big Six international CPA firms are household names in the business world:

- ✔ Arthur Andersen
- ✔ Coopers & Lybrand
- ✔ Ernst & Young
- ✔ Price Waterhouse
- ✔ Deloitte & Touche
- ✔ KPMG Peat Marwick

These six international CPA firms audit almost all the large publicly owned corporations in the United States. The federal securities laws of 1933 and 1934 require audits. For large publicly owned companies, the annual audit is a cost of doing business; it's the price that companies have to pay for going into public markets for their capital.

Banks and other lenders to private, closely held businesses whose owner-ship shares are not traded in any public marketplace may insist on seeing audited financial statements. I would say that the amount of a bank loan, generally speaking, has to be more than $5,000,000 or $10,000,000 before a lender will insist that the business pay for the cost of an audit. If outside, non-manager investors have this much invested in a business, they might also insist on an annual audit.

Instead of an audit, many smaller businesses have an outside CPA come in regularly to look over their accounting methods and give advice on their financial reporting. Unless a CPA has done an audit, he or she has to be very careful not to express an opinion of the external financial statements.

An audit, to be blunt, is often just a necessary evil that does not uncover anything seriously wrong with a business's accounting system and the accounting methods that it uses to prepare its financial statements. In the course of doing an audit, a CPA watches for procedures that could stand some improvement and for potential problems.

The CPA usually recommends ways in which the client's *internal controls* can be strengthened. For example, a CPA auditor may discover that accounting employees are not actually required to take their vacations and let someone else do their jobs while they're gone. The auditor would recommend that the internal control requiring vacations away from the office be strictly enforced. Chapter 2 explains that good internal controls are extremely important in an accounting system.

What an Auditor Does before Giving an Opinion

A CPA auditor does two basic things: examines evidence and gives an opinion of the financial statements. The lion's share of audit time is spent on examining evidence for the transactions and accounts of the business. A very small part of the total audit time is spent on writing the auditor's report, in which the CPA expresses his or her opinion of the financial statements.

This list gives you an idea of what the auditor does "in the field" — that is, on the premises of the business being audited:

- ✔ Evaluates the design and operating dependability of the business's accounting system and procedures

- ✔ Evaluates and tests the business's internal accounting controls

- ✔ Identifies and critically examines the business's accounting methods — especially whether the methods conform to GAAP, which are the touchstones for all businesses

- ✔ Inspects documentary and other evidence for the business's revenues, expenses, assets, liabilities, and owners' equities — for example, the auditor counts products held in inventory, observes the condition of those products, and confirms checking account balances directly with banks

The purpose of all the audit work (examining evidence) is to provide a basis for expressing an opinion of the business's financial statements, attesting that the company's financial statements and footnotes (as well as any directly supporting tables and schedules) can be relied on — or not, in some cases. The CPA auditor puts that opinion in the auditor's report.

The auditor's report is the only visible part of the audit process for financial statement readers. All the readers see is the auditor's one-page report (which is based on the evidence examined during the audit process, of course). For example, Deloitte & Touche spends thousands of hours auditing General Motors, but the only thing that GM's stockholders see is the final, one-page audit report.

What's in an Auditor's Report

The audit report, which is included in the financial report near the financial statements, serves two useful purposes:

- ✔ It reassures investors and creditors that the financial report can be relied upon or calls attention to any serious departures from established financial reporting standards and generally accepted accounting principles.

- ✔ It prevents (to a large extent, anyway) businesses from issuing sloppy or fraudulent financial reports. Knowing that your report will be subject to an independent audit really keeps you on your toes!

The large majority of financial statements audit reports give the business a clean bill of health, or a *clean opinion*. At the other end of the spectrum, the auditor might state that the financial statements are misleading and should not be relied upon. This negative audit report is called an *adverse opinion*.

That's the big stick that auditors carry: They have the power to give a company's financial statements an adverse opinion, and no business wants that.

Between these two extremes, the auditor's report may point out a flaw in the company's financial statements — but not a fatal flaw that would require an adverse opinion. The following section looks at the most common type of audit report: the clean opinion, in which the auditor "certifies" that the business's financial statements conform to GAAP and are presented fairly.

A clean opinion

If the auditor finds no problems, he or she gives the financial report a clean (or *unqualified*) opinion. The clean-opinion audit report runs about 200 words in three paragraphs, with enough defensive, legalistic language to make even a seasoned accountant blush. Table 15-1 cuts through the jargon and shows you what the audit report really says.

Table 15-1	What a Clean-Opinion Audit Report Really Says
Paragraph	*Explanation*
1st paragraph	We did the audit, but the financial statements are the responsibility of management; we just express an opinion of them.
2nd paragraph	We carried out audit procedures that provide us a reasonable basis for expressing our opinion, but we don't necessarily catch everything.
3rd paragraph	The company's financial statements conform with GAAP and are not misleading.

Other kinds of auditor opinions

An audit report that does *not* give a clean opinion may look very similar to a clean-opinion audit report to the untrained eye. Some investors see the name of a CPA firm next to the financial statements and just assume that everything is okay — after all, if the auditor had seen a problem, the Feds would have pounced on the business and put everyone in jail, right? Well, not exactly.

How do you know when an auditor's report may be something other than a straightforward, no-reservations clean opinion? *Look for a fourth paragraph;* that's the key. Many situations require auditors to add additional explanatory language to the standard, unqualified (clean) opinion.

In the most important modification to an auditor's report, the CPA audit firm expresses that it has substantial doubt about the capability of the business to continue as a going concern — in other words, that the business is in deep financial waters and may not be able to convince its creditors and lenders to give it time to work itself out of its present situation. The creditors and lenders may force the business into involuntary bankruptcy, or the business may make a preemptive move and take itself into voluntary bankruptcy. The equity owners (stockholders of a corporation) may end up holding an empty bag after the bankruptcy proceedings have concluded. (This in one of the risks that stockholders take.) If they exist, you find going-concern doubts in the fourth paragraph of the auditor's report.

Auditors also point out any inconsistent accounting methods from one year to the next, whether their opinion is based in part on work done by another CPA audit firm, on limitations on the scope of their audit work, on departures from GAAP (if they're not serious enough to warrant an adverse opinion), or on one of several other more technical matters. Generally, businesses — and auditors, too — want to end up with a clean opinion; anything less is bound to catch the attention of the people who read the financial statements. Every business wants to avoid that situation if possible.

Do Audits Catch All Fraud and Dishonesty?

Business managers and investors should understand one thing: Having an audit does not guarantee that all fraud, embezzlement, theft, and dishonesty will be detected. Audits have to be cost-effective; auditors cannot examine every transaction that occurred during the year. Instead, auditors carefully evaluate businesses' internal controls and rely on sampling — they examine only a relatively small sample of transactions closely and in depth. The sample may not include the transactions that would tip off the auditor that something is wrong, however. Perpetrators of fraud and embezzlement usually are clever in concealing their wrongdoing and often prepare fake evidence to cover their tracks.

Auditors look in the high-risk areas where fraud and embezzlement are most likely to occur and in areas where the company's internal controls are weak. But, again, auditors can't catch everything. High-level management fraud is extraordinarily difficult to detect because CPA auditors rely a great deal on management representations about the business. Top-level executives may lie to auditors, deliberately mislead them, and conceal things that they don't want auditors to find out about. Auditors have a particularly difficult time detecting management fraud.

Under standards adopted in 1997, CPA auditors have to develop a detailed and definite plan to search for indicators of fraud, and they have to document the search procedures and findings in their audit working papers. Searching is one thing, but actually finding fraud is quite another matter. Unfortunately, there have been far too many cases in which high-level management fraud went on for some time before it was discovered, usually not by auditors. The new auditing standard hopefully will lead to more effective audit procedures that will reduce undetected fraud, but only time will tell.

What Happens When Auditors Spot Fraud

When auditors spot fraud, they report it to one level higher in the organization than the level at which the fraud took place — all the way to the board of directors, if necessary. But auditors don't blow the whistle outside the client business. They don't take out an ad in *The Wall Street Journal* saying that they caught management fraud at XYZ Corporation, and they don't even report the fraud to the SEC. Everything the CPA auditor learns during the course of the audit must be held in the *strictest confidence,* according to the professional standards and ethics of the CPA.

When an auditor discovers fraud, a business has to clean up the fraud mess as best it can — which often involves recording a loss. Of course, the business should make changes to prevent the fraud from occurring again. And it may request the resignations of those responsible, or even take legal action against those employees. Assuming that the fraud loss is recorded and reported correctly in the financial statements, the auditor then issues a clean opinion on the financial statements. But auditors can withhold a clean opinion and threaten to issue a qualified or adverse opinion if the client does not deal with the matter in a satisfactory manner in its financial statements. That's the auditor's real clout.

The most serious type of accounting fraud occurs when profit is substantially overstated with the result that the market value of the corporation's stock shares are based on inflated profit numbers. When the fraud comes out into the open, the market value takes a plunge, and the investors call their lawyers and sue the business and the CPA auditor.

Another type of accounting fraud occurs when a business is in deep financial trouble but its balance sheet disguises the trouble and makes things look more sound than they really are. The business may be on the verge of financial failure, but the balance sheet gives no clue.

Investing money in a business or stock shares issued by a public business involves many risks. The risk of misleading financial statements is just one of many dangers that investors face. A business may have accurate and truthful financial statements but end up in the tank because of bad management, bad products, poor marketing, or just bad luck.

All in all, audited financial statements that carry a clean opinion (the best possible auditor's report) are reliable indicators for investors to use — especially because auditors are held accountable for their reports and can be sued for careless audit procedures. (In fact, CPA firms have had to pay many millions of dollars in damages over the past 30 years.) Make sure that you don't overlook the audit report as a tool for judging the reliability of a business's financial statements. When I read the auditor's report on the annual financial statements from my pension fund manager, believe me, I'm very reassured! This is my retirement money I'm talking about, after all.

CPA Auditors as GAAP Sleuths

Auditors are very good at one thing: They catch any accounting methods that violate GAAP, the approved and authoritative methods and standards that businesses must follow in preparing and reporting financial statements. All businesses are subject to these ground rules. An auditor calls to the attention of the business any departures from GAAP, and he or she helps the business make adjustments to put its financial statements back on the GAAP track. Sometimes a business may not want to make the changes that the auditor suggests because its profit numbers would be deflated. Professional standards demand that the auditor secure a change (assuming that the amount involved is material). If the client refuses to make a change to an acceptable accounting method, the CPA warns the financial report reader in the auditor's report.

CPA auditors do not allow their good names to be associated with financial reports that they know are misleading. Every now and then, I read in the financial press about a CPA firm walking away from a client ("withdraws from the engagement" is the official terminology). As mentioned earlier in this chapter, everything the CPA auditor learns in the course of an audit is *confidential* and cannot be divulged beyond top management and the board of directors of the business.

If a CPA auditor discovers a problem, he or she has the responsibility to move up the chain of command in the business organization to make sure that one level higher than the source of the problem is informed of the problem. But the board of directors is the end of the line. The CPA does not inform the SEC or another regulatory agency of any confidential information learned during the audit. If a CPA resigns from the audit of a public corporation, the CPA must file an information report with the SEC, but no confidential information is included. A *confidential relationship* exists between the CPA auditor and the client — although it is not equal to the privileged communications between a lawyer and a client.

CPA Auditors as GAAP Enforcers

I cannot exaggerate the importance of reliable financial statements that are prepared according to uniform standards and methods for measuring profit and putting values on assets, liabilities, and owners' equity. Not to put too fine a point on it, but the flow of capital into businesses and the market prices of stock shares traded in the public markets (the New York Stock Exchange and over the Nasdaq network) depends on the information reported in financial statements. Smaller privately owned businesses would have a very difficult time raising capital from owners and borrowing money from banks if no one could trust their financial statements. Generally accepted accounting principles, in short, are the gold standard for financial reporting. The sidebar "Setting financial reporting standards: The FASB and the SEC" presents a very brief overview of how financial reporting standards are established.

After financial reporting standards have been put into action, how are the standards enforced? To a large extent, the role of CPA auditors is to do just that — to enforce GAAP. The main purpose of having annual audits by CPAs, in other words, is to keep businesses on the straight and narrow path of GAAP and to prevent businesses from issuing misleading financial statements. CPAs are the guardians of the financial reporting rules. I think most business managers and investors would agree that financial reporting would be in a sorry state of affairs if auditors weren't around.

Other Services That CPA Firms Offer

CPAs have learned from experience that they have to offer *value-added services* to clients in addition to their traditional financial statements audit function. CPA firms offer one or more of the following professional services to both their audit and their non-audit clients:

✔ **Income tax compliance and planning services:** CPAs can advise on which accounting methods minimize taxable income (see Chapter 13) and which business ownership structure can reduce the tax bills of the business and its owners (see Chapter 11).

> # Setting financial reporting standards:
> # The FASB and the SEC
>
> I haven't counted the number of times in this book that I refer to generally accepted accounting principles (GAAP), but I'm sure that the number is large. These financial reporting standards have developed in a formal, authoritative way for about 60 years, starting in the 1930s. Since 1974, the Financial Accounting Standards Board (FASB) has been the highest authoritative source of pronouncements on generally accepted accounting principles that govern financial reporting by businesses and private nonprofit organizations.
>
> The FASB has been clipping along at the rate of more than five pronouncements per year. Most of these official accounting rules are very technical; you have to be a CPA to understand them. They are written by CPAs for CPAs.
>
> The FASB deserves a lot of credit for tackling some very difficult accounting problems. The business world objected to many of the solutions; in some cases the FASB prevailed, though in other cases the business lobby persuaded the FASB not to issue a pronouncement or to modify the final pronouncement.
>
> Some accounting standards have remained unchanged for more than half a century; they are tried-and-true accounting rules that are not likely to change in the future. But many accounting methods have been superseded by new methods. As new problems develop, new accounting pronouncements are sure to follow — though the time lag is bothersome. The FASB has a "let's listen to everyone" philosophy for its deliberations — which is good for allowing due process but bad for getting out prompt rulings on festering accounting problems. Many people feel that controversial issues have dragged on much longer than needed.
>
> One continuing issue concerns who should make the rules: the private sector or the public sector? Since 1934, the Securities & Exchange Commission (SEC) has had the legislative authority to establish accounting methods and financial reporting disclosure standards. But the SEC has delegated the authority to the FASB. The SEC retains veto power, which it uses now and then, though not very often. I don't see the SEC stepping in or taking over. But who knows?

- ✔ **General management consulting services:** These services might include helping the business to implement the ABC cost allocation technique (see Chapter 12) or to apply the best business practices to reduce costs and improve efficiency.

- ✔ **Internal control studies and recommendations:** Such recommendations might be to speed up collections from customers and reduce bad debts or to reduce inventory shrinkage.

- ✔ **Computer-based accounting systems consultation:** Examples include studying the types of demands the business places on its information systems, which hardware is available, which software is best for these demands, how to install networking, and so on.

> ✔ **A wide range of other services:** Other services include personnel searches, placement of executives, due diligence searches in business acquisitions, forensic services to investigate suspected employee fraud and embezzlement, and expert testimony when a business is involved in a lawsuit requiring technical testimony on accounting methods.

Some critics argue that providing these non-audit services to a business conflicts with the independence needed in an audit and in expressing an objective and unbiased opinion of the business's financial statements. However, people in the accounting profession, lenders, and investors, as well as government regulatory agencies, have accepted that CPA firms can provide these other services to their audit clients. CPA firms are very careful to maintain their audit independence.

Part V
The Part of Tens

In this part . . .

The Part of Tens contains two shorter chapters: one directed to business managers and the other to business investors. The former presents ten tools and techniques that are useful in running a business and getting the most from your accounting information. These top ten topics are summarized and condensed and present a quick summary and a compact accounting tool kit for managers. The latter chapter provides investors with a checklist of the top ten things they should do when reading a financial report in order to gain the maximum amount of information in the minimum amount of time.

Chapter 16

Ten Ways Business Managers Can Use Accounting

*S*o how can accounting make you a better business manager? This is the bottom-line question. Speaking of the bottom line, this is exactly the place to start. Accounting provides the financial information and analysis tools you need for making more-insightful profit decisions — and stops you from plunging ahead with gut-level decisions that may feel right but that don't hold water after due-diligent analysis.

Make Better Profit Decisions

Making profit starts with earning margin on each unit sold and then selling enough units to overcome your total fixed expenses for the period, a concept that I describe more fully in Chapter 9. I condense the accounting model of profit in the following equation:

```
[Margin per unit × sales volume] - fixed expenses = profit
```

Note: Profit here is *before* income tax. Some businesses are organized as *pass-through* tax entities that do not pay income tax; their owners pick up the taxable income of the business in their individual tax returns. Regular corporations pay income tax based on the amount of their taxable income; different rates apply to different brackets of taxable income. The bottom-line net income in the income statement of a business is after-tax income. A business — whether a pass-through entity or a taxable corporation — may distribute all, part, or none of its profit for the year to its owners.

Insist that your accountant determine the margin per unit for all products you sell. The margin is also called the *contribution margin* to emphasize that it contributes toward the fixed expenses of the business. Here's an example for determining the *margin per unit* for a product:

Margin Factors	Amount
Sales price	$100
Product cost	(60)
Gross margin	$40
Sales revenue–driven expenses	(8)
Sales volume–driven expenses	(5)
Margin per unit — which equals sales price less direct variable costs	$27

Warning: I'd bet you dollars to donuts that your accountant provides the gross margin (also called *gross profit*) on your products. So far, so good. But don't stop at the gross margin line. Push your accountant to determine the two variable expenses for each product. You don't make $40 per unit sold; you make only $27 from selling the product. Two products may have the same $40 gross profit, but one could provide a $27 margin and the other a $32 margin because the second one's variable expenses are lower.

Have your accountant differentiate between *revenue*-driven and *volume*-driven variable expenses for each product. Suppose you raise the sales price to $110.00, a 10 percent increase. The sales revenue–driven expense increases by 10 percent as well, to $8.80, because these expenses (such as sales commission) are a fixed *percentage* of sales price. Your margin increases not $10.00, but only $9.20 (the $10.00 sales price increases minus the $0.80 expense increase). In contrast, the higher sales price does not increase the sales volume-driven expenses (such as shipping costs); these expenses remain at $5.00 per unit.

You earn profit (or to be precise, profit before income tax) by selling enough products so that your total margin is higher than your total fixed expenses for the period. The excess of total margin over fixed expenses is profit. Setting sales prices to generate an adequate total contribution margin is one of the most important functions of managers.

When thinking about changing sales price, focus on what happens to the margin per unit. Suppose, for example, you're considering dropping the sales price 10 percent, from $100 to $90. You predict that your product cost and variable expenses will remain unchanged. Here's what would happen to your margin:

Margin Factors	After	Before
Sales price	$90.00	$100.00
Product cost	(60.00)	(60.00)
Gross margin	$30.00	$40.00
Sales revenue–driven expenses	(7.20)	(8.00)
Sales volume–driven expenses	(5.00)	(5.00)
Margin per unit	$17.80	$27.00

Your margin would plunge $9.20 per unit — more than one-third!

Suppose you sold 1,000 units of this product during the year just ended. These sales generated $27,000 total margin. If you drop the sales price, you give up $9,200 total margin. Where will the replacement come from for this $9,200 contribution margin? You'd better have a good answer. The profit model directs attention to this critical question and gives you the amount of margin sacrificed by dropping the sales price.

Understand Why a Small Sales Volume Change Has a Big Effect on Profit

Is that big push before year-end for just 5 percent more sales volume really that important? You understand that more sales mean more profit, of course. But what's the big deal: Five percent more sales volume means just 5 percent more profit, doesn't it? Oh no. If you think so, you need to read Chapter 9. Because fixed expenses are just that — fixed and unchanging over the short run — seemingly small changes in sales volume cause large swings in profit. This effect is called *operating leverage.*

The following example illustrates operating leverage. Suppose your $12.5 million annual fixed expenses provide the personnel and physical resources to sell 625,000 units over the year. However, you didn't hit capacity; your company's actual sales volume was 500,000 units for the year, or 80 percent of sales capacity — which isn't bad. Your average margin across all products is $30 per unit. Using the basic profit equation, you determine profit before income tax as follows:

$$[\$30 \text{ margin per unit} \times 500{,}000 \text{ units}] = \$15{,}000{,}000 \quad \text{contribution margin}$$
$$- \underline{12{,}500{,}000} \quad \text{fixed expenses}$$
$$= \$2{,}500{,}000 \quad \text{pretax profit}$$

Now, what if you had sold 25,000 more units, which is just 5 percent more sales volume? Your fixed expenses would have been the same because sales volume would still be well below the sales capacity provided by fixed expenses. Therefore, the profit increase would have been the $30 margin per unit times the 25,000 additional units sold, or $750,000, which is a 5 percent gain in contribution margin. But compared with the $2,500,000 pretax profit, the additional $750,000 is a 30 percent gain — from only a 5 percent sales volume gain, which is a 6 to 1 payoff!

Operating leverage refers to the wider swing in profit than the smaller swing in sales volume. In this example, a 5 percent increase in sales volume would cause a 30 percent increase in profit. Unfortunately, operating leverage cuts both ways. If your sales volume had been 5 percent less, your profit would have been $750,000 less, which would have resulted in 30 percent less profit.

A quick explanation of operating leverage is this. In this example, total margin is 6 times profit: $15.0 million contribution margin ÷ $2.5 million profit = 6. So a 5 percent swing in contribution margin has a 6-times effect, or a 30 percent impact, on profit. Suppose a business had no fixed expenses (highly unlikely). In this odd situation, there is no operating leverage. The percentage gain or loss in profit would equal the percentage gain or loss in sales volume.

The fundamental lesson of operating leverage is to make the best use you can of your fixed expenses. If your sales volume is less than your sales capacity, the unsold quantity would have provided a lot more profit. Most businesses are satisfied if their actual sales volume is 80 to 90 percent of their sales capacity. But keep in mind one thing: That last 10 or 20 percent of sales volume would make a dramatic difference in profit!

Fathom Profit and Know Where to Find It

Profit equals sales revenue minus expenses — you don't need to know much about accounting to understand this definition of profit. However, business managers should dig a little deeper. First, you should be aware of the accounting problems in measuring sales revenue and expenses. Because of these problems, profit is not a clear-cut and precise number. Second, you should know the real stuff of profit and know where to find profit in your financial statements.

Profit is not a politically correct term. Instead, business financial reports call profit *net income* or *net earnings*. Don't look for the term *profit* in external financial statements. So remember, net income (or net earnings) = bottom-line profit after income tax.

Profit accounting methods are like hemlines

Profit is not a hard-and-fast number but is rather soft and flexible on the edges. For example, profit depends on which accounting method is selected to measure the cost of goods sold expense, which is usually the largest expense for businesses that sell products. The rules of the game, called *generally accepted accounting principles* (or GAAP for short), permit two or three alternative methods for measuring cost of goods sold and for other expenses as well. (Chapter 13 discusses accounting methods.)

In evaluating the profit performance of your own business and when sizing up the net income record of a business you're considering buying, you should carefully look at whether profit measurement is based on conservative or generous accounting methods. You can assume that profit is in the GAAP ballpark, but you have to determine whether profit is in the right field or the left field (or perhaps in center field). Businesses are not required to disclose how much different profit would have been if different accounting methods had been used, but they do have to reveal their major accounting methods in the footnotes to their annual financial statements.

The real stuff of profit

Most people know that profit is a gain, or an increase in wealth, or how much better off you are. But managers and investors hit the wall when asked to identify the *real stuff* of profit. To make my point, suppose that the latest annual income statement of your business reports $10 million sales revenue and $9.5 million expenses, which yields $500,000 bottom-line net income. Your profit ratio is 5 percent of sales revenue, which is about typical for many businesses. But I digress.

My question is this: *Where is the half-million dollars of profit?* Can you find and locate the profit earned by your business? Is it in cash? If not, where is it? If you can't answer this question, aren't you a little embarrassed? Quick—go read Chapter 5!

Profit accounting is more complicated than a simple cash-in, cash-out measure. Sales for cash increase cash, of course, but sales on credit increase an asset called accounts receivable. So *two* assets are used in recording sales revenue. Usually, a minimum of four assets and two liabilities are used in recording the expenses of a business. To locate profit, you have to look at all the assets and liabilities changed by revenue and expenses. The *measure* of profit is found in the income statement. But the *substance* of profit is found in assets and liabilities, which are reported in the *balance sheet.*

As your accountant, I have determined that your $500,000 net income consists of the following three components:

```
$500,000 profit = $320,000 cash + $290,000 net increase
          in other assets - $110,000 increase in liabilities
```

This is a very typical scenario for the makeup of profit — I don't mean the dollar amounts but rather the three components of profit. The dollar amounts of the increases or decreases in assets and liabilities vary from business to business, of course, and from year to year for your business. But hardly ever would the profit equation be

```
$500,000 profit = $500,000 cash
```

Cash is only one piece of the profit pie. Business managers need accounting to sort out how profit is divided among the three components — in particular, you need to know the cash flow generated from profit.

Govern Cash Flow Better

My youngest son, Tage, a CPA and business consultant, has a favorite saying: "If we're in the black, where's the green?" Being *in the black* means making a profit, as you probably have heard. By "green," Tage means, "Where's the cash? Where's the money to show for the profit?" Making profit does not generate immediate cash flow. Seldom does $1 of profit equal $1 of immediate cash flow, as Chapter 7 decribes in full detail.

A business wants to make profit, of course, but equally important, a business must convert its profit into *usable cash flow.* Profit that is never turned into cash or is not turned into cash for a long time is not very helpful. A business needs cash flow from profit to provide money for three critical uses:

- ✔ To distribute some of its profit to the equity (owner) sources of capital, to provide a cash income to them for their capital investment in the business

- ✔ To grow the business — to invest in new fixed (long-term) operating assets and to increase its inventory and other short-term operating assets

- ✔ To meet its debt payment obligations and to maintain the general liquidity and solvency of the business

One expense, depreciation, is not a cash outlay. Rather, depreciation expense for a period is an allocated amount of the cost of the business's fixed assets that were bought and paid for in previous years. More importantly, depreciation recovers part of the cost invested in fixed assets. The sales revenue collected by the business includes money for its depreciation expense. Thus the business converts back into cash some of the money that it put in its fixed assets years ago. So a business has two sources of cash from its profit-making activities — depreciation (cost recovery) and net income.

To illustrate this critical point, suppose a business did not make a profit for the year but did manage to break even. Even in this zero-profit situation, there is cash flow from profit because of depreciation. The company would realize cash flow equal to its depreciation for the year — assuming that it collected its sales revenue. Depreciation is a process of recycling fixed assets back into cash during the year, whether or not the business makes a profit. The problem is that net income does not usually turn into cash flow immediately.

In the example in the preceding section, the business earned $500,000 net income (profit). But its cash increased only $320,000. Why? The *cash flow statement* provides the details. In addition to reporting the depreciation for the year, the first part of the cash flow statement reports the short-term asset and liability changes caused by the sales and expenses of the business. These changes either help or hurt cash flow from profit. An increase in accounts receivable hurts cash flow from profit because the business did not collect all its sales on credit for the year. An increase in inventory hurts cash flow from profit because the business replaces the products sold and spends more money to increase its inventory of products. On the other hand, an increase in accounts payable or accrued liabilities helps cash flow from profit. These two liabilities are, basically, unpaid expenses. When these liabilities increase, the business did not pay all its expenses for the year — and its cash outflows for expenses were less than its expenses.

Generally speaking, growth hurts cash flow from profit. To grow its sales and profit, a business usually has to increase its accounts receivable and inventory. Some of this total increase is offset by increases in its accounts payable and accrued liabilities. Usually, the increase in assets is more than the increase in liabilities, and therefore cash flow from profit suffers. When a business suffers a decline in sales revenue, its bottom-line profit usually goes down — but its cash flow from profit may not drop as much as net income, or perhaps not at all. A business should decrease its accounts receivable and inventory at the lower sales level, and these decreases help cash flow from profit. Even if a business reported a loss for the year, its cash flow from profit could be positive because of the depreciation factor and because the business may have reduced its accounts receivable and inventory.

Call the Shots on Your Accounting Methods

Business managers too often defer to their accountants — who are not called "bean counters" and "digitheads" for no reason at all — in choosing accounting methods for measuring sales revenue and expenses. You should get involved in making these decisions. The best accounting method is the one that best fits the operating methods and strategies of the business. As a business manager, you know these operating methods and strategies better than your accountant. Chapter 13 gives you all the details on the various accounting methods.

For example, consider sales prices. How do you set your sales prices? Many factors affect your sales prices, of course. What I'm asking here concerns your general sales pricing policy relative to product cost changes. For example, if your product cost goes up, do you allow your "old" stock of these products to sell out before you raise the sales price? In other words, do you generally wait until you start selling some of the higher-cost products before you raise your sales price? If so, you are using the first-in-first-out sales price method. You might prefer to keep your cost of goods sold expense method consistent with your sales pricing method. But the accountant may choose the last-in-first-out expense method, which would mismatch the higher-cost products with the lower sales price products.

The basic point is this: Business managers formulate a basic strategy regarding expense recovery. Sales revenue has to recoup your expenses to make a profit. How do you pass along your expenses to your customers in the sales prices you charge them? Do you attempt to recover the cost of your fixed assets as quickly as possible and set your sales prices on this basis? Then you should use a quick depreciation method, which is called *accelerated* depreciation. On the other hand, if you have to take longer to recover the cost of your fixed assets through sales revenue, then you should probably use the longer-life *straight-line* depreciation method.

In short, I encourage you to take charge and choose the accounting methods that best fit your strategic profit plan. You need to speak some of the accounting language and know which accounting methods are available. This is comparable, for example, to deciding which type of retirement income plan to provide for your employees — a traditional pension (defined benefit) plan or the 401(k) (defined contribution) plan. You'd carefully compare the two alternatives, listen to the experts, and make a decision. You should do the same in deciding the key accounting methods for measuring profit. The bonus is that you will have a much better appreciation of how your profit measure depends on which accounting methods are used to measure sales revenue and expenses.

In short, business managers should take charge of the accounting function just like they take charge of marketing and other key functions of the business.

Build Better Budgets

Budgeting (description in Chapter 10) provides many important advantages — first, understand the profit dynamics and financial structure of your business, and second to plan for changes in the coming period. Budgeting forces you to focus on the factors that have to improve in order to increase profit and helps you prepare for the future. The basic profit model provides the framework for the profit budget. A good profit model is the essential starting point for budgeting. To develop your profit plan for the coming year, focus on

- ✔ Margins
- ✔ Sales volume
- ✔ Fixed expenses

The profit budget, in turn, lays the foundation for changes in your operating assets and liabilities that are driven by sales revenue and expenses. Suppose you project a 10 percent rise in sales revenue: How much will your accounts receivable asset increase? Suppose your sales volume target for next year is 15 percent higher than this year: How much will your inventory increase? The budgeted changes in sales revenue and expenses for next year lead directly to the budgeted changes in operating assets and operating liabilities. These changes, in turn, direct attention to two other key issues.

First, if things go according to plan, how much cash flow from profit will be generated? Second, will you need more capital, and where will you get this money? The budgeted cash flow from profit for the coming year is needed for three basic financial planning decisions:

- ✔ *Cash distributions from profit* to owners (cash dividends to stockholders of corporations and cash distributions to the shareholders of LLCs and to partners)

- ✔ *Capital expenditures* (purchases of new fixed assets, to replace and upgrade old fixed assets and to expand the resources of the business)

- ✔ *Raising capital* from borrowing on debt and, possibly, raising new equity capital from owners

The higher your budgeted cash flow from profit, the more flexibility you have in having money available for cash distributions from profit and for capital expenditures, and the less pressure to go out and raise new capital from debt and equity sources of capital.

To sum up, your profit budget is dovetailed with the assets and liabilities budget and the cash flow budget. Your accountant takes your profit budget (your strategic plan for improving profit) and builds the budgeted balance sheet and the budgeted cash flow statement. This information is essential for good planning — focusing in particular on how much cash flow from profit will be realized, and how much capital expenditures will be required, which in turn lead down to how much additional capital you have to raise and how much cash distribution from profit you are able to make.

Optimize Capital Structure and Financial Leverage

To make profit, you must make sales. And you must invest in operating assets, which means that you must raise capital. Where do you get this money? Debt and equity are the two basic sources. *Equity* refers to money owners invest in a business with the hopes that the business will turn a profit. Profit builds the value of owner's equity; profit fundamentally is an increase in assets that accrues to the benefit of the owners. Chapter 11 discusses ownership structures; Chapter 6 covers debt and equity.

The return of the owners' equity interest in the business consists of two quite distinct parts:

✔ Cash distributions from profit to the owners

✔ Increases in the value of their ownership interest in the business

In contrast, lenders are paid a *fixed* rate of interest on the amount borrowed. This fixed nature of interest expense causes a *financial leverage* effect that either benefits or hurts the amount of profit remaining for the equity investors in the business.

Financial leverage refers in general to using debt in addition to equity capital. A financial leverage gain (or loss) refers to the difference between the earnings before interest and tax (EBIT) that a business can make on its debt capital and the interest paid on the debt. The following typical example illustrates a case of financial leverage gain.

Your business earned $2.1 million EBIT for the year just ended. Your net assets are $12 million — recall that net operating assets equal total assets less non-interest-bearing operating liabilities (mainly accounts payable and accrued liabilities). Thus your total capital sources equal $12.0 million. Suppose you have $4.0 million debt. The other $8.0 million is owners' equity. You paid 8 percent annual interest on your debt, or $320,000 total interest.

Debt furnishes one-third of your capital, so one-third of EBIT is attributed to this capital source. One-third of EBIT is $700,000. But you paid only $320,000 interest for this capital. You earned $380,000 more than the interest. This is the amount of your pretax *financial leverage gain*.

Three factors determine financial leverage gain (or loss):

- ✔ Proportion of total capital provided from debt
- ✔ Interest rate
- ✔ Rate of EBIT the business can earn on its total capital

In the example, your business made 17.5 percent on its capital — $2.1 million EBIT ÷ $12.0 million total capital) — and your interest rate was 8.0 percent, which gives a favorable 9.5 percent spread (17.5 percent – 8.0 percent). The 9.5 percent favorable spread times $4 million debt equals the $380,000 leverage gain for the year.

Business managers should watch how much financial leverage gain contributes to the earnings for owners each year. In this example, the after-interest earnings for owners is $1,780,000 (equal to EBIT less interest expense). The $380,000 financial leverage gain provided a good part of this amount. Next year, one or more of the three factors driving the financial leverage gain may change. Savvy business managers sort out each year how much financial leverage impacts the earnings available for owners.

A financial leverage gain enhances the earnings on owners' equity capital. The conventional wisdom is that a business should take advantage of debt that charges a lower interest rate than it can earn on the debt capital. Looking at the bigger picture, however, the long-run success of a business depends mainly on maintaining and improving the factors that determine its profit from operations (EBIT) — not taking maximum advantage of financial leverage.

Develop Better Financial Controls

Experienced business managers can tell you that they spend a good deal of their time dealing with problems. Things don't always go according to plan. Murphy's Law (if something can go wrong, it will, and usually at the worst possible time) is all too true. To solve a problem, you first have to know that you have one. You can't solve a problem if you don't know about it. Managers are problem-solvers; they need to get on top of problems as soon as possible. In short, business managers need to develop good *financial controls*.

Financial controls act like trip wires that sound alarms and wave red flags for a manager's attention. Many financial controls are accounting-based. For example, actual costs are compared with budgeted costs or against last period's costs; serious variances are highlighted for immediate management attention. Actual sales revenue for product lines and territories are compared with budgeted goals or last period's numbers. Cash flow from profit month by month is compared with budget. These many different financial controls don't just happen. You should identify the handful of critical factors that you need to keep a very close eye on and insist that your internal accounting reports highlight these operating ratios and numbers. (See Chapter 10 for more on budgets.)

Only you, the business manager, can single out the most important numbers that you must closely watch to know how things are going. Your accountant can't read your mind. If your regular accounting reports do not include the exact types of control information you need, sit down with your accountant and spell out in specific detail what you want to know. Don't take no for an answer. Don't let your accountant argue that the computer doesn't keep track of this information. Computers can be programmed to spit out any type of information you want.

The accounting profit model discussed in Chapter 9 is a good place to start. You absolutely must closely watch the margins on your products. Any deviation from the norm — even a relatively small deviation — needs your attention immediately. Remember that the margin per unit is multiplied by sales volume. If you sell 100,000 units of a product, a slippage of just 50 cents causes your total margin to fall $50,000. Of course, sales volume must be closely watched, too; that goes without saying. Fixed expenses should be watched in the early months of the year to see whether these costs are developing according to plan — and through the entire year.

Accounts receivable collections should be monitored closely. Average days before collection is a good control ratio to keep your eye on, and you should definitely get a listing of past-due customers' accounts. Inventory is always a problem area. You should watch closely the average days in stock before products are sold and get a listing of slow-moving products. Experience is the best teacher. Over time, you learn which financial controls are the most important to highlight in your internal accounting reports. The trick is to make sure that your accountants provide this information.

Minimize Income Tax

The first decision regarding income tax concerns which type of legal ownership structure to use for carrying on the activities of the business, as discussed in Chapter 11. When two or more owners provide capital for the business, you have four basic choices:

- ✔ A *partnership* — a specific contractual agreement among the owners regarding division of management authority and profit

- ✔ A *limited liability company* (LLC), which has many characteristics of a partnership but is a separate legal person, like a corporation

- ✔ An *S corporation,* which has fewer than 75 stockholders (owners)

- ✔ A *regular* or *C corporation* that cannot qualify as an S corporation or that could qualify but its stockholders do not elect to do so

Partnerships, LLCs, and S corporations are *pass-through* tax entities. A pass-through business entity pays no tax on its taxable income but passes the obligation to its owners, who pick up their shares of the taxable income in their individual income tax returns. In contrast, stockholders of regular (C) corporations pay tax only on the amount of actual cash dividends from profit distributed by the corporation. However, the corporation pays an income tax based on its taxable income. Except for very small and very large businesses, the basic corporate tax rate in 1997 is 34 percent of taxable income. Factors other than income tax affect the choice of ownership structure. The advice of tax professionals and financial consultants is needed.

Regardless of the ownership structure, you should understand how accounting methods affect taxable income. Basically, the choice of accounting methods allows you to shift the timing of expenses — such as depreciation and cost of goods sold — between early years and later years. Do you want more expense deductions this year? Then choose the last-in-first-out (LIFO) method for cost of goods sold expense and an accelerated method for depreciation. But keep in mind that what you gain today, you lose tomorrow. The higher expense deductions in early years cause lower deductions in later years. Also, these income-tax-driven accounting choices make your inventory and fixed assets in your balance sheet look anemic. Remember that expenses are asset decreases. You want more expense? Then lower asset values are reported in your balance sheet.

Think twice before jumping on the income tax minimization bandwagon. Knowing about accounting methods and their effects in both the income statement and the balance sheet helps you to make these important decisions.

Explain Your Financial Statements to Others

On many occasions, a business manager has to explain his or her financial statements to others:

✔ When applying for a loan — especially when the loan officer asks specific questions about your accounting methods and items in your financial report

✔ When talking with people or other businesses who may be interested in buying your business — and they ask questions about the book values of your assets and your accounting methods to measure profit

✔ When dealing with the press — large corporations, of course, but even smaller business are profiled in local news stories

✔ When dealing with unions or other employee groups in setting new wages and benefit packages, who may think that your profits are very high so you can afford to increase wages and benefits — who generally have little appreciation for the cost of capital

✔ When explaining the profit-sharing plan to your employees — who may take a close interest in how profit is determined

✔ When putting a value on an ownership interest for divorce or estate tax purposes — a difficult time, but the lawyer or executor of the estate needs these values, which are based on the financial statements of the business

✔ When reporting financial statement data to national trade associations that collect this information from their members — you should make sure that you're reporting the financial information consistent with the definitions used in the industry

✔ When presenting the annual financial report before the annual meeting of owners — who ask very penetrating questions and expect you to be very familiar with the financial statements and basic accounting methods used to prepare them

Knowledge of financial statement reporting and accounting methods also is extremely useful when you sit on a bank's board of directors, or a hospital board, or any of several other types of oversight boards (university regents, for example). In the preceding list, you're the "explainer," the one who has to do the explaining. As a board member, you're the "explainee," the person who has to make sense of the financial statements and accounting methods being presented. A good accounting foundation is invaluable.

Chapter 8 shows you how to understand finanical reports. In brief, you need a good grip on the purpose, nature, and limitations of each of the three primary financial statements reported by a business:

✔ **The income statement:** Many people think that bottom-line profit is cash in the bank, but you know better than this.

✔ **The cash flow statement:** Many people just add back depreciation to net income to determine cash flow from profit, but you know better than this.

  ✔ **The balance sheet:** Many people think that this financial statement
   reports the current values for assets, but you know better than this.

I'll tell you one disadvantage of knowing some accounting: The other
members of the board will be very impressed with your accounting smarts
and will want to elect you chair of the board.

A Short Word on Massaging the Numbers: Don't!

I'm an accounting professor who teaches the business managers and CPAs
of tomorrow. I don't encourage profit smoothing, window dressing, and
other techniques for manipulating accounting numbers to make a
company's financial statements look better — no more than my marketing
professor colleagues encourage their students to engage in deceptive
advertising tactics. Yet these things go on, and I expose my students to
these pratices as a warning that accountants face difficult moral decisions.
In a similar vein, I caution you, the business manager, that you will surely
face pressures from time to time to massage the accounting numbers — to
make profit look smoother from year to year, or to make the short-term
solvency of the business look better (by window dressing).

You can always excuse this practice by saying that the other guys do it. Yes,
some big corporations do it, and some small companies do, too. Accountants know how to do it, and you can give them orders to make the accounting numbers look a little better. When taking a hard look at some other
business's financial statements, you should be on guard that the accounting
numbers have been massaged a little. My father-in-law calls this "fluffing the
pillows." I hope that you take the high ground and don't do it.

Chapter 17

Ten Questions Investors Should Ask When Reading a Financial Report

*Y*ou have only so much time to search for the most important signals in the financial report of a business. You could read a financial report like a book, from the first to the last page, but this approach is not very practical. For a quick read through a financial report — one that allows you to decode the critical signals in the financial statements — you need a checklist of key questions to ask. I advise you to look for answers to the following basic questions, which definitely help you understand what sort of investment you may be getting into — or, if you already have money invested in the business, the answers tell you how the company is doing, and whether you should consider pulling your hard-earned money out of the business and putting it in another investment.

Before reading the annual financial report of a business, you should get up to speed on which products and services the business sells — automobiles, computers, airlines, and heavy equipment manufacturers are quite different businesses, for example — and you should learn about the history of the business and any current problems facing the business. Is the business presently the target of a hostile takeover attempt? Is the business looking for a new CEO? Has the company recently shifted its strategy? One place to find much of this information is the company's annual 10K form filed with the Securities & Exchange Commission, which is a public document available to everyone. Company profiles are prepared by securities brokers and investment advisors, and they are very useful. *The Wall Street Journal* and other national newspapers, such as *The New York Times,* are good sources of information about larger corporations. Last but not least, annual financial reports often present an overview of the products and services sold by the business, although some businesses are stingy in presenting this information.

Did Sales Grow?

Ron, a friend of mine who owns a flower business in Denver, made a good comment to me one night: He said that a business makes profit by making sales. This statement hits the nail right on the head (although you do have to take controlling expenses into account). Sales growth is the key to long-run sustained profit growth.

Start reading a financial report by comparing this year's sales revenue with last year's, and with all prior years included in the report. A company's sales trend is the most important factor affecting its profit trend. I dare you to find a business that has had a steady downward sales trend line but a steady upward profit line — you'd be looking for a long time.

Did the Profit Ratios Hold?

Higher sales from one year to the next don't necessarily mean higher profit. You also need to look at whether the business was able to hold its profit ratio at the higher sales level. Recall that the *profit ratio* is net income divided by sales revenue. If the business earned, say, a 6 percent profit ratio last year, did it maintain or perhaps improve this ratio on its higher sales revenue this year?

Also look at the company's *gross margin ratios* from year to year. Cost of goods sold expense is reported by companies that sell products. Recall that gross margin equals sales revenue less cost of goods sold expense. Any significant slippage in a company's gross margin ratio (gross margin divided by sales revenue) is a very serious matter. Suppose that a company gives up two or three points (one point = 1 percent) of its gross margin ratio. How can it make up for this loss? Decreasing its other operating expenses isn't easy or very practical — unless the business had allowed its operating expenses to become bloated.

In most external financial reports, profit ratios are not discussed openly and frankly, especially when things have not gone well for the business. Usually, you have to go digging for these important ratios and use your calculator. Articles in the financial press on the most recent earnings of public corporations focus on profit ratios — for good reason. I always keep an eye on profit as a percentage of sales revenue, even though I have to calculate this key ratio for most businesses. I wish that all businesses would provide this ratio.

Were There Any Unusual Gains or Losses?

Every now and then, a business records an *unusual,* or *extraordinary,* gain or loss. The first section of the income statement reports sales revenue and the expenses of making the sales and operating the business. Also, interest and income tax expenses are deducted. Be careful: The profit down to this point may *not* be the final bottom line. The profit to this point is from the business's ongoing, normal operations before any unusual gains or losses are recorded. The next layer of the income statement reports these extraordinary, nonrecurring gains or losses that the business recorded during the period.

These gains or losses are called unusual or extraordinary because they do not recur — or at least should not recur, although some companies report these gains and losses on a regular basis. These gains and losses are caused by a *discontinuity* in the business — examples are a major organizational restructuring involving a reduction in the workforce and paying substantial severance packages to laid-off employees, selling off major assets and product lines of the business, retiring a huge amount of debt at a big gain or loss, and settling a huge lawsuit against the business, to name just a few such unusual developments. Generally, the gain or loss is reported on one line, but a brief explanation can be found in the footnotes to the financial statements.

Investors have to watch the pattern of these items over the years. A gain or loss now and then is a normal part of doing business and is nothing to be alarmed about. However, a business that reports one or two of these gains or losses every year or every other year is suspect. These may be evidence of past turmoil and future turbulence. I classify these businesses as high-risk investments — because you don't know what to expect in the future.

In any case, I advise you to ask whether an unusual loss is the cumulative result of poor accounting for expenses in previous years. A large legal settlement, for example, may be due to the business refusing to admit that it is selling unsafe products year after year; its liability finally catches up with it.

Did Earnings Per Share (EPS) Keep Up with Profit?

Suppose you own stock in a public corporation that reports bottom-line net income that is 10 percent higher than last year's. So far, so good. But you know that the market price of your stock shares depends on *earnings per share* (EPS) — which is equal to [total net income ÷ total number of stock shares]. You should ask: What happened to EPS? Did it also go up 10 percent? Not necessarily. You have to check.

Public corporations whose stock shares are traded on one of the national stock exchanges (New York Stock Exchange, Nasdaq, American Stock Exchange, and so on) are required by generally accepted accounting principles (GAAP) to report EPS in their income statements, so you don't have to do any computations. (Closely held businesses whose shares are not traded do not report EPS.)

EPS increases exactly the same percentage that net income increases only if the total number of stock shares remains constant. Usually, this is not true. If you look in the owners' equity section of a company's balance sheet, you'll often find that the business increased (or perhaps decreased) its total number of stock shares during the year. For example, some executives may have exercised their stock options during the year and bought some shares. Or employees may have bought shares under the company's stock purchase plan. Or the business may have issued stock shares in the acquisition of other businesses during the year.

Many public corporations have a fair amount of activity in their stock shares during the year. So they include a schedule or table of changes in stockholders' equity during the year. Look on this schedule to find out how many shares were issued during the year. Also, corporations may purchase some of their own stock during the year, which is reported in this schedule. If net income increases, say, 10 percent but EPS increases only 5 percent, you should definitely look into the reasons why so many additional shares of stock were issued. This may happen again next year and the year after.

 By and large, public corporations do not comment on whether EPS was diluted or dilated by an increase or decrease in its total number of stock shares during the year. You have to ferret out this information on your own, which I advise you to do.

 An increase in EPS may not be due entirely to an increase in net income, but rather to a decrease in the number of stock shares. Cash-rich companies often buy their stock shares to reduce the total number of shares that is divided into net income, thereby increasing EPS. You should pay close attention to increases in EPS that result from decreases in the number of stock shares. The long-run basis of EPS growth is profit growth, not a decrease in the number of stock shares.

Did the Profit Increase Generate a Cash Flow Increase?

Increasing profit is all well and good, but you also should ask: Did *cash flow from profit* increase? Cash flow from profit is found in the first section of the cash flow statement, which is one of the three primary financial statements included in a financial report. (The cash flow statement begins with an explanation of cash flow from profit.)

Accountants use the term *cash flow from operating activities* — which, in my opinion, is not nearly as descriptive as *cash flow from profit*. The term *profit* is avoided like the plague in external financial reports; it's not a politically correct word. So you may think that accountants would use the phrase *cash flow from net income*. But no, the official pronouncement on the cash flow statement mandated the term *cash flow from operating activities*. *Operating activities* refers simply to sales revenue and expenses, which are the profit-making operations of a business. I'll stick with *cash flow from profit* — please don't report me to the accounting authorities.

To start with, depreciation expense is not a cash outlay; depreciation is a cost recovery. Each year, a business converts some of the cost of its fixed assets back into cash through the cash collections from sales made during the year. Over time, fixed assets are gradually used up, so each year is charged with part of its fixed assets' cost by recording depreciation expense. And each year a business retrieves cash for part of the cost of its fixed assets. Thus depreciation expense decreases profit but increases cash flow. But net income plus depreciation does not equal cash flow from profit. Sorry, it's not that simple. The problem is that net income does not immediately increase a business's cash account by the same amount.

For example, some of a company' sales revenue for the year may still be in accounts receivable at year-end, so not all its sales revenue was collected by year-end. The business may have increased its inventory, which uses up cash. A business may have run up the balances of its unpaid expenses at year-end, which conserves cash. The first section of the cash flow statement summarizes these changes that affect cash flow from profit.

The key question is: Should cash flow change about the same amount as net income changed, or is it normal for the change in cash flow to be higher or lower than the change in net income?

As a general rule, sales growth penalizes cash flow from profit in the short run. A business has to build up its accounts receivable and inventory, and these increases hurt cash flow — although, during growth periods, a business also increases its accounts payable and accrued liabilities, which helps cash flow. The asset increases, in most cases, dominate the liability increases, and cash flow from profit suffers.

I strongly advise you to compare cash flow from operating activities (see, I use the officially correct term here) with net income for each of the past two or three years. Is cash flow from profit about the same percentage of net income each year? What does the trend look like? For example, last year, cash flow from profit might have been 90 percent of net income, but this year it may have dropped to only 50 percent. (You have to pull out your calculator and divide cash flow from profit by net income; businesses do not report this ratio.) In this situation, the company's profit is not being converted into cash flow at the same pace as it was the preceding year. Don't hit the panic button just yet.

A dip in cash flow from profit in one year actually may be good from the long-run point of view — the business may be laying down a good foundation for supporting a higher level of sales. But then again, the slowdown in cash flow from profit could present a short-term cash problem that the business has to deal with.

A company's cash flow from profit may be a trickle instead of a stream. This drains its cash reserves. The business may have to curtail its cash distributions to owners. And it may have to raise capital from debt and equity to provide money for replacing and expanding its fixed assets. Low cash flow from profit, in an extreme case, may even raise questions about the *quality of earnings,* which refers to the credibility and soundness of the net income reported by a business. Cash flow from profit is low, in most cases, because accounts receivable from sales haven't been collected and because the business has made large increases in its inventories. These large increases raise questions whether all the receivables will be collected and whether all the inventory will be sold at regular prices. Only time can tell. But, generally speaking, you should be more cautious and take the net income number that the business reports with a grain of salt.

Are Changes in Assets and Liabilities Consistent with the Business's Growth?

This question is at once apparent, yet investors often overlook it. The purpose of presenting a two-year comparative balance sheet is to make it relatively easy for you to evaluate the increases and decreases of assets and liabilities over the year and to compare these changes with the growth (or decline) of sales revenue. Businesses report a two- or three-year comparative income statement so that you can observe the trend of sales revenue and expenses from year to year. But don't stop there. You also should ask whether the increases of the company's operating assets and liabilities reported in its balance sheet are consistent with the sales growth of the business.

Suppose the business grew 10 percent last year. This doesn't mean that every operating asset and liability should increase precisely 10 percent. But then again, if the increase is too far off 10 percent, you should look more closely. Check to see whether the company's accounts receivable are growing at a faster rate than its sales revenue. If so, the company may be having trouble getting its customers to pay up, possibly because the customers aren't happy with the company's products or services. Or a big blimp in accounts receivable might mean that the business gave its customers more liberal credit terms this year.

Suppose inventory went up, say, 30 percent, but sales revenue increased only 10 percent. The business obviously bought or manufactured more products than it sold — quite a bit more. At the next annual stockholders meeting, I would definitely ask the CEO about this. And I would ask what the company plans to do next year to bring inventory back into line with sales.

Unusually large increases in assets that are greatly out of line with the company's sales revenue growth put pressure on cash flow and could cast serious doubts on the company's solvency — which I discuss next.

Are There Any Signs of Financial Distress? Can the Business Pay Its Liabilities?

A business can build up a good sales volume and have very good profit margins, but if the company can't pay its bills on time, its profit opportunities could go down the drain. *Solvency* refers to the prospects of a business being able to meet its debt and other liability payment obligations on time. Solvency analysis asks whether a business will be able to pay its liabilities, looking for signs of financial distress that could cause serious disruptions in the business's profit-making operations. In short, even if a business has a couple billion bucks in the bank, you should ask: How does its solvency look?

To be solvent does not mean that a business must have cash in the bank equal to its total liabilities. Suppose, for example, that a business has $2 million in non-interest-bearing operating liabilities (accounts payable and accrued liabilities), $1.5 million in short-term notes payable (due in less than one year), and $3.5 million in long-term debt (due over the next five years). Thus its total liabilities are $7 million. To be solvent, the business does not need $7 million in its checking account. In fact, this would be foolhardy.

A business uses the money from its liabilities to invest in *non-cash* assets that are needed to carry on its profit-making operations. For example, a business buys products on credit and holds these goods in inventory until it sells them. It borrows money to invest in its fixed assets. There's no point in having liabilities if all the money were kept in the bank. The purpose of having liabilities is to put the money to good use in assets other than cash.

Solvency analysis asks whether assets can be converted quickly back into cash so that liabilities can be paid on time. Will the assets generate enough cash flow to meet the liability payment obligations of the business as they come due?

Short-term solvency analysis looks two or three months into the future of the business. It focuses on the *current* assets of the business relative to its *current* liabilities, which are reported in the balance sheet. A rough measure of a company's short-term liability payment ability is its *current ratio* — current assets (cash, accounts receivable, inventory, and prepaid expenses) are divided by current liabilities (accounts payable and accrued liabilities for unpaid expenses, plus interest-bearing debt coming due in the next twelve months). A 2 to 1 current ratio usually is a reasonable benchmark for a business — but don't swallow this ratio hook, line, and sinker.

The current ratio does not have to be 2 to 1 for many businesses. Much depends on the products a business sells and the established financing practices in the industry. For example, auto dealers rely on very heavy short-term borrowing to carry their huge inventories of cars and light trucks. They survive and remain solvent on very low current ratios. Lenders know the financing needs of businesses they deal with, and they judge current ratios accordingly. A 2 to 1 current ratio is fairly conservative. Many businesses can get by on a lower current ratio without alarming their sources of short-term credit.

Business investors and creditors also look at a second solvency ratio called the *quick ratio*. This ratio includes only a company's quick assets — cash, accounts receivable, and short-term marketable investments (if the company has any). Quick assets are divided by current liabilities to determine the quick ratio. It's also called the *acid-test ratio* because it is a very demanding test to put on a business. More informally, it's called the *pounce ratio,* as if all the short-term creditors pounced on the business and demanded payment in short order.

Many consider a safe acid-test ratio to be 1 to 1 — $1 of quick assets for every $1 of current liabilities. However, be careful with this benchmark. It may not be appropriate for businesses that rely on heavy short-term debt to finance their inventories. For these companies, it is better to compare their quick assets with their quick liabilities and exclude their short-term notes payable that don't have to be paid until inventory is sold.

The current and acid-test ratios are relevant. But the solvency of a business depends mainly on the ability of its managers to convince creditors to continue extending credit to the business and renewing its loans. The credibility of management is the main factor, not ratios. Creditors understand that a business can get into a temporary bind and fall behind on paying its liabilities. As a general rule, creditors are slow to pull the plug on a business. Shutting off new credit may be the worst thing lenders and other creditors could do. This might put the business in a tailspin, and its creditors might end up collecting very little. Usually, it's not in their interest to force a business into bankruptcy.

Are There Any "Unusual" Assets and Liabilities?

One thing I do in reading a balance sheet is to look for out-of-the-ordinary assets and liabilities. These may be very legitimate, but I want to know what they are and whether they affect the profit of the business. The usual assets (to name the major ones) include accounts receivable, inventory, and fixed assets. The usual liabilities include accounts payable, accrued liabilities, short-term and long-term debt accounts, and, of course, the owners' equity accounts for capital invested by the owners and for retained earnings. Once you get off this beaten path, you never know what you'll discover.

Most businesses report a miscellaneous, catch-all account called "other assets." Who knows what might be included in here? If the balance in this account is not very large, trust that the CPA auditor did not let the business bury anything important in this account.

Marketable securities is the asset account used for investments in stocks and bonds (as well as other kinds of investments). Companies that have more cash than they need for their immediate operating purposes put the excess funds to work earning investment income rather than let the money lie dormant in a bank checking account. The accounting rules for marketable securities are fairly tight; you needn't have any concern about this asset.

If you encounter an asset or liability you're not familiar with, you should look in the footnotes to the financial statements, which present a brief explanation of what the accounts are and whether they affect profit accounting. (I know, you don't like reading footnotes; neither do I.) For example, many businesses have large liabilities for unfunded pension plan obligations for work done in the past by their employees. The liability reveals that the business has recorded this component of labor expense in determining its profit over the years. The liability will be a heavy demand on the future cash flow of the business.

How Are Assets Being Utilized?

Every business needs assets to make profit, and every business has to raise capital from debt and equity sources. Both have a cost — business managers should never lose sight of the *time cost of money*. Interest must be paid on debt, and net income must be earned on equity capital. A business has to make enough *earnings before interest and tax* (EBIT) to pay interest, pay income tax (unless it is a pass-through entity), and provide a residual net income that is sufficient for the amount of equity capital being used. Leaving land to lie fallow for a season or two may be smart farming, but business assets have to be put to good use all the time.

The overall test of how well assets are being used is the *asset turnover ratio*, which equals annual sales revenue divided by total assets. (You have to calculate this ratio; most businesses do not report this ratio in their financial statements, although a minority do.) This ratio tests the efficiency of using assets to make sales. Some businesses have low asset turnover ratios, less than 2 to 1. Some have very high ratios, such as 5 to 1. Each industry and retail sector in the economy has a standard asset turnover ratio, but these differ quite a bit from industry to industry and from sector to sector. There is no standard asset turnover ratio for all businesses. A supermarket chain couldn't make it if its annual sales revenue were only twice its assets. Capital-intensive heavy manufacturers, on the other hand, would be delighted with a 2 to 1 asset turnover ratio.

Financial report readers are wise to track a company's asset turnover ratio from year to year. If this ratio slips, the company is getting less sales revenue bang out of each buck of assets. If the company's profit ratio remains the same, it gets less profit out of each dollar of assets, which is not good news for equity investors in the business.

What Is the Return on Capital Investment?

I need a practical example to illustrate the *return on capital investment* questions you should ask. Suppose a business has $12 million total assets, and its accounts payable and accrued liabilities for unpaid expenses are $2 million. Thus its *net operating assets* — total assets less its non-interest-bearing operating liabilities — are $10 million.

I won't tell you the company's sales revenue for the year just ended. But I will tell you that its earnings before interest and tax (EBIT) were $1.32 million for the year. The basic question you should ask is this: How is the business doing relative to the total capital used to make this profit?

EBIT is divided by assets (net operating assets, in my way of thinking) to get the *return on assets* (ROA) ratio. In this case, the company earned 13.2 percent ROA for the year just ended:

```
$1,320,000 EBIT ÷ $10,000,000 net operating assets =
           13.2% ROA
```

Was this rate high enough to cover the interest rate on its debt? Sure; it's doubtful that the business had to pay a 13.2 percent interest rate. Now for the bottom-line question: How did the business do for its *owners,* who have a lot of capital invested in the business?

The business uses $4 million total debt, on which it pays 8 percent annual interest. Thus its total owners' equity is $6 million. The business is organized as a regular corporation that pays a combined 40 percent federal and state income tax on its taxable income.

Given the company's capitalization structure, its EBIT (or profit from operations) for the year just ended was divided three ways:

- ✓ **$320,000 interest on debt:** [$4,000,000 debt × 8% interest rate = $320,000]

- ✓ **$400,000 income tax:** [$1,320,000 operating earnings – $320,000 interest = $1,000,000 taxable income × 40% tax rate = $400,000 income tax]

- ✓ **$600,000 net income:** [$1,320,000 operating earnings – $320,000 interest – $400,000 income tax = $600,000 net income]

Net income is divided by owners' equity to calculate the *return on equity* (ROE) ratio, which in this example is

```
[$600,000 net income ÷ $6,000,000 owners' equity] = 10% ROE
```

Some businesses report their ROE ratios, but many don't — generally accepted accounting principles do not require the disclosure of ROE. In any case, as an investor in the business, would you be satisfied with the 10 percent return on your money?

You made only 2 percent more than the debtholders, which is not much of a premium for the additional risks you take on as an equity investor in the business. But you may predict that the business has a bright future and over time your investment will increase two or three times in value. In any case, ROE is a good point of reference — although this one ratio does not give you a final and conclusive answer regarding what to do with your capital. Reading Eric Tyson's *Investing For Dummies* (published by IDG Books Worldwide, Inc.) can help you make the best decision.

P.S. What Does the CPA Auditor Say?

One quick final postscript: What does the CPA auditor say? Large publicly owned businesses are legally required to have their annual financial reports audited by independent CPA firms who are elected by the stockholders. Many private businesses have their annual reports audited, even if the audit is not legally required. Smaller businesses may not have an audit but instead have a CPA review or compile their financial statements — in these cases, the CPA does not express an opinion of the financial statements. The business pays a lot of money for its audit, and you should read what the auditor has to say.

The auditor's report is attached to the financial statements, sometimes right before the statements or, alternately, following the footnotes. I'll be frank: The wording of the auditor's report is tough going. Talk about jargon! In any case, the last of the three paragraphs is the one to read.

Look for the key words *fairly present*. These code words mean that the auditors have no serious disagreement with how the business prepared its financial statements. If the auditors cannot give this so-called clean opinion, they say so in a fourth paragraph explaining their concerns. A fourth paragraph is the tip-off; read the fourth paragraph. Only in the most desperate situations would the auditor give an adverse opinion, which in essence says that the financial statements are misleading. But short of this, the auditor may have reservations about the financial statements that you should take note of. In particular, the auditor may express some doubt about the business being able to continue as a going concern. The solvency ratios discussed earlier should have already tipped you off. When the auditor mentions it, things are pretty serious.

Appendix A

Glossary: Slashing through the Accounting Jargon Jungle

· ·

accelerated depreciation: One of two basic methods for allocating the cost of a *fixed asset* over its useful life and estimating the useful life. Accelerated depreciation means taking a greater amount of depreciation in early years and lower amounts in later years, and also using shorter life estimates. See also *straight-line depreciation*.

accounting: The procedures for recording, accumulating, and analyzing relevant information about the financial activities of a business and preparing summary reports of these activities. Business managers and owners use summary accounting reports called *financial statements* to make intelligent and informed business decisions.

accounting equation: Assets = Liabilities + Owners' Equity. This basic equation is the foundation for *double-entry accounting* and reflects the relationship between a business's assets and the sources of its assets, which are liabilities and owners' capital.

accounts payable: Short-term liabilities representing the amounts owed to vendors or creditors for the purchase of products, supplies, parts, or services that were bought on credit, which do not bear interest (unless the business takes too long to pay).

accounts receivable: A short-term asset representing the amount due for the credit sale of products and services to customers. Customers are not normally charged interest, unless they do not pay a bill when it is due.

acid-test ratio: See *quick ratio*.

accrued liabilities: Short-term liabilities that arise from the gradual buildup of unpaid expenses, such as vacation pay earned by employees or profit-based bonus plans that aren't paid until the following year.

accumulated depreciation: Refers to the total, cumulative amount of annual depreciation expense that has been recorded since the fixed asset being depreciated was acquired. The amount in this account is deducted from the cost of the fixed asset in the balance sheet. The purpose is to report how much of the total cost of fixed assets has been depreciated over the years. Be careful of this term.

accrual basis accounting: The accounting method that records revenues at the time sales are made (rather than when the cash is actually received from customers) and records expenses when they're incurred (rather than when the liabilities for the expenses are paid). Profit measurement demands accrual basis accounting for almost all businesses. A business that sells products and holds inventory must use this basis of accounting.

annual percentage rate (APR): The annual interest rate that you pay for credit or for borrowing money. You use the APR as a starting point for determining the *effective interest rate*.

asset turnover ratio: The measure of how effectively assets are used during a sales period. To find the asset turnover ratio, divide annual sales revenue by net operating assets, which are total assets less short-term, non-interest-bearing operating liabilities.

bad debts: An expense that arises from a customer's failure to pay the amount owed to the business from a prior credit sale. Tax law requires a business to show clear-cut evidence that the customers will not pay the debt, after which the bad debt is recorded against the specific customer's receivables and the amount is written off.

balance sheet: The financial statement that summarizes the assets, liabilities, and owners' equity of a business at a specific moment in time. Prepared at the end of each profit period, and whenever needed, the balance sheet shows a company's overall financial position.

book value (of assets): Refers to the recorded balance (amount) of an asset — usually to emphasize that the amount in the accounts maintained by the business may be less than the current replacement cost of the assets.

book value (of owners' equity, in total or per share): Refers to the *balance sheet* value of owners' equity, either in total or on a per-share basis for corporations. Book value of owners' equity is not necessarily the price someone would pay for the business as a whole, but it is a useful reference point.

break-even point: The annual sales volume at which total *contribution profit margin* from profit margin per unit times sales volume equals total annual *fixed expenses* (that is, the sales volume at which the business has covered its fixed expenses and begins to earn profit on additional sales). An important point of reference for management analysis.

budgeting: The process of estimating expenses and revenues and adopting a profit strategy for the coming financial period, as well as estimating the assets, liabilities, and cash flow for the forecast level of sales and expenses. Actual performance during the period can be compared against budgeted goals to determine progress or lack of progress; or the budget can be used only for general planning purposes, especially regarding additional capital that will be needed for growth.

burden rate: A key product cost component for manufacturers. The burden rate is the fixed manufacturing cost allocated to each unit produced, calculated by dividing the total fixed manufacturing costs for the period by the total production output.

capital expenditures: The total amount spent for the purchase and construction of new fixed assets to replace old ones, or to expand and modernize a business's long-term operating assets. Fixed assets have useful lives from 3 to 39 (or more) years, depending on the nature of the asset and how it's used in the operations of the business.

capital stock: The certificates of ownership issued by corporations for capital invested in the business by owners, which is divided into units called *shares of capital stock.* Holders of capital stock shares participate in cash dividends from profit, voting in board member elections, rights to asset liquidation proceeds, and several other rights. A business corporation must issue at least one class of capital stock called *common stock.* It may also issue other classes of stock, such as *preferred stock.* Both common and preferred capital stock shares of public corporations are traded on the New York Stock Exchange and over NASDAQ.

cash flow: In general, refers to cash inflows and outflows during a financial period. Frequently used as a shorthand phrase for *cash flow from profit.* The *cash flow statement* classifies cash flows into three different categories. Cash flow comes from *operating activities* (that is, profit-making activities), from *investing activities,* or from *financing activities.*

cash flow from profit: Also called *cash flow from operating activities.* Equals *net income* for the period, adjusted for changes in short-term operating assets, liabilities, and depreciation expense. Some people call this *free cash flow* to emphasize that this source of cash is free from the need to borrow money, issue capital stock shares, or sell assets. The term *free cash flow* is also used to denote cash flow from profit, less *capital expenditures.* (Some writers deduct cash dividends also, so be careful when you see this term; usage has not completely settled down yet.)

cash flow statement: This financial statement summarizes cash inflows and outflows that occur during a period according to a threefold classification: *cash flow from profit* (operating activities), investing and disinvesting activities, and financing activities, which refers to borrowing and repaying debt, raising and retiring capital from owners, and distributing profit to them.

certified public accountant (CPA): The CPA designation is a widely recognized and respected badge of a professional accountant. A person must meet the educational and experience requirements and pass a national uniform exam to get a state license to practice as a CPA. Many CPAs are not in public practice; they work for business organizations, government agencies, and nonprofit organizations. CPAs in public practice do audits of financial statements and also provide tax and management consulting services.

chart of accounts: The official, designated set of accounts used by a business that constitute its *general ledger,* in which the transactions of the business are recorded. These accounts must be used, unless the chief accounting officer of the organization (the Controller) authorizes new accounts to be added to the list.

common stock: The class of capital stock that must be issued by business corporations. It has the most junior, or residual, claim on the business's assets in the event of liquidation, after all liabilities and any senior capital stock, called *preferred stock,* are paid. Common stock has voting rights in the election of the board of directors, although a business may issue both voting and nonvoting classes of common stock. Common stock receives dividends from profit after preferred stockholders (if any) are paid.

compound interest: Interest *compounds* when you don't withdraw interest income but instead add it back to your account (into a savings account, for example). Thus you have a bigger balance on which to earn interest the following period. Interest also compounds on money that you owe: Each month, any unpaid interest is added to your loan or credit balance, on which next month's interest is computed.

contribution profit margin: Equals sales revenue minus the cost of goods sold and all *variable expenses* (contribution profit margin is calculated before *fixed expenses* are deducted). On a per-unit basis, contribution profit margin equals sales price less *product cost* per unit and less variable operating expenses per unit. Contribution profit margin is an exceedingly important profit measure for analyzing profit behavior and for making sales price decisions.

Controller: The chief accounting officer of a business organization. The controller may also serve as the chief financial officer, although in larger corporations the two jobs are usually split.

cooking the books: Refers to any one of several different fraudulent accounting schemes used to overstate profit and to make one's financial condition look better than it really is. Cooking the books is different from *profit smoothing* and *window dressing,* which are tolerated in financial statements. Cooking the books for income tax is just the reverse: It means overstating, or exaggerating, deductible expenses or understating revenue to minimize taxable income. *Warning:* Cooking the books for income tax can lead to a criminal conviction for tax evasion, which is a felony.

cost of capital: The *interest* that you pay on debt capital; also refers to the net income goal that a business should earn to justify the owner's equity capital that it uses. Interest is a contractually set amount of interest; no set amount of net income is promised to owners.

current assets: The sum total of a company's cash, *accounts receivable, inventory,* and *prepaid expenses* (and marketable securities if the business owns any). These assets can be converted into cash during one *operating cycle.* Current assets are compared with current liabilities to calculate the *current ratio.*

current liabilities: The sum of *accounts payable* and *accrued liabilities,* plus any *short-term notes payable*, *income tax payable*, and the portion of long-term debt that falls due within the coming year. This group includes both non-interest bearing and non-interest-bearing liabilities that must be paid in the short-term, usually defined to be one year or less. Current liabilities are divided into current assets to calculate the *current ratio.*

current ratio: Ratio that assesses a business's short-term solvency (debt-paying capability). Find the current ratio by dividing *current assets* by total *current liabilities.* (See also *quick ratio.*)

debits and credits: Refer to the decreases and increases recorded in assets, liabilities, owners' equity, revenue, and expenses. When recording a transaction, the total of the debits must equal the total of the credits. The rules for what's a debit and what's a credit stem from the *accounting equation.* "The books are in balance" means that the sum of debit balance accounts equals the sum of credit balance accounts. Even so, accounting errors happen when transactions are not recorded or are recorded with the wrong amounts.

depreciation expense: Allocating (or *spreading out*) a fixed asset's cost over the estimated useful life of the asset. Each year of the asset's life is charged with part of its total cost as the asset gradually wears out and loses its economic value to the business. For income tax purposes, an *accelerated depreciation* method is generally preferred over the *straight-line depreciation.* Both are acceptable methods; a choice must be made. ***Note:*** Only the straight-line method is allowed for buildings.

dilution of stock share value: An increase in the number of stock shares issued by a business corporation (such as stock options granted to managers) that causes the value per share to decrease or to be lower than it would be without the higher number of shares.

dividend yield: A measure of the cash income component of the return on investment in stock shares of a corporation. The dividend yield equals the most recent 12 months of cash dividends paid on a stock, divided by the stock's current market price. If a stock is selling for $100.00 and over the last 12 months has paid $3.00 cash dividends, its dividend yield is 3.0 percent.

double-entry accounting: Keeping accounts for both sides of the *accounting equation,* that is, both the assets of a business and the sources of the assets (which are also claims on the assets of one sort or another). Every business accounts for its assets (which are reported on the left or top side of the balance sheet) and its liabilities and owners' equity (which are reported on the right or bottom side).

earnings before interest and tax (EBIT): Sales revenue less cost of goods sold and all operating expenses — but before deducting interest on debt capital and income tax expenses. The measure of profit also is called *operating earnings, operating profit,* or something similar; terminology is not uniform.

earnings per share (EPS): Equals *net income* (bottom-line profit) for the year divided by the number of capital stock shares of a business corporation. EPS is a key reference point for judging the market value of stock shares issued by publicly owned corporations.

effective interest rate: The true interest rate per period — which is that rate multiplied by a loan or savings balance to determine the amount of interest for that period. The effective interest rate is determined by dividing the quoted *annual percentage rate* (APR) by the number of periods for which interest is computed during the year. For example, if the APR is quoted at 12.0 percent and interest is figured quarterly, the effective quarterly interest rate is 3.0 percent.

equity capital: See *owners' equity.*

external financial statements: The financial statements included in financial reports that are distributed outside the business to stockholders and debtholders (who are entitled to a periodic accounting on the financial performance of the business). Internal financial statements, although based on the same accounting methods, are prepared differently and disclose more detail, which management needs for control and decision-making.

Financial Accounting Standards Board (FASB): The highest authoritative standard-setting body of the accounting profession in the United States. The FASB issues statements that establish new *generally accepted accounting principles (GAAP)* and that modify previous standards. These pronouncements on accounting standards and accounting methods are very technical and are written by CPAs for other CPAs. CPA firms offer digests of new FASB statements in their client newsletters, and many are covered in articles in *The Wall Street Journal.*

financial leverage: Refers to using debt in addition to equity capital to provide the money for a business's *net operating assets.* The strategy is to earn a rate of *return on assets (ROA)* higher than interest rate on the borrowed money. A favorable spread between the two rates generates *financial leverage* gain. The term *financial leverage* is applied generally to mean using debt capital on top of equity capital.

financial statement: The generic term for *balance sheet, cash flow statement,* and *income statement,* all three of which present summary financial information about a business (or other type of organization). Sometimes financial statements are called simply "financials."

first-in-first-out (FIFO): One of two widely used accounting methods by which costs of products as they are sold are charged to cost of goods sold expense in chronological order, so the most recent product costs are in ending inventory. However, the reverse order also is acceptable, which is called the *last-in-first-out (LIFO)* method.

fixed assets: The shorthand term for the long-life (generally three years or longer) operating assets used by a business, which includes land, buildings, machinery, equipment, tools, and vehicles. The most common account title for these assets in a balance sheet is *property, plant, and equipment.*

fixed expenses (costs): Any expense or cost that remains the same over the short run and does not vary with changes in sales volume or sales revenue — building rent under lease contracts, salaries of employees, property taxes, and monthly telephone bills are common examples. Fixed operating expenses provide *capacity* for carrying out operations and for making sales. Fixed manufacturing costs provide production capacity.

free cash flow: Cash flow from profit (operating activities) less capital expenditures for the period. *Caution:* This term is relatively new, and not everyone uses it in exactly the same way; some people equate it with cash flow from profit and do not deduct capital expenditures.

generally accepted accounting principles (GAAP): The authoritative standards and approved accounting methods used by businesses and private nonprofit organizations to measure and report their revenue and expenses (and therefore profit) and to present their assets, liabilities, and owners' equity in their financial statements.

going-concern assumption: The assumption that a business will continue in operation and will not be forced to liquidate its assets.

goodwill: Goodwill has two different meanings, so be careful. The term can refer to the product name recognition and excellent reputation of a business that provide a strong competitive advantage. Goodwill in this sense means the business has an important but invisible "asset" that is not reported in its balance sheet. Second, a business may purchase and pay cash for the goodwill that has been built up over the years by another business. Only in this case does purchased goodwill show up as an asset in the balance sheet.

gross margin (profit): Equals sales revenue less cost of goods sold for the period. On a per-unit basis, the gross margin equals the unit sales price less the per-unit product cost.

imputed cost: An hypothetical cost used as a benchmark for comparison. One example is the imputed cost of equity capital. No expense is recorded for using owners' equity capital during the year. However, in judging net income performance, the company's rate of *return on equity (ROE)* is compared with the rate of earnings that could be earned on the same amount of capital if it were invested elsewhere. This alternate rate of return is an imputed cost.

income statement: The *financial statement* that summarizes sales revenue and expenses for a period and reports one or more *profit* lines. Also, unusual gains and losses are reported in this financial statement. The income statement is one of the three primary financial statements of a business.

internal (accounting) controls: Additional accounting forms and procedures established to detect and deter errors and fraud (beyond what would be required for normal accounting record-keeping). Common internal control procedures include requiring the signature of two managers to approve a transaction, conducting searches at entry and exit points, using surveillance cameras, and conducting surprise inventory counts.

internal financial statements: The *financial statements* prepared for use by managers to help them carry out their decision-making and control. The detailed information needed in these statements is confidential and is not circulated outside the business. Internal management income statements focus on *profit margin* and sales volume and separate variable from fixed expenses.

last-in-first-out (LIFO): One of two widely used accounting methods by which costs of products as they are sold are charged to cost of goods sold expense in *reverse* chronological order, so the ending inventory consists of the costs of the first goods purchased or manufactured. However, the opposite order is also acceptable, which is called the *first-in-first-out (FIFO)* method. The actual physical flow of products seldom follows a LIFO order. The method is justified on the grounds that the cost of goods sold expense should be the cost of replacing the products sold, and the best approximation is the most recent acquisition costs of the products.

LIFO liquidation gain: A unique result of the *last-in-first-out (LIFO)* method, that happens when fewer units are replaced than sold during the period. The inventory decrease requires the accountant to go back into the old cost layers of products for some of the cost of goods sold expense. Thus, there is a one-time windfall gain in *gross margin,* roughly equal to the difference between the historical cost and the current replacement cost of the inventory decrease. A material LIFO liquidation gain is disclosed in a footnote to the financial statements.

lower of cost or market (LCM): A special rule applied to inventory, that can result in a write-down and charge to expense for the loss in value. The costs of products in ending inventory are compared with their current replacement costs *(market price)*. If the market price is lower, the recorded cost is written down to this lower cost value. ***Note:*** Inventory is not written up when replacement costs rise after the inventory was acquired.

margin of safety: Equals the excess of actual sales volume over the company's *break-even* sales volume; often expressed as a percent. This information is used internally by managers and is not disclosed in *external financial statements.*

net income: Equals sales revenue less all expenses for the period; also includes any extraordinary gains and losses for the period. All revenues and expenses are taken into account to compute net income, which is commonly called the *bottom line.* Alternate titles are *net earnings* or just *earnings.*

net operating assets: The total assets used in operating a business, less *accounts payable* and *accrued liabilities* (and less income tax payable, if any). Suppose a business's total net operating assets are $25 million. Thus, the company must have raised $25 million total capital from interest-bearing debt and equity sources of capital. (See also *return on assets [ROA]* and *return on equity [ROE].*)

operating assets: The several different assets used in the profit-making operations of a business. Includes cash, *accounts receivable* from making sales on credit, *inventory* of products awaiting sale, *prepaid expenses,* and various *fixed assets.* The company's short-term, non-interest-bearing operating liabilities are deducted from its total operating assets to get its *net operating assets.* A business may have other assets not essential to its mainstream sales and expense operations. For example, a business may invest its excess cash in marketable securities or real estate.

operating cycle: The sequence of producing or acquiring inventory, holding it, selling it on credit, and finally collecting the account receivable. It also refers to the "cash-to-cash" cycle — investing cash in inventory, then selling the products on credit, and then collecting the receivable. A business wants to end up with more cash than it started with.

operating earnings (profit): See *earnings before interest and tax (EBIT).*

operating liabilities: Short-term liabilities generated spontaneously in the profit-making operations of a business. The most common ones are *accounts payable, accrued liabilities,* and income tax payable — none of which are interest bearing unless a late payment penalty has to be paid, which is in the nature of interest.

opportunity cost: An economic concept that refers to the *alternative* use of money, time, or talent foregone by taking a particular course of action. Suppose you earn $100,000 on your money, time, and effort. Suppose you could have earned, say, $85,000 if you had followed the next best alternative.

The opportunity cost is the $85,000 that you gave up by following the course of action you did. Your "real" economic profit is the $15,000 you gained by choosing the best alternative.

overhead costs: Those sales and administrative expenses or manufacturing costs that have two main characteristics: (1) They are _indirect_ and cannot be matched or linked with a particular product, revenue source, or organizational unit — such as the annual property tax on the building in which all the company's activities are carried out; and (2) With few exceptions, they are _fixed_ and cannot be decreased over the short run — such as the general liability insurance carried by a business. Although they are indirect and fixed, _manufacturing_ overhead costs must be allocated among products produced during the period in order to account for the full cost of each product. Non-manufacturing overhead costs may be allocated, but they do not have to be unless the allocation helps management in some way.

owners' equity: Refers to the ownership capital invested in a business. Owners' equity derives from two sources: investment of capital in the business by the owners (for which _capital stock_ shares are issued by a corporation) and profit that has been earned by the business but not distributed to its owners (called _retained earnings_ for a corporation). (See also _accounting equation._)

pass-through tax entity: Taxable income from a business _passes through_ to its owners, who include their respective shares of taxable income on their personal income tax returns. Sole proprietorships and partnerships are pass-through tax entities. Limited liability companies (LLCs) and corporations with 75 or fewer stockholders (called S corporations) can elect to be treated as a pass-through tax entity.

preferred stock: A second class or type of capital stock that may be issued by a business corporation in addition to its _common stock._ Preferred stock derives its name from the fact that it has certain preferences over the junior common stock — preferred stock is paid cash dividends before any can be distributed to the common stockholders, and in the event of liquidating the business, preferred stock is redeemed before any money is returned to the common stockholders. Preferred stock usually does not have voting rights, however.

prepaid expenses: Expenses that are paid in advance. The cash outlay for these future expenses is entered in the _prepaid expenses_ asset account. For example, a business writes a $60,000 check today for fire insurance coverage over the following six months. The cost is first entered in the asset account; then, each month, $10,000 is taken out of the asset and charged to expense. Though significant, prepaid expenses are smaller than the balances in a business's inventory and accounts receivable asset accounts.

price/earnings (P/E) ratio: The current market price of equity (capital stock) shares divided by *earnings per share (EPS)*. A low P/E may signal an undervalued stock or a pessimistic forecast by investors. A high P/E may reveal an overvalued stock or may be based on an optimistic forecast by investors.

product cost: Equals the purchase cost of goods for retailers and wholesalers (distributors). In contrast, a manufacturer factors in three different types of production costs to determine product cost: direct materials, direct labor, and manufacturing *overhead costs.* Overhead costs are allocated to different products in order to account for the full cost of making products.

profit: A general term that is not that well defined. It may mean gains less losses, or inflows less outflows, or some other kinds of increases minus decreases. In business, the term means sales revenue (or other sources of operating income) minus expenses for a period of time, such as one year. In an *income statement,* the final or bottom line of profit is called *net income,* which equals sales revenue (plus any extraordinary gains) less all expenses (and less any extraordinary losses) over the period.

profit and loss statement: An alternate title for the *income statement,* which may be used internally by a business but not in its external financial reports to investors. The title was used in external financial reports some years ago, but it is not used today. Also, the term *P&L* is tossed around loosely to refer to the profit or loss aspects of a venture or when referring to the profit performance of a product line or a specific investment.

profit ratio: Equals *net income* divided by sales revenue. Measures bottom-line net income as a percentage of sales revenue. A closely watched ratio by both business managers and investors.

profit (income) smoothing: A practice for manipulating the timing of recording sales revenue and/or expenses on the books in order to report a smoother profit trend from year to year. Investors prefer steady trend lines instead of fluctuating ones.

quick ratio: Also called the *acid-test ratio.* Ratio of the total of *cash, accounts receivable,* and *marketable securities* (if any), divided by total *current liabilities.* This ratio measures the capability of a business to pay off its current short-term liabilities with cash and near-cash assets. Note that inventory and prepaid expenses, the other two current assets, are excluded from assets in this ratio.

retained earnings: One of two basic sources of owners' equity for a business (the other being the capital invested by the owners). Annual profit *(net income)* increases this account and distributions of profit to owners decreases the account. ***Caution:*** Retained earnings does not refer to cash or any particular asset. This is a common misconception. In fact, a business could have a small cash balance but a very large retained earnings balance — you often see this situation.

return on assets (ROA): Equals *earnings before interest and tax (EBIT)* divided by the *net operating assets* (or by total assets, for convenience) and is expressed as a percentage. The ROA rate is the basic test of how well a business is using its assets so that it can pay the interest rate on its debt and can generate a satisfactory rate of *return on equity (ROE)* for its owners.

return on equity (ROE): Equals *net income* divided by the total *book value* of owners' equity. ROE is expressed as a percent. ROE is the basic measure of how well a business is doing in providing a return on the owners' capital investment in the business.

return on investment (ROI) ratio: This term refers to the income, profit, gain, or earnings on capital investment, expressed as a percentage of the amount of invested capital. The most relevant ROI ratios for a business are *return on assets (ROA)* and *return on equity (ROE)*.

sales revenue–driven expenses: Operating expenses that vary in proportion to changes in total sales *revenue* (total dollars). Examples are sales commissions, credit card discount expenses, and rent expense and franchise fees based on total sales revenue. (Compare with *sales volume–driven expenses*.)

sales volume–driven expenses: Operating expenses that vary in proportion to changes in sales *volume* (quantity of products sold). Examples include delivery costs, packaging costs, and other costs that depend mainly on the number of products sold or the number of customers served. (Compare with *sales revenue–driven expenses*.)

straight-line depreciation: Spreading the cost of a fixed asset to depreciation expense over its useful life by allocating an equal amount to each year. Depreciation is the same amount every year by this method. Although this method has a lot of intuitive appeal and must be used to depreciate the cost of buildings for income tax, for their other fixed assets many businesses select an *accelerated depreciation* method both for income tax and financial reporting.

variable expenses (costs): Any expense or cost that changes in direct proportion with changes in sales volume or sales revenue. (See also *sales revenue–driven expenses* and *sales volume–driven expenses*.) In contrast, *fixed expenses (costs)* do not change over the short run in response to changes in sales activity.

window dressing: Accounting techniques that can make the short-term liquidity and solvency of a business look better than it really is. One common trick is to hold the books open a few business days after the close of the accounting year in order to record additional cash receipts (as if the cash collections had occurred on the last day of the year).

Appendix B
Accounting Software

*L*arge business organizations write their own computer accounting programs, which contain thousands and thousands of lines of instructions and computer code. Fortunately, those of you who don't have computer programmers on your staff (or the money to pay for outside professional programmers) can buy a simple, ready-to-use accounting program right off the shelf. You can find accounting software at your favorite computer store or in your favorite mail-order computer catalog. That's the good news.

The bad news is that you have to decide *which* accounting software package is best for your particular business. Because quite a few good programs are on the market, you should consider your business needs in order to narrow down your choices. For example, if you have three kids and two dogs to haul around, you probably steer clear of the snazzy sports-car section of the car lot. Likewise, if you run a no-frills, straightforward business operation, you probably don't need many of the features that the fancy software packages offer.

The following list gives you some general pointers for narrowing down your choices and deciding which accounting software package is right for your business:

✔ **Get your bookkeepers or accountants involved in the selection process early on.** They know which features are most critical for your business, even though they may not know all the technical points about computers and software. They're the ones who will have to use the software and make it work for your business. Input from your accounting people can help you decide what features you need from an accounting software package.

✔ **Make a list of the features that you need.** Some accounting programs intended for small businesses are designed around a "typical" business and may not support the accounting needs of a particular business. For example, if you collect sales taxes, you need to make sure that the software program supports sales tax collection and remittance to the tax agencies. Or if you're a contractor who bases each job on a custom order, you need an accounting program that includes *job order* accounting.

✔ **Get a software recommendation from your business friends and associates who are already using an accounting program (or have your accountant talk with their accountants).** This step is possibly the most important. Try to get a feel for how much work *they* went through in picking out, setting up, and actually using the software. Zero in on the particular strengths and weaknesses that they've discovered in the accounting program that they're using. (There's no substitute for their actual, on-the-job experience.) Keep your ears peeled for any problems they've had that may be particularly troublesome in your own business.

✔ **Pay attention to the features and flexibility of the accounting program.** For example, how much customization of source documents and financial statements does the program allow? You want a certain amount of flexibility to tailor forms and formats to your needs. On the other hand, you may be intimidated by the idea of customizing accounting forms, so a program with plenty of ready-made forms may be right for you. Also, the program's capability to leave good *audit trails* (documentation that you'd need if audited) is important.

✔ **Check whether the software comes with a good user's manual and other documentation.** The trend these days is to put most or all of the help information in the software itself, meaning that the program needs to be up and running in order for you to access the help information. That can be a little intimidating to people who aren't all that comfortable with computers. Consider your staff members who will be using the software and decide how important an old-fashioned paper manual is to your business.

✔ **Consider how simple or difficult the program is to set up.** Although the initial cost of the software may not be a factor for you (all the accounting programs that I list here sell for a couple hundred bucks or less), be sure to consider the cost and time required to get the software up and running. Don't underestimate how daunting the task of entering all your company's accounts into a new software program can be. Some accounting programs get higher marks than others for ease of setup.

Some authorized software dealers offer setup assistance. Of course, you have to pay for the assistance — either in the price of the software or as an add-on fee.

Some software comes on CD-ROM (compact disc) rather than floppy disks, which saves you time installing the software — but it doesn't do you much good if your computer system doesn't have a CD-ROM drive, so make sure that you get the right format for your computer.

One option is to use a computer consultant (such as a CPA with the appropriate experience) to help you choose the right software package and to help you with the initial setup of the software. This option is certainly less expensive than hiring professional programmers to write a program based on your business's needs, but you may want to try a do-it-yourself approach first, before paying for outside help. You can find computer consultants in the Yellow Pages. The best consultant for your needs is a qualified expert who has experience in implementing accounting software in businesses like yours.

Here's a list of seven popular accounting software programs (for Windows 3.1 or Windows 95 operating systems) to get you started on your search for the perfect program for you. I include the name of the software company, its Web address (which is in a font like this), its toll-free telephone number, and the suggested retail price of the program. (Prices may vary, so check with the manufacturer for the current price.) Some manufacturers have Macintosh versions, but you have to inquire:

- **DacEasy Accounting & Payroll 95:** DacEasy; www.daceasy.com; phone 800-322-3279: $150

- **Mind Your Own Business Accounting (MYOB):** BestWare; www.bestware.com; phone 800-322-6962; $134.95 (includes payroll functions)

- **One-Write Plus:** NEBS Software; www.nebs.com; phone 800-388-8000; $89.95

- **Peachtree Accounting for Windows:** Peachtree Software; www.peachtree.com; phone 800-228-0068; $129

- **Profit:** Great Plains; www.gps.com; phone 800-926-8962; $99 to $299 (depending on the version of software and level of technical support that you purchase)

- **QuickBooks and QuickBooks Pro:** Intuit; www.intuit.com; phone 800-224-0991; $99.95 for QuickBooks; $199.95 for QuickBooks Pro

- **Simply Accounting:** ACCPAC International; www.accpac.com; phone 800-773-5445, $129

Before taking the accounting software plunge, you or your accountant should check out any of the popular personal computer magazines for reviews of the latest versions of accounting software packages. These reviews are generally the best place to start — they point out the strengths and any serious limitations of the various programs, any special hardware requirements, and the program's relative ease of installation.

Index

• *C* •

• *J* •

• S •

Notes

Notes

WWW.DUMMIES.COM

Discover *Dummies*™ Online!

The *Dummies* Web Site is your fun and friendly online resource for the latest information about *...For Dummies*® books on all your favorite topics. From cars to computers, wine to Windows, and investing to the Internet, we've got a shelf full of *...For Dummies* books waiting for you!

Ten Fun and Useful Things You Can Do at www.dummies.com

1. Register this book and win!
2. Find and buy the *...For Dummies* books you want online.
3. Get ten great *Dummies Tips*™ every week.
4. Chat with your favorite *...For Dummies* authors.
5. Subscribe free to *The Dummies Dispatch*™ newsletter.
6. Enter our sweepstakes and win cool stuff.
7. Send a free cartoon postcard to a friend.
8. Download free software.
9. Sample a book before you buy.
10. Talk to us. Make comments, ask questions, and get answers!

Jump online to these ten fun and useful things at
http://www.dummies.com/10useful

SURF THE NET

WWW.DUMMIES.COM

For other technology titles from IDG Books Worldwide, go to
www.idgbooks.com

Not online yet? It's easy to get started with *The Internet For Dummies*®, 5th Edition, or *Dummies 101*®: *The Internet For Windows*® *98*, available at local retailers everywhere.

IDG BOOKS WORLDWIDE

Find other *...For Dummies* books on these topics:

Business • Careers • Databases • Food & Beverages • Games • Gardening • Graphics • Hardware
Health & Fitness • Internet and the World Wide Web • Networking • Office Suites
Operating Systems • Personal Finance • Pets • Programming • Recreation • Sports
Spreadsheets • Teacher Resources • Test Prep • Word Processing

IDG BOOKS WORLDWIDE
BOOK REGISTRATION

We want to hear from you!

Visit **http://my2cents.dummies.com** to register this book and tell us how you liked it!

- Get entered in our monthly prize giveaway.

- Give us feedback about this book — tell us what you like best, what you like least, or maybe what you'd like to ask the author and us to change!

- Let us know any other ...*For Dummies*® topics that interest you.

Your feedback helps us determine what books to publish, tells us what coverage to add as we revise our books, and lets us know whether we're meeting your needs as a ...*For Dummies* reader. You're our most valuable resource, and what you have to say is important to us!

Not on the Web yet? It's easy to get started with *Dummies 101*®: *The Internet For Windows*® *98* or *The Internet For Dummies*,® 5th Edition, at local retailers everywhere.

Or let us know what you think by sending us a letter at the following address:

...*For Dummies* Book Registration
Dummies Press
7260 Shadeland Station, Suite 100
Indianapolis, IN 46256-3917
Fax 317-596-5498

BESTSELLING
BOOK SERIES